Nights of Fury

*

Writing as 'Jason Fury'

Screams of Pan
Naked Fury
The Secret of Jimmy X and Other Stories of the Macabre
His Eyes Were Dark, He Licked His Lips
The Kiss of King Kong
The Rope Above, the Bed Below
Eric's Body

*

Writing with 'Big' Bill Jackson

Eighth Wonder

*

Writing as 'Jerry Tucker'

Daddy, My Love

*

Writing as 'Andrea D'Allasandra'

The Creaking Door and Other Stories of Madness and Horror
Horror House
The Master of Hell Mountain
Death House

Coming in 2004/2005!

Jason Fury

The Sex of Angels

Andrea D'Allasandra

House of the Screaming Clowns
Swamp Mama

* * *

By Kandy Khristmas

Doofus, the Little Christmas Boy

Nights of Fury

Jason Fury

iUniverse, Inc.
New York Lincoln Shanghai

Nights of Fury

iUniverse, Inc.

For information address:
iUniverse, Inc.
2021 Pine Lake Road, Suite 100
Lincoln, NE 68512
www.iuniverse.com

Cover photo courtesy of Kandy Kristmas

ISBN: 0-595-32356-1

Printed in the United States of America

In memory of those heroic firemen and law enforcement officers who perished September 11, 2001 in New York City—and showed us just who our real heroes were

Contents

Part V   *Manhattan Twilight*

Author's Note

Over the past twenty-five years, readers have many times asked me to write my memoirs.

Nights of Fury is my attempt to fulfill this wish. These vignettes are based mostly on my daily journals that I've kept from the 1950s to the present.

To avoid any embarrassment to the living or the dead, I've changed the identities of all primary figures described here and have transfigured only a few. I've also taken the creative liberty of re-arranging some happenings and dropped many men who played pivotal roles in my life. Those singled out here are the ones who profoundly affected my life—for better or for worse.

As for the days before and after September 11, 2001, I've relied on first hand experience. I was there and saw it all.

Jery Tillotson
Manhattan

New York City
Autumn ~ 2004

3:15 a.m.

No more sleep tonight. I know the signs only too well.

I watch the bar of streetlight beneath my window shade. I've watched its arrival and departure for nearly twenty-five years.

In just an hour or more, the charcoal glow of dawn will slowly replace the silver illumination.

I wish it were a living thing so that we could console each other on these many nights without sleep.

My nightstand totters beneath a mish-mash of sleeping aids. A stack of well-worn Nancy Drew mysteries, a collection of old ghost stories, videos like *Night Monster, Dark Victory* and *Since You Went Away.*

The lonely wail of a fire truck pierces the silence. It travels in the darkness somewhere out there along Third Avenue before fading away. A police siren follows close behind and then another one.

For me, that uneasy cry evokes images of two men who lie buried tonight somewhere in Ground Zero. The cold wind of early autumn sweeps over their anonymous graves within that deep pit.

Roberto and Kevin had described to me a week before all the things they wanted to do with their lives. Marriage. Kids. They wanted to settle down in Queens or Long Island near their families. Neither could afford Manhattan.

All ashes now. September 11, 2001 terminated those dreams with brutal finality.

After the great AIDS epidemic of the 80s and then the massacre of thousands of my fellow residents here in New York that autumn morning, the world is a place I prefer to watch only on the telly.

I drag out from my nightstand a large envelope that bulges with old, yellowing photos from the past. Each of them is embedded with men in eras long gone.

There's Scotty, my first newspaper editor from 1965, as he mugs for the camera in the newsroom of a building that was torn down nearly half a century ago.

His face is square and too large for his body and he sports an old-fashioned 50s crew cut, but—his blazing charm shines through the camera lenses. I remember how each month he demanded that I resign from "his" newsroom because he didn't want to have a fag working with him. That changed, though, and no one knows of his private demons and what happened to us the day I left him.

1

Here's the badly developed Polaroid of Billy Dragon from 1962, the sultry, half-Indian with full lips and troubled eyes and his hair slicked up into a 60s pompadour. Even in this blurred image his dark eyes smolder with blazing sexuality. To the left is the corner of our marriage bed.

A handsome, beefy man, stands behind a church podium in this picture from 1971. He's shouting and ranting and in another magazine snapshot, he's on his knees with his hands clasped in prayer.

That's the Reverend Luther Landau of Alabama. His heyday as the blazing hot evangelist has long passed. His earthly appetites finally destroyed him.

So many more photos…a slender, young-looking priest, caught putting on his collar while he winks at me…a rugged Irishman in sleeveless hard hat and tank top, mocking me with a black cigar clenched between white teeth…naked, sweaty men, smoking cigarettes and bellowing Chic's disco hit, "Good Times," behind stage in 1980 at the notorious Show Place Theater off Broadway and Times Square.

I would soon join them on that small wooden stage and do my best to whip the audience of men into a sexual lather.

That photograph was taken at the big Christmas show, right on the eve of the Great Plague that mowed down Manhattan's great male beauties from the disco scene.

And there's Eric, the mental patient, who I cared for in 1963, and whom everyone thought was a dead ringer for Clark Gable without the moustache. Stunning, mysterious, doomed, he showed to me that love comes in different forms.

An old magazine article features the sexiest of the Wall Street Tigers back in the early eighties. Gene Adair is shown in half-naked splendor. He offered me money and an apartment if I would stay with him and only him and no one else.

Being kept by anyone was alien to me and I went my own way.

My former Wall Street stallion is now a grandfather of three.

I try not to study the picture of my two Manhattan cops—one black haired, the other with lockets the color of brick. Their remains are buried along with thousands of others at Ground Zero.

There's my box of journals. From the fifties on up to the present, I've been a faithful little diarist. But if I started browsing through those old relics, I would certainly receive no visit from sleep.

Much like the men who no longer pay their visits to me. I'll never see them again that's for sure.

Death has visited many in their former playgrounds here in the big city and left others to be buried in lonely graveyards in the South. Disease, old age and physical abuse did them in. They were loners, even with me, and we knew their ends would come quietly and with no fanfare. No surprises there.

Before I moved to Manhattan in 1978, our affairs had to be committed behind locked doors, in secret locations and we had to pretend to the outside world that we barely knew each other.

While "queer" people are everywhere on the tube today and are part of mainstream America, I remember vividly those decades when suspicion of even being that way could result in violent death. If not murder then at least torture, job termination, ejections from hotels, restaurants and apartments. Entrapment by the law was a fact of life.

Beatings from mobs of gay-hating hoodlums were rarely reported to police. If they were, the victims would be made the villains because "they asked for it." Because they were faggots, then they deserved nothing but contempt.

In that era, queers were the white niggers—creatures that could be spat upon in public, beaten up and violently disposed of and no one gave a damn. Fags were even lower than blacks, according to these psychos. Because you were white and you were suspected of doing the forbidden dirty with other men, then that made you into a loathsome monster.

Death was too good for you. Violent mutilation had to be your fate, with your privates rammed down your throat and your body split open with an axe.

In this hidden little world I knew while growing up, suicide was commonplace. Marriages of convenience often ended in alcoholism, physical abuse and misery for everyone. I've often wondered how many millions of homosexual men and women felt doomed as they walked down the aisle to marry—and how many hated themselves for the rest of their lives?

For those who chose to live alone and unmarried, we knew our peculiar path could be a lonely one. Especially if you lived in small towns where everyone was expected to marry, produce children and raise a family.

Single men and women were tolerated just as long as they gave no cause for gossip.

The men I knew intimately were all straight. A few were bisexual. While I was a friend to many homosexual men, I very rarely bedded down with them. Butch, natural, virile guys were always my poison.

Here, on this small isle of Manhattan, I visited one of my ancient flames last year in his six-floor walkup rooming house in Harlem. On the sidewalk below his window crowded Discount Stores with plastic flip-flops selling for .99

cents…plastic tablecloths for $1.00 and old packages of Hunan Noodles—4 for $1.00.

This small, dingy home of my once passionate steady resembled more the cell of a monk than a former libertine: a narrow bed hugged the flyspecked wall painted bilious mustard. A pale spread the color of Pepto-Bismol covered the thin mattress. A plastic crucifix of Christ hung above the single, flat pillow. He has renounced sex and drink.

He coughs a lot. Within reach from his bed sits a folding table missing one leg. Neatly arranged on its surface are his hot plate, his plastic bowls and plastic forks and a nearly empty jar of Maxwell House Instant Coffee.

A religious calendar showing Jesus with red cheeks and crimson lips and Walt Disney lamb in his arms fill up the page for December.

He has, indeed, changed from those days of the Disco hysteria.

In this sweltering steam bath of a home, he wanted to talk about God and how he played too hard and too fast back then and now he's paying for it. Coughs interrupt his words as he chain smokes Basic Cigarettes and sips the tepid black instant coffee from a stained Dixie Cup.

As I study him—emaciated, the color of old candle wax, with his hair dyed a blue-black and matted in strands around his face—I try to remember that earlier image of him when we met in the gay baths.

His torso was slender and hard and healthy. His eyes sparkled with sexual fever and he emanated an intoxicating aroma of clean flesh, a touch of *Halston Cologne*, tobacco and brandy.

I remember his stunning young body aquiver as he threw himself into the throes of sexual passion. And afterwards, in his strong, young arms we both dreamed of a future together—he, a famous movie star, and I, an internationally renowned writer.

He chose to play around the clock while I labored over my keyboard to create. As he coughed again into a Kleenex, he gasped: "What happened? I just never got the breaks!"

For me, the Great Plague of the eighties was the first big tragedy that suggested other unpleasant surprises awaited us down the road. This changed life forever. I never felt so free and good again. Men I thought the most beautiful in the world transformed into cadaverous zombies who didn't recognize me at the end.

Their deaths brought relief to us who held their hands to the grave.

All those beautiful, kicky clothes of the seventies vanished, too, because Disco was supposed to be a bastard music and so it ended. I still have Disco outfits I

loved to wear. *Royal Bain de Champagne* I spritzed on as my signature scent. A few golden drops that still remain in the sculpted bottle can still evoke those wild, fun days.

I remember the exhilaration of smelling my perfume mingling with the intoxicating scent of gin and tonic, sex and endless Salem Cigarettes.

What the plague didn't wipe away, September 11, 2001 exterminated the rest.

The only proof these old joys were actually experienced are now in the rapid scrawl found in my journals and on the pages of old gay magazines that showcased my many tales of feverish love between men.

I'll try to evoke those moments for you, too, as we drift back through all those nights of Fury.

Jason Fury

PART I
The Door Opens

THE FORTIES

"You started something,
Yes you did and you didn't even know it…"

—Betty Grable singing to Robert Cummings
In l941's *Moon Over Miami*

Chapter One
The Predator

In my memory, Dale is always naked.

He alone inhabits this mental room filled with rose and purple shadows. A lamp bathes his young torso with gold luster.

He lies there on his bed, relaxed, tanned and makes no attempt to cover up. From my child's face, his deceptively innocent eyes stare down at his uncovered lap and youthful arousal. A strange smile loosens his mouth.

Then he watches me again for he has plans for us both, only I don't know it yet. True pederasts never give away their secrets.

I'm only four and I approach his bed eagerly. He is the favorite person in my childhood world.

At sixteen, his clean smile startles against toasted skin.

A crew cut crowns the torso of a lean, tough body.

Those devious eyes are opened wide, as if in constant surprise, and his mouth has fallen open into a sweet, goofy grin. Now, he holds out his arms and laughs:

"Jason! My little boy, my favorite buddy in the whole wide world!"

I hurry toward him and he scoops me up and pulls me tight against him. That one embrace changes my life for he introduces me into a world that children are not supposed to visit. How many others did he escort through this forbidden door and reveal the dark secrets of life?

Daily he has ridden me on his bike around our neighborhood. I sit in front of him, leaning back. He whispers, "I love you more than anybody, Jason! You're so beautiful."

His teenage mouth nibbles my ears and neck and he rubs his chin in my curls. His tongue licks the back of my neck and my throat and I giggle. He laughs, too. He's only teasing me, you understand?

Even in the outside world, he wears no clothes, other than a skimpy pair of swim trunks.

With him holding me close, I delight in being held so secure between his warm thighs. He presses them tight against me so that we're already in a sexual position. His legs, his arms, his chest and his moist mouth envelope me and dissolve my boundaries. Already he conditions me for sacrifice to feed his uncontrollable libido.

He is strong and funny and he loves me more than anyone in our neighborhood.

The feeling of being loved was unknown to me until he came into my world. My parents and I lived in a modest house on that remote street in Newport News, Virginia.

The year was 1945. My father worked as a white-collar employee in the vast ship yards there. War was wounding down.

My mother was a bitter, scowling nightmare who I avoided even then. I remember her slapping me around and screaming that I was "a sissy! A little girl! Why were you born? You're a freak."

I didn't understand any of that, yet I can remember those glittering, black eyes, staring at me with sheer hatred. I was to see them all my life.

When my father came home from work, he had nothing to do with me either. After eating supper, he picked up his newspapers and magazines and listened to the radio.

He should never have had children—yet, within twenty years, he would help bore six more. One more thing I remember about him: when my mother wasn't around, my father would walk around me naked. If he came out of the shower, he made a point of coming up close to me and drying himself off just inches away from my face.

He ran his towel between his legs and buttocks, as if wanting to entice me. Once when I reached out to touch his tush, he shoved me roughly against the wall, hard enough to make my nose bleed. He left me there, weeping and watching blood spatter my child's body.

So when Dale found me playing outside alone with my kitten, he saw something that attracted him. He sensed that I was someone so desperate for affection that I would seize it greedily when offered to me.

I was like a puppy, desperate for a master. So I found one but this master would demand more than soulful looks and a slobbering tongue on his hand. He expected a child's tongue and mouth to taste his young torso. And then he would repeat the favor on his obedient victim.

For already I was a beautiful child. My pictures from that period reveal a boy with a gleaming helmet of yellow curls. Large, dark eyes peer upward, shyly, from a face that is fair and unusually feminine.

My mouth suggests a delicious smile that none of the pictures reveal. Already I was fearful of my mother's eager slaps. She liked to come upon me quietly and then strike me hard across my face because I was not evolving into her fantasy creation of what an All-American boy of four should be.

So suspecting this, or sensing what might be happening to me in my dark household, Dale invited me to sit in front of him on his bike and he would whiz me around our neighborhood.

My mother was thrilled to have the "freak" taken off her hands. Like the other mothers in the small neighborhood of working couples, she approved of Dale.

He was the all-American boy. His parents also worked in the shipyards so he stayed home those summer days to clean up his small house.

Then he was free to play baseball with his buddies, attend Boy Scout meetings, or go swimming in the nearby ocean. He and his friends loved to go to see Tarzan and Abbott and Costello movies and return home to imitate those film characters.

I remember Dale buying me Royal Crown drinks at the nearby little grocery store. He gave me chewing gum and strawberry suckers. At some point, he adopted me as his "little brother" because he didn't have any.

So, anyone seeing us thought it was so great and touching that this bigger, handsome boy had decided to make that shy, weird little Jason Fury his surrogate sibling.

I remember the sky as always a washed-out, glassy blue. The sun burned down in pure white light. Shade was a rarity. Everyone stayed in doors during the hottest part of the day.

My mother liked to listen to the soap operas that came on the radio during the afternoon. Television was nonexistent.

A group of other small kids did live up and down our block, though, and they clamored for Dale's attention. He was sweet when he joked to them that I really was his brother.

"Jason vanished from my house when I was little," he told them, "and we found out he was kidnapped by a bunch of Nazi spies. I went over there to Germany and fought like crazy to get him back here."

The children giggled or made sounds of disgust. They were jealous of me because I had been chosen by their golden boy to be his very own companion.

When he herded a group of us the few blocks to the beach, his own buddies were already there.

They cut up, some smoked cigarettes, and they tried to pull each other's trunks down.

They did this to Dale a lot. We got used to seeing his naked butt. They grabbed each other in the crotch, too. I didn't know why they did this. He laughed and howled with them, with his face becoming a bright pink.

One time I watched them standing in a circle. Now and then one would glance over his shoulder as if they were doing something dirty. Their hands were hidden in front of them. Shorts were lowered over their hips. Their shoulders trembled as they did what they were doing in secrecy. Dale's face looked up, he saw me and grinned. His face was flushed and strange looking.

And then someone whooped, the others laughed loudly.

"Dale, you did it again! You win!"

I waited impatiently for him to come and pick me up and take me into the water. When he did, the front of his shorts jutted out slightly. His buddies watched him and laughed and whooped again. He threw them a grin as he stared down at me.

"I was thinking of you," he winked. "All the time I was having some fun, I was thinking of you."

I didn't know what he meant. He took my hand and pressed it briefly to that bulge in his crotch and he made a groaning sound.

Then he led me into the waves. I came to his waist and he suddenly held me close. I clutched his strong, young neck tightly.

"We're going a little bit deeper," he explained. "Just hold on to me now. I won't let you get hurt."

Those words were magical for in Dale's arms, I knew he would never let me become harmed.

Water came up to his chest now. He buried his face against my hair and kissed my ears and cheeks as the waves floated close to our shoulders.

"Wow, if you were a girl, Jason! If you were only a girl!"

He lowered me slightly and I felt something stiff and long beneath me. I looked down and saw that Dale had lowered his trunks. From his hips, jutted a big stick like object.

Up and down he raised me with the weird hard thing between my thighs. I didn't know what it was but that was okay. I was in the arms of my Prince Charming.

He gasped and smiled. He reached down and pulled up his shorts.

"That felt soooo good! One day, you'll know what I did. But don't tell anybody."

On the nearby shore, I watched his gang of buddies studying us, as if awaiting a signal. Dale saw them and thrust his fist in the air.

"Did it! Did it!" he shouted.

His pals laughed and doubled over in laughter. He had done something that they knew about—but which left me mystified.

I was fearful of the water. Dale had me clamber onto his broad back as he swam back to shore. When we left the water, he took my hand and led me to his friends.

"Guys, here's my little buddy, favorite buddy, Jason."

They said nothing. They moved closer, all of them staring down at me and several pulled at their crotches. All I saw were big bodies and faces watching me with strange expressions—as if waiting for me to do something.

"You want a sucker?" one boy asked me. "I got a big sucker."

"Yeah, you want a lollipop to suck on?" another one giggled. "I've got a real big one."

All of them began pulling at themselves and snickering and nudging each other.

"Not here, you jerks!" muttered Dale and pulled me away.

I didn't know what was going on—but their faces scared me. They all looked so big and serious looking with red splotches on their cheeks.

When a new Tarzan movie played at the theater, our neighborhood kids tried to imitate our jungle hero. Dale delighted in rolling down the waist of his trunks so that you nearly saw his wee-wee.

Then we'd go to a group of trees along the beach and Dale would swing from one limb to another. The other kids tried it, too. Most fell to the soft sand below.

He picked me to play Boy, the son of Tarzan. He told me to hang onto his neck as he swung from limb to limb. I clung tight as the other kids cheered. When he jumped to the ground, he held me close against him.

"Hey, that was fun, right?"

The other kids wanted him to carry them, too, but he shook his head.

"You're too big. Jason's perfect."

I had already fallen in love with his strong, tanned neck, his smell of teenage boy and that dazzling smile of his.

And one momentous day that summer, I finally saw Dale completely naked and he proved his love for me.

He lived two houses down from my family.

One day, he told me he was going into the hospital. He was to have his tonsils removed. He would be gone for a whole day. I wasn't to worry.

When he returned, his parents asked my mother if she would mind looking in on the patient. He was to stay in bed for several days.

My mother let me accompany her to Dale's house. She took him hot soup and Jell-O.

He looked like a beautiful prince, propped up in his bed with pillows and wearing blue pajamas. I didn't want to leave him there and then Dale wondered if I had any comic books he could read.

"I'll let Jason bring you some of his."

Comic books were a passion all of us kids shared back then. We saved up our money and brought gobs of them every month. *Little Lulu. Donald Duck. Superman. Captain Marvel. Tarzan. Captain America.*

"I'll read him some comic books, Mrs. Fury," Dale smiled. "Don't worry. I'll look after him."

"Well, if you're sure you don't mind."

"I'd be happy to. I'll bet Jason makes a great nurse."

I still remember grabbing a stack of comic books from my collection and telling my mother I was going to Dale's house. She was already laying down for her afternoon nap.

The street was empty. No one was around beneath that white ball of fire. Like my mother, most stay-at-home wives took naps at this time. The kids were mostly indoors, listening to the radio or reading their comics.

I knocked on the screen door of Dale's home.

He came to the door, wearing his pajamas. I was on a lower step and he loomed way above me like a majestic young giant.

"Dale! Comic books" I cried out.

"Hey, it's my favorite kid brother, Jason! You brought me something?"

He took the comics from me and picked me up. He kissed my cheeks and buried his face in my curls.

"I've missed seeing you," he said. With me still hugging his neck, he carried me into his bedroom. The house was empty of other people and very quiet. I sniffed ghosts of toast and bacon from that morning's breakfast.

That profound little chamber is a blur of images in my memory. Thick shadows lay everywhere, except for the lamp that glowed on his nightstand.

Football, baseball and basketball pennants decorated his wall. He turned the key in the lock of his door.

"Don't want nobody to bother us," he winked. "My parents are gone all day. And yours don't care where you go, do they?"

I nodded my agreement. My mother was always only too glad for me to leave her alone.

"Did they tell you what they did to me in the hospital?" he smiled, in a playful manner. "They did all kinds of things to me. They gave me a shot in my arm."

He took off his pajama top. His young flesh gleamed and he touched his forearm. Then he lay down on his bed.

"Wow, it hurt!" he joked. "I cried and said, 'don't do it anymore! That hurts!'"

I laughed as he feigned great pain.

"Then," he said more quietly, "a nurse came in with a real big needle. And she gave me a shot in my butt. Want me to show you where she stuck the needle in?"

I nodded and he swiftly turned on his side, pushed his bottoms down over his hips, and showed me his bare butt.

"Right there," he said. "Feel of it, Jason. That's where she put the needle in."

I touched his buttock. This was such fun. I had seen glimpses of his bare rear but now here it was, right beneath my hands. I slid my fingers over into his cleft.

I heard him gasp. And then he rolled over onto his stomach and pushed his bottoms down further.

"Then—then the nurse, she put fingers inside my crack, and she put the needle in my hole. See it. Feel of it, Jason."

His fingers parted his buttocks and I saw his opening. I touched it. It moved slightly. I put a finger on it. And again, he squeezed it.

This was fun. And exciting.

Dale turned over on his back. He had tossed aside his pajama bottoms so that he lay there completely naked. He dazzled with his nudity. Those long, strong legs, the flat stomach and the broad chest, with nipples hard like thimbles—I can still see it in my mind.

He had pulled me close beside him on the bed so that our bodies touched. Then he took my hand and guided it over his chest.

"See how big my nipples are? Squeeze them, Jason."

I remember them as being unusually large. Both were hard and erect and he used both his palms to rub them. He made his biceps bulge and I squeezed them. Dale wanted me to see what a powerful torso he had.

Taking my hand, he guided it down his flat stomach. He took my second finger and inserted it into his deep navel.

"One day, your belly button will be as big as mine."

He seemed to like the sensation of a fingertip sliding into the shallow cavity.

From there, still smiling, he took my fingers and brought them at last to his young manhood.

"When you're a grown man," he smiled, "you'll have one as big as mine."

His looked so different from my father's.

Dale's young manhood sprouted up white and strong, with a pink tip. It made me think of taffy candy—and it jutted up from his hips.

He guided my hand up and down his phallus. I was amazed. His wee wee, like my father's, had grown so big.

"In the hospital," he grinned, "the nurse liked to pretend this was a sucker—and she put her mouth on it. Let's pretend I've got a sucker between my legs and you want to taste of it. Come closer."

His voice had become hoarse and urgent as he urged me to think of his organ as a lollipop. I liked lollipops, didn't I? Then pretend he had one right there jutting up from between his thighs.

He told me that everyone wanted his special lollipop but he wouldn't give it to them. He was saving it for one beautiful, little boy named Jason.

Many times he had wanted me to enjoy and suck on it but it was never the right time. Now, the time was right.

"Now, you can't tell anybody about this or they'll get really mad at me because they all want it so bad. I'm going to let you lick it and taste it. Would you like that? Nobody in the world can do this except you. Do you understand?"

I nodded my head. His right arm lay protectively around me as he pulled me closer to his nude torso.

His left hand was gentle as his fingers entwined with my curls. He murmured encouragement and he uttered a string of joyful endearments: "Wow...just like the nurse...you've got a wonderful sucker in your mouth...you can have it anytime you want it!"

I felt wonderful because this was my most beloved person in the world who presented me with this unique gift.

His "sucker" felt smooth and pleasant in my mouth. I was thrilled to see that this present swelled up from between his thighs and that it belonged only to him.

He arched his hips and slipped his fingers into my curls and guided my head. He was too big for me to do anything but under his direction, I used my tongue to taste him and formed my hands into fists to grasp him.

His own hands skimmed over his body and between his thighs. His breathing quickened and he writhed like he was in pain.

Then he arched his hips and I watched his source of power pulse suddenly and suddenly there it was. Sex was presented to me with unblinking gaze.

I drew back, astonished that his boy thing was doing all of this. I only thought that thing between your leg was to use for pee pee only. He gasped loudly and opened his mouth wide.

"Hurt?" I asked fearfully.

He shook his head and grinned. "Big boys and men do that when their lollipop feels real good. One day you'll do that, too, Jason."

I couldn't take my eyes off his candy cane. It kept changing. I had watched it go from soft to rubbery to hard to limber in just a few minutes. Because it belonged to Dale, I imbued it with magical prowess. His magical boy toy had done all kinds of wondrous things. It spewed out white pee, it felt like hard rubber and now it was warm and soft again.

I pulled at it and he chuckled.

"Now, in the hospital, they made me wash up a special way," he said. "Let me show you."

He held my hand and led me into the bathroom. He took a small hand towel from the rack and held it under the water.

"Here, you wash off my lollipop and make it clean and shiny."

This was proving to be fun and I liked the sensation of holding a forbidden thing in my hands and covering it with water and then drying it off.

"Don't forget these round things we call balls," he suggested. His groin had become bigger, too. He joked about his two baseballs and said that when I became as old as he, I would have them, too.

He instructed me on how to use to use the towel and then my tongue to make certain his "man things", as he called them, were clean and dry.

Still naked, he sat on the toilet.

"My nurse made me do this every hour," he informed me. "She got behind me and made sure I did it. You get behind me now and I'll prove to you I'm doing it."

This was another taboo ritual in our family. I was potty trained by now and I was told many times that I should always close the door and make sure no one saw me.

"Real boys don't do dirty stuff in their pants," my mother had warned me.

He half stooped over the toilet and I saw him do the dirty stuff. He did this for several minutes. I was fascinated. I didn't think of how it looked when I did it.

Now, I saw the whole process and if possible, this made Dale even more of an immortal. He was using his beautiful young body to teach me everything about how the human torso functioned.

"I'll show you how wonderful you are," he gasped and he arched his hips slightly. Once more, I was amazed to see how large his toy had become—and what it could do.

After he cleaned himself with his dirty cloth, his young arms pulled me next to him. I felt wonderful to be embraced by someone who was so young and nice to me.

His lips traveled over my face and covered my mouth. He pushed my shorts down and his mouth made me giggle. He covered my own boy's privates and he savored this for many minutes.

Then he pulled me close to him again and kissed my face, my ears and chest and my boy's organ. He turned me over and he repeated on me what I had done to him. He licked and kissed and gasped and I laughed because it all tickled me so much.

Naked and embraced by his arms, he licked me so thoroughly I felt sticky. From my face to my toes, his tongue traveled thoroughly. His hungry mouth stayed on my own childish privates and then my tush for a long time. He groaned and I saw his right hand moving faster over his rigid organ.

I heard him gasp and he stopped suddenly, quivering and making loud breathing sounds. Quickly, he helped me get dressed. I sensed that he had changed because he was quiet and serious.

Dale went to one wall of his small room and he removed an American Indian dagger from a beaded holster. It had hung there beneath a bow and arrow.

"Now, we're going to keep this a secret," he said. "Don't you tell anybody or I'll have to cut you with this dagger. You understand me?"

I nodded and was puzzled by this sudden change. He looked serious and a little scary, not like the warm, smiling friend I had enjoyed.

"You want some more of my lollipop?" he asked. I nodded. He held it out to me but when I went to put my hands around it, he pushed my fingers away.

"You can have it again when nobody's around. You'd better get on home. Don't you tell your Mamma about this! Or you won't get anymore of my special candy."

Again I reached for it because I wanted to put it in my mouth and I wanted to see it go through all these magical changes.

He let me squeeze it with my hands and lick it, and then he stepped back and said I should be going home.

I went home and thought of all the fun I had with Dale's lollipop. I couldn't understand why he let me have fun with him but my own father wouldn't?

Dale said all men had what he had. I would be like him, too, as I got older. That meant my own Daddy could make his toy do all the things that Dale's did. I had seen it dark and mean looking and didn't believe it could do all the wonderful things that Dale's own organ did.

When my Daddy came home from work at dusk, I watched him with unusual interest. He always changed into his swim trunks and after supper that evening he washed our car.

I sat on the steps and studied him. His briefs were skimpy and I could imagine his lollipop getting all hard and swollen like Dale's. Did he make it get wet and sticky, too?

But Dale had warned me to be careful and not to breathe a word. If anything slipped out, he would never look at me again. I was terrified of that happening. I desperately wanted him to hold me close and kiss me and let me have fun with his body.

When Daddy took me and Mama and my sisters to a movie that night, hundreds of men in uniforms swarmed the lobby of the theater.

I looked at them and thought: they've all got a lollipop like Dale. What if I went up to one and asked him if I could put his sucker into my mouth? When I went into the men's bathroom after the movie, the place was jammed with military guys.

I stood at a urinal to do pee. A man in a uniform joined me. I looked up. His male thing was just inches away from my head. It looked huge! I watched him tinkle and he winked at me.

When he finished, he flipped it several times so that it was more like a dark balloon than a human sucker. His lollipop didn't look like either Dale's or Daddy's. It was bigger and scary looking.

I opened my mouth to ask him if I could lick his male thing but he moved away.

Several days passed and I didn't see Dale anywhere. I heard his mother tell mine that the doctors had wanted him to stay indoors for a few more days.

Then when I came in one day with an older sister who had taken me with her to the nearby post office, I was thrilled to see Dale in the kitchen with my Mother. She had made him a glass of iced tea and he looked stunning.

He wore a green jersey and brown shorts and tennis shoes. His smile lit up his boyish face when he saw me.

"Hey, there's my little buddy, Jason. We've been waiting for you."

"Oh, boy!" I cried and he picked me up right there and squeezed me tight.

"You miss me?" he said quietly. "My doctor didn't want me to get outside much after my tonsil operation. But now I'm ready to go."

"Dale's getting rid of some his comic books," my mother said. "If you want to go and get some, go on along."

"I saved a big stack of them for you," Dale smiled.

But my older sister said she wanted some, too. She loved *Little Lulu.*

"I don't have any of those," Dale said. "They're mostly *Donald Duck* and *Superman.*"

She had no interest in those.

"We'll see you in a little while, Mrs. Fury," Dale called out.

"I know Jason's safe with you," she called out. He was one of the few people who could actually make her smile.

"Don't worry. I'll take care of him."

Dale took my hand and walked with me to his house.

No one was there. He locked the door and took my hand and led me into his bedroom.

That incredible bedroom. Ever since that time, a bedroom fascinates me. So much of life's joys and horrors occur in this special place in every house and apartment.

I clapped my hands when he stripped all of his clothes off and he lay back on the bed. I had thought and thought about our game and this time he didn't have to encourage me to make him feel good.

To me, I had no idea of what sensual meant. This was like a fun game that was a secret between my wonderful friend and me. I thought then that this was the type of private fun all older boys and men enjoyed.

I still remember that soft smile, those hot eyes as he told me what a wonderful little boy I was. When he held me in his arms again and used his mouth on me like I had him, this was a wonderfully warm moment.

It was like he was doing all the things my father wouldn't do.

I remember that boyish aroma of his—clean, sweaty, slightly woodsy. He held me close and kissed my naked body so intensely that I heard him groaning and gasping. He ground his hips hard against the bed and panted.

He used his "dirty cloth" to wipe away the wetness. Then he lay on his stomach and parted his buttocks. It was time for me to use my tongue to make him clean again.

I was greedy now to use my mouth on his boy stick because I had thought constantly about it.

"Never ever tell anyone," he repeated. No smile lit up his face. "You're the only one who plays with my body."

I wonder. Was he also playing his games with other little boys and girls in the neighborhood?

Because this was the last time I visited Dale.

Perhaps he grew nervous or maybe someone in the neighborhood had grown suspicious. He suddenly vanished from my memories of those childhood days.

Maybe I let something slip about the games I played with Dale or maybe he revealed something to his buddies.

From a shimmering figure of power and beauty, he abruptly vanished from my memory.

Our family moved from Virginia to North Carolina soon after that. But two years later, I was amazed when I came into our house and found a group of people visiting us.

My Daddy said: "Jason, remember our neighbors—the Windbergs? There's your friend, Dale."

I was so shocked I think I just stared. This was Dale?

In pictures from that era, I'm usually shown with my hands behind me and my face lowered in shyness. It was around this time that my mother had begun to beat me for being "a sissy." I remember keeping my face lowered so her hands couldn't strike me.

The tall, slender young man looked nothing like my childhood god. For one thing, he wore clothes.

This mature youth sported loose slacks, a short-sleeved shirt and his hair was long and parted on the side.

He wore no smile for me. He didn't hold out his arms anymore.

"Remember how Jason used to follow Dale around everywhere?" Mother continued.

"Well, Jason," he said quietly. "You've not grown too much, have you?"

"He stays indoors all the time, acting like a little sissy girl," my mother explained. "He's gotten worse. I don't know what we're going to do with him. Or her."

My eyes couldn't feast enough on this ghost from the past. I looked at his crotch and then at his face. It was between his legs that I had thrilled to making contact with another person. As if sensing where my thoughts lay and possibly frightened of what I would say, he crossed his legs and looked away. He remained sitting stiffly with his parents.

They were remembering those days in Virginia and gossiped about old neighbors and Dale was saying something about starting college the next year.

They ignored me.

I went outside and hid behind some bushes. Why had this golden Adonis changed so much? He didn't even look like the bedroom playmate that had shown me the joys of human contact.

When they went to their car, I appeared and stood with my older sister as we waved goodbye. Dale gave me a brief glance from the back window and then he stared straight ahead. Their dusty Ford glided down the neighborhood street and vanished.

My mother grabbed my hair and slapped me hard against the face several times.

"Why did you act so silly when the Windbergs were here?" she yelled at me. "You acted so stupid. I thought you'd be glad to see Dale again. He was always so nice to you."

My father watched this scene of tenderness while smoking quietly his pipe. He said nothing and went to sit in his rocking chair on the front porch. Nothing stopped him from reading the Sunday newspapers.

"Why don't you ever slap him some?" my mother screeched. "He needs a whipping to knock that sissiness out of him?"

"Let's try to have a good afternoon," my father said absently. He had already learned how to tune this psychopath out. "That was nice of the Windbergs to come by, wasn't it?"

"I had to do all the talking," Mother seethed while glaring at me. "You never say anything. And then this sissy had to come into the living room and embarrass the hell out of me. Look at him? He looks like a little girl! Maybe I should make some dresses for him. Put some of my make-up on him."

"His nose is bleeding," my father said dully. "Better get some ice for it. You hit him too hard."

"He can get his own damned ice," growled Mother. "I hope he bleeds to death. You'd think he'd be glad to see that Dale. Now that's the kind of boy I wish I had for a son."

My sister took me into the kitchen and put some ice cubes into a cloth and held it to my nose.

My mother had followed us. Now, she shoved me against the wall and got a broom and began to beat me with it. I ran into a corner and she followed me, screaming and beating me. I tried to get past her but she trapped me.

She kept beating and beating me until her arms became tired.

No one did or said anything. She terrified everyone and could quickly use her broom on anyone in her path. In those terrifying moments, I thought: one day I'm going to kill you.

I thought of those rare minutes I had spent with Dale and compared those to what was happening to me then.

No wonder I wept.

◆   ◆   ◆

Many times I've wondered where my youthful satyr picked up all of his sexual tricks at so young an age.

True, he and his buddies probably did "horse" around but Dale acted so experienced in bed—with his way of touching and kissing and using his fingers to make your body feel good.

Perhaps his own father had taught him such skills for several times during our encounters, he had blurted out: "Pretend I'm your Daddy and only your Daddy knows how to make it all feel so damn good!"

If he is still alive, then he's already an old man, an old codger nearing seventy. Then what does it matter?

Monsters never die.

THE FIFTIES

"Oh, man, I wuz crawlin',
A just-a bawlin'…"

—*"Crawlin"*
The Clovers

Chapter Two
The Sadist

❖

Summer ~ 1956

From behind the curtain, I watched him.

Sweat glistened on his powerful shoulders, chest and arms. Thinning dark hair was slicked back from his face.

The swimming trunks clung to the incredible roundness of his buttocks. His cleft sucked in the material so that it looked as if his rear-end had been spray painted blue.

An azure tattoo darkened his right forearm. He was a former Navy man.

With every movement, his muscles danced in an unforgettable rhythm beneath his bronzed skin.

I already knew that when Dick Grubb smiled, a missing tooth near the front of his mouth gave him the rakish, brutal quality of a boxer.

I wanted to go out there and make an excuse to talk to him. He had visited us briefly but there was never a chance for him to notice me. Since he had moved in a month before, I already knew his daily schedule.

His fat, slob of a wife, Chrissie, had a day job as cashier at our town's only grocery store. I watched her waddle down the street every morning. Her clothes never changed from the uniform of skin-tight jeans, a tent of a white tee shirt and her hair hanging in a greasy ponytail.

How in the world did such a stunning slab of beefcake wound up with a fat pig of a woman? She arrived home in the afternoon right after her husband went off to his job.

This left her hunky, sexy husband alone all day. His job at the chair factory a mile away didn't start until late afternoon. He always walked there. I'd see him leave the house, swinging his lunch pail, and dressed in snug jeans, a cotton jersey of black or white.

His body-clinging clothes emphasized the muscularity of our new neighbor. In the small town of Carson City, the population of 300 boasted only the average male, with many of these paunchy and shapeless.

Nearly all the men were hard-bitten farmers with stooped shoulders and heavily lined faces. Even their younger cohorts looked broken and exhausted from dawn-to-dusk days.

If the men weren't farmers, they worked in the chair factory like Dick Grubb. They made me think of animated masses of potatoes, the food they thrived on.

They had no incentive to look good or handsome. Those days ended in high school.

So Dick Grubb was a real novelty in our whistle-stop of a town.

Their house, like ours, was located on the tiny Main Street of Carson City, North Carolina. While our residence glowed with white paint and blooming roses and sunflowers, the next-door house was hideous beneath a cover of pale green paint.

To an eerie degree, it resembled exactly all the houses of that grim street in Newport News, Virginia.

No trees or shrubbery enhanced the square box of old wood.

Instead of curtains, bed sheets and blankets covered the windows.

Previous tenants had chopped up the Evergreen bushes that someone long ago had planted there. Now they looked identical to the battered tin trashcans that were put out on the curb each Tuesday and Thursday for the garbage collectors.

No one stayed there long. Couples rented this house until they brought their first trailer and moved to Trashville. That's the area of Carson City filled with white trash.

On this sultry summer afternoon, my mouth had parted in longing as I continued feasting my eyes on this dazzling Hercules who was on full display just a few feet away.

My curtain hid me but if the wall suddenly vanished, I could take about ten steps and I would be there—in his powerful arms, being held tight against that all-powerful, sweaty body.

And then I could once more play the lollipop game that Dale had exposed me to. I would make this new man feel so good that he would want it all the time. And maybe, he would leave his wife and he and I would go to New York City and live.

There, I could be a woman for real, dressed up in stunning outfits I had seen in movies and I'd wear a blonde wig. Dick would only be one of my lovers.

I really believed those fantasies could come true. I accepted completely the fact that I was a woman. Mother Nature had made a slight error in putting me into a male body.

Why couldn't people accept this and not become hysterical about it? It didn't bother me. I was a beautiful youth and I was wasting away in this whistle stop of 300 rednecks.

For eight years we had lived here. My father was a traveling salesman now. Living in this cemetery didn't bother him. My mother continued to scream at me, to ridicule me and tear me down daily.

I had learned to avoid her. If I were home, I cleaned up the house, which allowed her to remain in bed and read her magazines.

My older sister, Nan, and I prepared most of the meals, too, because Mother hated to cook.

I did all these things to prevent a mauling and to keep her from having me committed to the state mental hospital. This was a threat she often made.

This was no idle warning. Everyone in our tiny community knew of the case where Mrs. Powers had simply picked up her phone and had asked that her husband be committed to the state mental hospital.

He was picked up that afternoon by sheriff deputies and driven to the nut house in nearby Raleigh, North Carolina. He was just as quickly released since there was nothing wrong with him. His wife simply didn't him like drinking beer and smoking cigars.

Mother threatened to do the same to me and she would see that I stayed locked up there.

Several times a week, she came up to me and said:

"If I ever hear of you doing sissy, perverted stuff with any boy in town," she threatened, "I'll call up the sheriff's office without blinking an eye."

The boys in school certainly wanted to discover if I would "do it." At first, their sexual propositions came everyday. They wanted to show off their manhood and describe to me what fun we'd have in their Daddy's pickup trucks.

Some of these guys were hot looking in their skin-tight denims. In the hallways, they'd grab themselves and outline their tool boxes for me while making panting noises like, "Hey, come' ere and get it, Miss Jason!…I got a fuckin' foot of love for you, Miss Sissy."

My desire to take them up on their sexual invitations was powerful and I'd become dizzy. I knew they would most definitely let me swing on their equipment—but I also knew the real danger of its aftermath.

They were testing me, attempting to be the first to spread the news that the Town Sissy really did suck cock. And then my life really would be in danger as the tougher bullies decided it was time to give me my punishment.

Because no one could prove that I gave blowjobs, they finally decided I was an asexual freak. They came to tolerate me but they avoided me. I was the town queer, the town sissy, and the boy-girl mistake.

Later, one of these persistent admirers admitted that if I had taken any of them up on their sexual offers, they would have let me have my fun—and then they and their buddies would have dragged me out into the woods, gang raped me and then drowned me.

This had happened several times to male misfits, especially sissies, in that community over the decades. Nothing was ever done to the killers. That's because the sheriff was among the gang of murderers.

Not only did this knowledge safely prevent me from taking up these louts on their propositions, but also I knew full well how unstable my mother was.

If she heard even the hint of gossip that had me having some fun with the boys in their pick-up trucks, then her rage could destroy everything around her.

While I had resisted temptation so far, I felt like I would explode from sexual desire.

If I could just get Dick alone, then maybe I could do the things to him that Dale had taught me to do to him.

Since 1945, my first lover became an obsession of mythic proportions.

I drew pictures of him and spent much time sketching images of Dale's column of power.

By now, I discovered that I was becoming like him in some ways. My body was changing and my "wee wee" was also developing this terrifying habit of becoming rigid.

But I was a woman. A female was not supposed to be developing like this.

Dale had certainly sensed this even when I was five.

His whispers haunted me: "You're the most beautiful little girl I've ever seen…all the big boys want to do things with you…you make us all so hard…if they only knew I've got you in my arms right now…we made bets as to who would get your cherry first…and I did!"

Had he really said that? I had dramatized and re-imagined my time with him so many thousands of time that I couldn't be sure any longer what his real words were.

Every time I saw a halfway decent adult male, I would superimpose images of Dale on him. He revealed to me what every man had hidden in his britches. If they would only let me put my hands and mouth on it, they would be so happy!

Outside, the August sun baked everything beneath it.

Our new neighbor gleamed like he had just jiggled out of a shower.

Dick paused in his mowing. He took a few steps to his small, back porch and guzzled water from a pitcher. This simple movement caused the muscles of his gleaming torso to interlock.

Then he bent over to remove a large rock from the ground. In doing so, his briefs stretched over his buttocks, revealing a perfectly round derriere.

I could see the darkness of the sweaty cleft, which sucked in the thin fabric. When he resumed mowing, he reached down and pulled at his crotch.

My house was empty that morning in August, 1956.

Mother and Daddy had both gone to the mountains for the whole day. Daddy was a traveling salesman and often took Mother with him if it was only a day trip. She liked shopping and going to a movie and getting out of this hick town.

I was ordered to stay home and clean up the house. My two older sisters were visiting friends.

I did that quickly. I had nothing else to do. There were no summer jobs to be had. None of the kids would have anything to do with me.

I liked some of the girls at school and we talked about Elvis Presley and movie stars. But they all lived out in the country.

Some of the men in town were definitely interested in knowing me much better. Already I was attracted to the "Daddy" type. When I went to the local drugstore down the block, I'd check it for the latest comic books and order me a limeade.

The owner, a beefy man with hot, dark eyes, named Ralph would talk to me. So did the handsome instructor of health and phys Ed at school. Eddie was a husky looking coach, as well, for our girl and boy basketball team.

But later I realized why they never did more than flirt with their eyes and mouths. They could end up in the pen if they had sex with an underage kid. I was still only 15.

Also, if they had sex with another male, no matter the age, the scandal could ruin them. And everyone in that rural community had heard of the blonde-haired "sissy...queer...freak..."

I was pointed out to others when I walked down Main Street. While parents sat in cars waiting to pick up their kids, I'd hear someone say: "That's him. Or it! Look at how sissy he is! Lord, he looks like a little girl!"

My mother encouraged this brutal atmosphere. When friends visited her and I was nearby, she discussed me like I wasn't even there.

"I don't know what we're going to do it with It. Or Her. Jason won't play ball with the boys; he won't act like a real boy. I could put a dress on him and he'd pass for a little girl."

My own bedroom that day was so hot I felt dizzy. Mother wouldn't let me use a fan. She said only sissies used fans although she and my father had a big one in their bedroom.

From the closet, I pulled out an old cloth sack. I emptied it on my bed.

A sharp knife, a screwdriver and a column of wood lay there.

I was going to use one of these items to murder my mother. I knew I was going to do it one day and I had fantasized her last moments.

I caressed the handle of the knife and gripped the tool and hard wood. How solid they felt. I wanted to experience one of them sinking into my horrible Mother's throat or back.

Maybe I'd do it while she napped. Or, I might sneak up on her while she ate supper and just when she put a mouthful of green peas into her mouth, I'd jam the screwdriver into her throat.

I smiled at the image. No feelings of tenderness or love touched me when I thought of her. She was a human monster that I wanted to destroy.

I put these potential weapons back in their bag and hid them beneath a pile of old sweaters.

Now, it was time to really live. I couldn't resist it anymore.

Quickly, I put on some pink shorts and a blue jersey and took a pitcher of lemonade and some Nancy Drew books out into our backyard.

Dick Grubb couldn't help but notice me.

His backyard merged into ours with only a narrow driveway separating the two.

I dragged my lounge chair into the shade of a crepe myrtle bush. As I settled in, Dick glanced up, saw me and lifted a hand. I waved back.

As I pretended to concentrate on my favorite Nancy Drew mystery, *The Password to Larkspur Lane,* I suddenly noticed that our sexy neighbor had cut off the mower.

He picked up a grass cutter and slung it over some weeds. He had moved closer.

Then, he dropped it, turned, stretched his arms and came over to me.

My breathing increased at a breathless pace.

"Hey, there, Jason!" he grinned. "Kinda hot to be out here reading."

"It's worse indoors," I said. "You want some cold lemonade? I've made a lot."

"Wow, that'd sure be great!"

I had brought an extra glass just for this occasion. I poured him a big tumbler full and he held it to his full lips and guzzled it down. He had squatted down, resting on the balls of his feet.

He was so overpowering I nearly cringed. Close-up, sweat dripped from his face, over his stiff nipples. His flat stomach gleamed with wetness. The blue shadow of an American flag decorated his right forearm. I smelt his clean sweat, the cut grass that clung to his feet, the whiff of gasoline from his mower.

I briefly glimpsed that bulging area between his thighs. If I could just bury my face in that sacred area like Dale had taught me...

"What'cha reading?"

I handed him one of my Nancy Drews. His hands were so damned big. They held the book like it was a cookie.

"Pretty good book, uh?" he said and handed it back. "I don't have much time to read. I like to be doing stuff."

He stood up and swung his upper torso from left to right.

"I like to exercise and work out," he smiled. "Looka that? Ever see one that big?"

He had made his bicep bulge to the size of a soft ball. He leaned down so I could rub it.

"Wow!" I whistled. "That is sure big. You've got big muscles all over?"

"You think so, eh? Look at this."

He forced his pectorals to bulge out and his shoulders to tighten. His stomach sunk in.

"This is my prize winning pose," he grinned, relaxing now. "I got second runner up in the Mr. Myrtle Beach contest."

"Gee, you're kidding me? You look like that Charles Atlas ad in the back of magazines."

"I met him once," he grinned and I saw that missing tooth on the side of his mouth. But this made him look even cuter. Like a rough, gorgeous bulldog.

He stepped closer. Since I was sitting down, his crotch was just a few feet away from my face. Dick pointed to his stomach.

"Charles Atlas was at Myrtle Beach last summer when I was competing. He was a judge. He told me I needed to work on my stomach. See? I can make it dance. Feel of it."

I ran my hand over that warm, smooth surface and he caused his stomach to dance.

"Now hit it hard!" he commanded proudly. "Go on. Double up your fist. Pound it."

His hips were so close, the bulge in his briefs so prominent, I could sniff his sweaty crotch. I thought of Dale! This guy smelt just like him! This sensation was so overpowering I felt dizzy.

I obeyed and he giggled.

"That warn't no punch. A grown man could wallop me in the stomach and it'd break his fist."

"I would have voted you first place, Dick. You're the biggest guy in Carson City."

"You think so?" he said seriously. "My wife tells me that. This is a dead end place. Nothing to do. I'll bet you think so, too."

"You said it. I want to move to New York City or Hollywood and have some fun."

"You wouldn't stand out there like you do here," he said quietly. "I know some of the guys call you names. In those big cities, they wouldn't. You could even have some fun in those places."

He raised a brow and winked.

He knew! This was his way of conveying to me: I know what's going on in your mind and it doesn't bother me.

I managed to croak: "As soon as I get my high school diploma, I'm outta here."

"Way to go!" he laughed. "Well, I gotta finish trimming the backyard. I'll see ya later."

He started to turn away. No, no, I couldn't let him go like this!

"Do-do you have any pictures of your winning the Mr. Myrtle Beach contest?"

"Yeah, yeah, I sure do," he said with a smile. "I'll see if I can find'em and I'll show'em to you."

"Hurry up!" I said. "I'd love to see them."

"Maybe tomorrow."

He went indoors as I did. My face felt warm and good. I closed my eyes tight and giggled.

I had finally made contact with my Greek God. The vibes were unmistakable.

◆   ◆   ◆

That night, I read in my favorite books of erotica. They weren't the graphic stuff you read these days. These were from the old classics that we had in our own house. Balzac's *Nana* was one of my favorites. In this classic, the heroine, Nana, is a prostitute who appears totally nude on a French stage during the late nineteenth century.

I loved the idea of being a woman and coming out on stage totally naked.

Men would crowd around me and caress me and offer me their lollipops. I'd let them fondle my large breasts, that valley between my thighs—I'd let them do that in full sight of everyone.

Another spicy book was the unexpurgated *Arabian Nights* where handsome men thought nothing of going around in the nude while in public!

Nudity thrilled me. I remembered how Dale had lain there naked on his bed. He didn't apologize or try to cover up. He was proud of his body and wanted me to see him with no clothes.

And those incidents at the beach where Dale and his buddies yanked down the shorts of the others. It didn't bother them. They snickered and blushed but it was like they got a kick out of being exposed in front of others.

My father still enjoyed playing his bare ass routine with me when nobody else was home.

If I were there, he'd make a point of emerging from the bathtub without a stitch on.

Saying nothing, he would rub himself sensually just a few feet away. He dried off his boyish butt first and then his male things so that they would be fully aroused by the time he entered his bedroom and closed the door.

Neither he nor I said anything. I knew that if I tried reaching for him, he would brutally reject me. I knew he knew this which is why I hated him with nearly the same intensity I hated my mother.

My father knew what I was. He delighted in torturing me. The Gutless Marshmallow. This is the name I came up for him. He was just a beautiful shell of man. There was nothing within except goopy air and emptiness.

I couldn't enjoy exploring myself in my room. Mother made sure the lock didn't work. She enjoyed barging in unexpectedly, as if she hoped to find me doing something perverted.

I couldn't even imagine wearing just a bathing suit in my backyard. Since I considered myself a woman, I knew I shouldn't show off my bare chest. A woman did not expose her breasts!

Dick's near nudity thrilled me! It didn't appear to bother him that people saw his exposed chest, legs and nearly everything else in that thin little pair of bathing trunks.

While I prepared supper that evening, I thought of nothing but my new sexual obsession. I imagined myself on his bed and him pushing down his briefs and joining me.

Then, I would show him all the little sexual tricks that Dale had taught me.

Those hours with the long lost Dale haunted my memory. What was he doing now? Had there been others? How could I let the older men in town know I wanted to have fun with them?

I wish I could find some way of doing it without my mother finding out. But I knew nothing of conveying my desires.

◆   ◆   ◆

A week passed and during that times my parents and the Grubbs next door became better acquainted.

Daddy got out the charcoal grill and Mother invited our new neighbors to join us for hamburgers and watermelon.

While my two sisters and I brought out the potato salad and the deviled eggs that we had made, Daddy was talking to my dream lover.

I watched them compare their biceps, their stomachs and to my delight, Dick stripped off his tee shirt to demonstrate how he could make his pecs dance.

"Put your shirt on now Dick!" giggled his fat cow of a wife. She wore shorts and a white tee shirt that made her resemble a dumpling. Her long hair was pulled back into a greasy rope of matted hair. She smoked nonstop and sipped beer that she and Dick had brought over.

Dick regaled us with his adventures in the Navy and competing with Charles Atlas in physique contests.

My Father actually became animated as he and his new found buddy discussed physical training. They both stood on their hands and walked around. Then Dick had my father put his bare feet into his hands and raised him into the air.

My father did the same. Together, they were two beautifully proportioned males but my eyes were fixated on the fascinating, ravishing Dick Grubb.

Then, to my joy, Dick did the same to my two sisters and me. He had us each to put our bare feet into his hands and he held us aloft while we laughed and gasped. When he dropped us, we had to grab his neck.

Oh, what a feeling that was! That powerful, warm neck and all the strength it contained!

Later, I heard my Mother screeching at my Father for "making a spectacle out of yourself. That's perverted stuff. You and that man acting like a bunch of fools."

Then she turned her wrath on me. "And you—crying out like a girl! I saw you put your arm around that man's neck! I know what's going through your mind!"

"Do you?" I suddenly blurted. "You're just pissed because he didn't ask you!"

She and my father and my two sisters became suddenly still. Rarely had I fought back but the words just shot out.

"What did you say?"

"I saw you watching us and looking at Dick Grubb!" I yelled. "If he'd asked you, I'll bet you would have jumped at the chance!"

"Why you goddamned queer!" she screamed and lunged for me.

I dashed out the backdoor. It was dark and hot and my face was flushed. My pulse pounded because I had finally lashed back at the Monster.

Let her call the nut house. I was sick of everything I did being perverted by her and distorted through her sick mind.

I could hear her voice rising into a shrill screech as she screamed at my father and my sisters.

Suddenly, I noticed a slit of gold light in a window next door.

That must be the bedroom of my Roman God. The window was low to the ground.

I crept closer. A large bush grew in front of it. Closer I moved. The blanket that covered the window left several inches bare at the right hand corner.

I stooped down behind the bush. No one could see me from our house. I saw movements. A bed creaked. I sniffed cigarette smoke.

"Where's my beer?" Chrissie said. "You'd better not have drunk it all up!"

"Oh, shut up. Here's your damn beer. You drink so fuckin' much. Where's the 'maters?"

Maters? He used the term everyone in town did for tomatoes.

"I got'em right here and I'm gonna really use'em tonight. Oink! Oink!" Why was she making pig noises? Then she gibbered: "Slobber, slobber, mmmmm-good!"

"Rub my back. It's sore from all that lifting tonight."

"You made a big hit with those weirdoes. That Mr. Fury's got the hots for you."

"Yeah, that's what I think."

Mr. Fury? That was my father! I was amazed at the thought that my own father would be attracted to the handsome Dick Grubb as much as myself!

"I'm surprised he didn't pull your britches down and do you right there."

"I—"

I didn't hear the rest. The backdoor of my home had opened and closed. My older sister had come out to tell me that the coast was clear. Mother had taken her sleeping pill and was in bed.

I was happy to hear that but still shocked at what Dick and his wife had mentioned about my Father. It never entered my mind then that a married man with children could still be attracted to other men.

The next morning, my mother approached me from behind and yanked me around.

"You homo!" she screamed. "You queer!"

She slapped me hard across the face.

My sisters had already gone out for the day to visit friends while my father sat sipping his coffee and reading the morning papers.

Only this time I didn't cower and try to escape. I picked up a platter of scrambled eggs and threw them at her.

"Look at what he did!" screamed my mother. "He tried to attack me! Wally, do something!"

My father glanced up from his newspaper.

"Now, let's try to get along. Let's quiet down."

I grabbed a handful of silverware and threw them at her. She recoiled and made a threatening motion with her broom.

"I'm not going to stand this anymore!" she blubbered. "I'm calling up the state mental hospital right now. I'm calling them up—"

"—And I'll tell them how you've beat me up like a punching bag, Mother. I'll show them this scar over here on my foot—where you dumped boiling water on me that time? Remember? And all the times you beat me until my nose bled. They'd like to hear that!"

"That's all a damned lie!" she wailed. Her face curdled as she tried to figure out whether to cry or to scream. "You're a sick pervert! Everybody knows you are!"

"Yeah, thanks to you! You run around town telling everybody what a pervert I am! I think I'll call up the state mental hospital to come and pack you up!"

I ran to the telephone and picked it up.

She shouted: "Don't you dare! Don't you even think of it!"

I dropped the receiver and shoved the screen door open and went outside. Things were changing for me. A small flame flickered within me now. It was like a voice whispered: "You've only got two more years and then you'll be free. Just bide your time—and try to stay calm."

As if someone above was listening, that very afternoon, Mother had to travel to nearby Thomasville. One of her brothers was nearly killed in a car crash. My sisters visited friends and my father had left for work.

I put on a pair of white shorts and a black and white shirt.

Armed with a pitcher of lemonade and movie magazines, I took up my position beneath the shade of a large Mimosa Tree.

It was shortly after noon and the temperatures had zoomed past 100.

A door opened and closed.

My heart jumped. Stepping out of his backdoor was my Dream God.

He looked so much like a movie star in his brief, navy shorts, that I became breathless.

He saw me and raised a hand: "Hey, Jason. Pretty hot today, eh?"

"Yeah, sure is."

Why couldn t I think of something more clever? I smiled and sipped my lemonade and pretended to read my book. Maybe I should get up and go over there.

I arranged myself in a movie star pose. Reclining on my side, one leg was drawn slightly up to my waist.

He took a hoe and started digging up roots of weeds in his backyard. His body rippled with each movement of the hoe.

Then after a few minutes of this, he went to his barbells. He studied them and then I saw him coming towards me.

"You read too much!" he grinned. "Don't you get tired of reading? Wanna watch me work out? Maybe I could show you a few tricks and you can build yourself up. Like me! Feel of that?"

He bunched his bicep up and leaned down. I squeezed it with my hand.

"Wow, it feels like a rock. Is your other arm just as hard?"

"I sure hope it is. Here, feel of it."

He thrust his other arm closer and let me feel of his other bicep.

"It's so hard."

I felt dizzy. It was finally coming true. I was touching the bare flesh of my dream god. His muscles that I had dreamed about were just inches away from me.

Sweat already glistened on his tanned skin. His nipples were so thick and prominent that I could barely resist sucking on them. He rubbed them absently as he grinned down at me.

"You have to keep working at it to keep it hard. Come on. I'll show you."

"You want some lemonade before we start."

"Sure. That'd be nice."

"Just drink it from pitcher. I don't want anymore."

He took the pitcher with the hand painted carnations on it and held the rim to his mouth. His lips looked so pink and hungry as he gulped down the beverage.

"Mmmmmm! That was good. You make it?"

"Oh, sure. I know how to cook and make iced tea and lemonade."

"You'd make some guy a good wife!"

He winked and laughed.

"I'm just waiting for the right man to come along."

There. I'd actually said it. I let him know how I thought. He laughed softly and raised his brow.

"Maybe it'll happen one day. Come on."

Walking behind him, I glimpsed the top of his jock strap hugging his right hip above the waistband of his briefs. He's nearly naked. It would take no time to for him to pause, slip his fingers beneath the waistband and strip off that thin little pair of shorts.

Then, he would be completely bare assed. His buttocks moved from side-to-side like they were bowling balls, held together by that dark cleft.

He picked up a heavy weight and raised it several times.

When he finished, he gasped and pretended to pound his chest.

"Me, Tarzan! What'd ya think? You ever see a chest as big as mine? Feel of it!"

I ran hands eagerly over the enormous pillows and rubbed his nipples. I expected him to jump back and object—like my father did. But he continued to grin and let me caress his pectorals for a long time.

"You like those?" he said softly. "I can tell you do. Women always want to rub my tits. They want to rub other things, too."

He giggled and his dark eyes flashed. He began breathing harder.

"Let's see if you can raise this weight."

"Oh, no. It looked pretty heavy for you. I know I couldn't raise it."

"No, no, now give it a chance. You can't just read all the time. I'll help you. Put your hands around the rod."

I stooped down and grabbed the iron column. He stood directly behind me. Then his body pressed against mine as he also grasped the steel bar.

"Okay, now. Raise it up. I've got it, I've got it."

I was too startled to realize what I was doing. His wet body was pressed against mine from behind as he helped me raise and lower it. His hips squeezed against mine. His chest rubbed against my back. I could even feel his stiff nipples caressing my back.

Then he instructed me to leave the weight on the ground.

"Come on inside for a sec. I'll show you some pictures of me at the competitions that I don't usually show other people. Eh, your Mama's not home, is she?"

"No, no! That bitch is in Thomasville for a few days. I hope she dies there."

Dick threw his head back and laughed. "Oh, my God! You're too much, Jason. My wife and I noticed how your Mama acts towards you. She acts a little bit—uh—crazy?"

"Worse than that. She thinks I'm the crazy one."

He chuckled again. At last, I was in his own cocoon.

His kitchen was dull and nearly bare. A trashcan brimmed over with beer and soup cans. Cockroaches raced around on the floor.

In his small den, it was nearly as empty. An old sofa was draped with a pink bedspread.

"We don't use this room much," he explained. "We never have any company. Here, sit down here beside me."

We both sat down on the sofa. He was not more than two inches away. I smelt his sweaty flesh and felt the heat from his body.

He lifted a heavy scrapbook from the coffee table. He opened it to reveal countless color photographs of him in physique contests. Glistening with oil, clad only in black tights, sometimes white, he posed either grinning or scowling at the camera in muscle man poses.

"You look better now," I said. "A lot bigger than in those pictures."

"You think so?" he asked, grinning. "Hey, that's nice to hear. Now here's some photos I don't usually show to just anybody. See?"

He picked up another narrow album and flipped open the plastic pages.

I was amazed to see him wearing just a black cup over his privates as he posed for the photographer.

"I'm naked here—except for that stupid little posing cup. The photographer takes pictures of Charles Atlas and all the other big time body builders. I told him I didn't want anything to cover me. But he said I need this thing over my pecker or he might be arrested for taking dirty pictures."

In the striking color photos, dramatic lighting set off his impressive physique. His posing strap merely whetted one's appetite to gobble up this Greek god.

"It—it didn't bother you to pose like this?" I stammered. "Nearly naked?"

"Hell no. That's why I work out. To look good to everybody. To show all the gals what I've got. When I show some of them these pictures, they want to know what I've got hidden behind that black posing strap. Ha!"

"You look just like Charles Atlas!"

"Hey, you think so? That's really nice to hear!"

He stood up and stretched, so that muscles all writhed together in a spellbounding display of male beauty.

"You know what, I'm burning up. If you don't mind, I'm taking my shorts off and I'll show you some more of my poses."

Staring at me intently, he slipped his fingers beneath the waist of his briefs and peeled them down.

Only a white supporter hid his equipment. But this was even more exciting to me. I knew that beneath that thin strap, nestled the type of toys that Dale had revealed to me.

He turned around. His ass was completely exposed. He playfully made his buttocks dance. And I saw that dark cleft that Dale had introduced me to. I could clearly see myself burying my face in there and rediscovering heaven again.

"You should have worn that in your competitions instead of a bathing suit," I blurted.

He giggled. "Yeah, that would have brought the house down, wouldn't it? Everybody says my butt is my best feature. What do you think?"

He stuck it out slightly, in my direction. I couldn't resist sliding my hands along its white, smooth surface.

"It really is a knockout."

I could hardly talk. I had never thought my fantasy would come true, of getting close to this glorious Hercules.

"Stay there," he said softly. "I'll show you something."

He went into the kitchen and came back with two large tomatoes. He sat down on the sofa again, this time turned towards me. Then he put his fingers beneath the waistband of his supporter and peeled it off.

I was stunned to see his dark manhood flow out. Moist, glistening, heat had made his equipment loose and aromatic.

He pulled at his impressive phallus and did the same to his groin. His testicles were enormous. They bulged against the delicate skin of his sac like two softballs.

I watched him arrange a dark towel beneath his male package.

Beneath these twin beauties, he placed the tomatoes.

"See?" he whispered, smiling strangely. "My balls are as big as these tomatoes! My wife—she loves tomatoes. Sometimes I'll put two of them beneath my balls, and make her use her mouth to get to them."

I could say nothing. My eyes were fastened on this bizarre sight—of two luscious globes of pinkness resting on twin balls of crimson.

Flowing over this mass of luscious rose was his impressive phallus. It could have been a water hose painted ivory. The oval tip had slid out of its fleshy covering and touched the sofa cushion.

He talked rapidly, in a whisper, about how his wife was a sex addict and that she went absolutely, totally crazy over this game.

Dick said she made pig like sounds and she pretended to be that animal as she rooted her face around until she had consumed the vegetables and then lashed her tongue over his flesh.

"I have to constantly warn her to be careful," he grinned, "because she gets so carried away! She keeps on groveling and snorting and gobbling on my balls like she's really eating those durn tomatoes! Ha, ha, that's what makes it so damn fun! She tells me she could gobble up my balls so easily, like she was eating steak!"

He said she sometimes cried hysterically when he withheld his goodies from her. It was all a game, see? And when he eventually rewarded her efforts, she again went so crazy he had to grab her head and bring her under control.

"Woo!' he gasped, grinning bigger. "You oughta see this gal go absolutely ape shit over my balls and my cock! She don't like me to fuck her pussy. She just wants to gobble me. That's all she ever wants."

I listened, dizzy and intoxicated with this idea that there were others in the world who thought of completely uninhibited sex where you made noises and snorted and cried.

"You wanna try and get these 'maters with your mouth?" he asked quietly. "I've seen you looking at me like you want to swallow me alive. You stare at my box all the time and I thought to myself: I'll bet he knows how to handle a cock and balls like mine. Ain't that true, Jason? Huh? Ain't that true?"

"Yeah," I whispered. "You're right. I want to do it really bad."

Even now I remember the syrupy heat that coated everything in that that dull, dark room. No breezes entered the cracked window. No fans or air-conditioner cooled the air.

Dick gleamed all wet and golden and gleaming like a movie god whose suddenly jumped off the screen and wandered into that dull, nothing little room.

He sat with his arms stretched out along the back of the sofa. His powerful thighs were parted. Nestled there between them was a pink and ivory mass of flesh and muscle.

He glanced down proudly and then stared at me.

"Go ahead. I won't tell nobody. Everybody's gone for the day. My wife won't be home until four this afternoon. Your parents are gone. We're here all alone. Nobody will bother us. You can have as much fun as you want. I'm used to it. Lotta guys and girls have had fun with ole Dick's equipment. Let's see what you can do. Get closer."

He had placed a washed out blue towel beneath him.

I edged closer and felt his blazing body heat. Sweat sparkled on his skin. It dripped from his thick nipples, down to this rippled stomach and slid lower between his thighs.

I lowered my head and started to lick his testicles—but he quickly covered them with his hand.

"Get those 'maters first. Grab'em with your mouth."

The tomatoes he chose were over ripe and red and soft.

I bit into the left tomato and brought it out from beneath his groin. Then I went back for the second one. Each time I tried to lick his groin but his hand securely covered it.

Dizziness made me nearly faint, for on either side of my face raised those muscular thighs—arranged to let me slack my lust on the treasure they enclosed.

I didn't care how I looked or how I sounded. I sank my teeth into the mushy vegetables, swallowed the pulp, all the time fantasizing that these were Dick's balls I feasted upon.

Now and then he made sounds like a pig, "Oink! Oink!…uh huh. Uh huh. You're getting there, little piggy."

I glanced up once and saw his mouth parted in a big grin. His missing tooth gave him a sinister quality: this perfect body, like something out of a magazine muscle ad, and that thin-lipped grimace.

After I gnawed the vegetables into red pulp, I licked the back of his sticky hands that gleamed pink and wet.

I tried to use my face to remove his hands that guarded the ultimate treasure but they remained clasped firmly over his manly jewels.

His thighs tightened so that my face was caught in a narrow space but I loved it. I smelt him, felt his body heat and aroma and felt protected by this young giant.

His fingers would playfully part just a little, so I could dart my tongue between but I could never reach his prized possession. I could glimpse the moist surface of that object which I sought and which he protected so zealously.

My hands slid over his thigh and down over his to forcefully move them—but Dick suddenly stood up.

"Hey, I just forgot, Chrissie's getting home earlier than usual today. I'd better get dressed. You'd better get on home before she gets here."

"What-what—? I thought we were going—?"

"We'll get together again. Aw, I'm sorry. I know you really wanted to get it on. I could tell. Guys have offered me lots of money to just lick me. I could be living in a penthouse somewhere. Guys watched me at these physique contests and they came back stage and they offered me a fortune. But I clean forgot about Chrissie getting home early today."

I felt like he had literally slapped me. I stood up unsteadily. I swayed and I remember my mouth hanging open in shock.

I wanted to scream and say a lot. He had changed completely. He used the old towel beneath him to wipe away the sticky pinkness left from the gutted vegetables.

Quickly, he pulled on his jock strap, his briefs in brisk motions and wadded up the messy, glistening towel.

He glanced at me and gave me a cool smile.

"You'd better be going on," he said flatly. "I've got to dress for work. You'd better wipe your face off. Looks like you've been busted up in a car wreck."

He threw me the sticky towel he had sat on. I wiped my face clean of tomato pulp. I could smell his maleness most intently now.

"You missed a spot right there," he grinned, as if we had played a game and he won. I touched a spot on my chin with the dirty cloth and threw it at him.

"You played a trick on me," I blurted. "You were just playing with me."

"Aw, come on now," he smirked. He couldn't restrain his mouth from quivering and then he burst into laughter. "I wasn't making fun of you. Now, you'd better get on. I'll see's ya."

What happened? Had I done something that made him hate me? Mother told me most people hated me because I was a sissy. I thought it was mostly the school kids.

I thought: The adults hate me, too. I'm not a human. I'm a freaky thing.

My breathing had become faster and I stayed there, staring at him, my mouth working. I wanted to scream and kill this muscle-headed slob!

With him studying me with a pitying smile, I turned around and returned to my house and washed my face at the sink. I studied my reflection in the mirror. I was beautiful. My hair was as naturally gold as Marilyn Monroe's. Eyes stared back at me that were striking in their rich brown and long lashes.

Even a teacher one day had complimented me on my eyes after we had school pictures made and I showed her mine.

"You're such a beautiful boy, Jason. I wish I had your eyes."

One of the thugs overheard her and the favorite taunt became: "Ohhh, Jason, we just love those beautiful, girly eyes! Wooooo! Will you kiss me?"

None of that had done me any good. If Dick Grubb wouldn't give me his body, then nobody would. It was such perfect time and place. We were alone and I could tell he was aroused.

My shock turned to rage, though. It was a trick. He had created this little game and he knew exactly what he was doing. He had gotten his kicks from seeing me literally pant for his body.

And then I wondered if my Mother had put him up to this? As a test. To see what I would do. I wouldn't put this past her. She was obsessed with punishing me for proving a disgrace of a son to her.

My theory was strengthened when Mother suddenly returned from Thomasville that night.

Her relative had miraculously not been seriously injured.

While I put supper on the table, she came up to me and slapped a Life magazine article in front of me. The photo showed a group of white bigots from the 40s as they surrounded the corpse of a black man. They had lynched him. His neck lay at a grotesque angle on his shoulder. His clothes were ripped off and the men had set fire to them.

The article went on to say that incidents like these still occurred in the Deep South.

All those grinning, pig-like white men, whooping and laughing at their triumph over the undesired.

"That's going to happen to you one day if you don't shape up," she said tersely. "They do this to queers, too."

I stared up into those black, glittering eyes. Hate and lunacy made them burn like the eyes of a Cobra.

"Will you head the mob, Mama?" I asked. "You'd like that wouldn't you? What if I turned the mob on you? Would you like that? I hear that even bigots don't like child beaters and killers."

Her black eyes gleamed even more dangerously.

"I hate to think of how you're going to end up," she muttered, studying me.

"A lot better than you!" I shot back.

Her mouth fell open. Her eyes widened in shock.

"What—what are you saying? I've always been a good mother!"

"To who? Not to me. You look just like the men in this picture. You've got the same expression. I can see you at the head of a lynch mob!"

Her mouth worked to form words and then she spat: "I'm calling up the state mental hospital. I'm calling them tomorrow morning."

"Great! When you do, I'll tell them to bring another straitjacket for you."

Quickly I escaped through the backdoor and sat down on the backyard lounge chair. Things were changing for me. I shook from all that was going on but that sudden burst of warmth within I had experienced earlier shot up again.

If these monsters were trying to destroy me, then I wouldn't go down without a fight. I had to find a way of getting rid of both of them: my Mother and the monster next door.

◆　　　◆　　　◆

My mother didn't carry out her threat, not because of any hurt it might bring to me but because she "didn't want people to talk," as I heard her tell one of her gabby old friends on the phone.

That took care of Monster Number One. I sensed then that she would never call up the nut house. She had her reputation to maintain. The opinion of a town full of rednecks was more important to her than the opinion of her family.

As for Monster Number Two, he acted like nothing had happened.

From my bedroom window, I'd see him come out in his swimming trunks to work in that horrible looking little yard.

Now, I knew he wasn't really working. He was just showing off his lousy body for whoever might be passing by. He'd strut around and flirt and preen and if it was a woman, then she might get lucky. For poor perverts like myself—and maybe even my father—it'd be just a miserable joke.

We had a cookout again and once more, our neighbors were invited.

I caught Chrissie staring at me, while she smoked one of her long, long Pall Mall Cigarettes. Her lumpy, white dough body was stretched out on a lounge chair. She wore shorts and a white tee shirt that exposed all that dripping fat.

She sneered and flipped her wrist. A few minutes after she did this, I passed her by with a large glass of tea. I pretended to trip and the tea splashed all over her.

"You clumsy idiot!" snarled my mother.

"Say!" sputtered the fat Chrissie. She stood up and shook the tea from her jersey and face. "Look where you going?"

"What happened?" Dick said. He looked from his sputtering wife to me.

"I tripped," I said flatly.

"How could you trip?" he demanded.

"Well, I wanted to get some more of those great tomatoes you brought over here? Remember, Mr. Grubb? Tomatoes. Mmmmmm, good. Oink, oink."

"What is he talking about?" snapped my mother.

The face of my demon boyfriend tightened. He didn't look like the usual grinning, chuckling neighbor we were used to.

I went indoors and I heard my father saying, "He didn't mean to do that. Let's get over it."

"He can act a little strange," Dick said. "He needs to get out more. Not read so much."

"That's what I tell everybody!" Mother hissed. "You can't make him budge. Stubborn as a mule."

Dick muttered: "Maybe he needs to see one of those head doctors. A psychiatrist. There's something a little wrong with him. I could tell it right off."

"You think so?" asked my mother. "I'm going to do something."

Oh, so now my muscle god had joined forces with my mother. I was on the very verge of marching outside and telling everyone what had happened next door with this monster and his tomatoes.

Something warned me to keep my cool. My mother and father would refuse to believe me. Dick could prove dangerous. Because I sensed that he and my mother were very much alike.

My intense hatred for him grew.

There had to be a way of getting revenge on him. And then I thought of something that would definitely do the trick.

In my closet was an old BB gun my father had brought me one Christmas. This was a real boy's toy. All the guys in town had BB guns. You hunted with it, you could target practice. I showed zero interest. And so my BB gun had remained in its box in my closet.

Why hadn't I thought of this before? I'd shoot the bastard in the balls! That's where I'd really hurt the prick!

Maybe I could even use it on my mother. I'd aim for her eyes—those horrible, black eyes that terrified me!

◆   ◆   ◆

On the last night of August, 1955, the time had come.

I would get my revenge on the greasy bastard next door.

I didn't care what happened anymore. I'd probably be arrested or sent to the nuthouse. At least that'd get me out of this cage. I'd be with all those rough, lusty convicts I'd read about.

Think of all the sex I'd have. And imagine the scandal that would destroy my mother?

Thus, I rationalized my lunatic plot to seek revenge.

I crept up to the big Crepe Myrtle bush that grew outside the Grubb's bedroom window. The light was on. The sheet was still sloppily secured and a space to the right allowed me to peer directly into the room.

My right hand grasped my BB gun. Dick couldn't shuttle me aside like some mental retardate or freak. And he thought he had.

Now, I caught my breath at the sight of Chrissie who waddled into the room. She wore metal curlers in her hair. Fat bulged around her white bra and nylon panties. She smoked a cigarette and had a beer in her hand.

"Hurry up, Dick!" she called out. "We ain't got all night."

She curled up on the dull, pink sheet and I thought how much she resembled a slug that crawled all over our back porch in early morning. Shapeless, white, dripping rolls of fat, Chrissie could have been the monster in a sci-fi movie.

There was nothing else in that bedroom. A cheap, wood chair in the corner was covered with old clothes. White walls held no pictures or dime store paintings. Dirty socks, silk panties and wadded bags of potato chips littered the floor.

I heard the shower faucets being turned off.

He appeared completely naked. His hands grasped a white towel that he moved over his powerful chest. He dried his tools.

His rich brown body was startling against that drab backdrop but I was relieved that I felt no more desire for him. Without the illusion of lust, I saw him as he really was.

His mouth was small and round. His thinning hair brought out the reddish tone of his tan. His upper body danced with muscles. His thighs and legs were spindly. His feet were too big and I could even see his overgrown toenails.

He looked ugly.

"Maybe I should let Miss Faggot come over here and gobble me up."

"You let that fucking homo over here and I'll kill you. You'd better not let him touch you, you understand? I coulda killed him when he threw that tea on me. I was afraid he'd start blabbing about you and that game you played on him. If he does, you're in deep shit. He's not even sixteen."

"You shoulda seen him that day I had him going—"

"I'm sick of hearing about that. Shut up already. If he told anybody, you could get the pen. There's been cases of men being sent up for playing around with jail-bait. And this kid's nutty enough to—"

"He wanted me so bad he was shaking. His mouth had fallen open."

He imitated me by letting his thin little mouth hang open.

"I said to shut the fuck up. I'm surprised you didn't let him suck you. You told me those days were over. Guys slobbering all over you. You'd better not let it happen with him. If he talks—"

"I was just about to let him have it. You know something, he really did get me hard. He's a beautiful kid. Like a girl. I'll bet he could have gobbled me good. And I'll bet if I had fucked him—"

"You sonofabitch! Now, cut it out. I'm the only one who gets your goober and balls. Don't you keep joking with me about this."

"You got the 'maters?"

"Fuck the 'maters. I'm tired of that game. Let's just do it. Let me just eat you without any games. I want it right now, Dick."

"We're playing the 'mater game. That really gets me hard. Just keep thinking of gobbling my balls and cock like you do those 'maters."

He lie on his back and spread his legs. At that moment, the emotional veil lifted even more from my vision and I saw this bastard without any teenage lust.

His face was hard and flat. An accident had broken his nose and it sloped sharply to a tip that pointed upwards. How big his nostrils were! Except for his muscles, he was like all the other rednecks I saw around town. It was easy to see why he'd never be anything more than a factory worker.

When he grinned, he halfway stuck his tongue out. Grinning made his small eyes recede so that he resembled a pig.

He placed a rubber pad on the bed and lay down on top it.

Then he positioned two large tomatoes beneath his testicles. Then he put his arms behind his head and smiled.

"Start eating'em, Miss Piggy. Oink! Oink!"

Chrissie rolled over on her fat stomach and threw her face down on the area right before his equipment. Her head bobbed up and down. Once she glanced up at Dick. Her ass looked like two shapeless pillows.

Tomato pulp and juice glistened in gobs on her face. Her eyes glittered with lust and then her mouth worked on her husband's equipment. She had turned into a bobbing, grunting, groveling mass of blubber.

Metal curlers glinted in the light as her head frantically jiggled, like she were lunging for apples in a barrel of water. Curds of tomato pulp flicked upon Dick's flat stomach. Her red, sticky hands grabbed both his thighs so she could bore her face down tighter into his lap.

Tomato pulp glowed on his legs now and whenever Chrissie turned her face slightly, it was like she'd been in a train wreck. Her features were coated with shimmering puddles of overripe tomatoes.

"Aw!" he gasped and raised his hips upwards. "Yeah, yeah. You're doing great, hot Mama. Eh, just a second, Chrissie—not too hard."

If possible, she became even more frenzied. I listened to her gulping and snorting and her face dug harder against her husband's equipment.

Dick sat up.

"Hey, cut it out, hon, you're too hard. Your teeth are cutting me—"

She was beyond hearing. Her hands grasped his hips and her head went sideways and moved crazily. I listened to her loud gulps and snortings.

"Stop it!" hollered Dick.

Her panting sounded like a dog. She whined and groaned as she groveled and chewed and sucked.

I nearly burst out laughing when Dick used both hands to grab her tomatoe covered face and head.

"Ouch!" he screeched. "Stop it, stop it, stop it! Oh, sweet Jesus, Dear God, what've you done? Stop it, stop it, you fucking bitch!"

He used his fist to hit her face and then used both hands to tear her head away.

She lay on her side, quivering and moaning and panting. Her face was slathered with puddles of crimson pulp. Her eyes blinked as she wiped the wetness away.

Her husband stared down at his lap. His wife's face looked like she'd been busted up from a chainsaw. Scarlet, glistening tomato matter slathered her features and her hair.

On the mushy rubber pad, more gobbets of scarlet gleamed.

"Jesus!" groaned Dick. "You—you bit my balls! Looka what you did! Jesus H. Christ! You bit my balls! You chewed them bad! Look! They're bleeding. You ruined me!"

"Aw, no, no, no, I didn't, I didn't, I was real careful, honey bunch, I couldn't have now let me—"

His lap was a red mass of tomato pulp, piled up between his legs and on him. His hands moved carefully down to his manhood and he stared, with bulging eyes, at what had been done to his most precious possession.

"Awwww!" he gulped. "Oh, Jesus, God, have Mercy, what've you done, you fuckin' bitch? You—you done gone bit my balls really bad! They're—they're bleeding. Looka the blood!"

He fell back against the headboard and closed his eyes as he wailed: "Oh, Lordy, oh, Lordy you done ruined me! I tol' you to stop biting me, and you didn't! You didn't do it, you fuckin' cunt!"

"Now, Dick, now Dick," babbled his wife as she, too, stared at his glistening package of goodies. She wiped away the tomato pulp with a dirty towel very carefully. She studied something and then—

"Oh, noooo!" she hollered. "We need to go to the clinic!"

She pressed the towel up against the wound and Dick sat there like an old man, his legs spread wide, red splotches of tomato still glistening all over the bed.

He tried to stand up. He cried out and fell back hard on the bed. His spouse galloped back into the room. She had thrown on old gray shorts and a tee shirt and she handed him some clothes. Splotches of red pulp criss-crossed her face.

"You ruined me!" he sobbed. "Looka what you did, you bitch! I warned you to stop it!"

I fell back and scuttled back to my house. Both Grubbs were hollering and screeching now. She was yelping about, "Oh, God, I didn't mean to!"

"I gotta get to the clinic!"

◆   ◆   ◆

I had expected the whole town to be talking about the scandal next door.

The Grubbs kept it very quiet. Mother told someone on the phone the next morning that our next-door neighbor had an appendicitis attack overnight. It was so severe, he was transferred to High Point General Hospital, which was about thirty miles away.

So, I smiled, it wasn't just a little nip in his balls after all.

At supper that night, Mama told my father about Dick Grubb and his appendicitis. Mama had even forgotten about me because she thrived on anything unusual that happened on our block.

"Oh, Lord! I had mine out when I was sixteen. Thought I'd die."

"How do you know Dick Grubb had appendicitis?" I asked.

"Because I saw Chrissie this morning. Her husband's going to be in the clinic for awhile."

"I'll bet it wasn't appendicitis," I smiled. "I hope it was something a lot, lot worse."

"Listen to him!" screamed my mother. "Can you believe this? This freak is smiling! Smiling, I tell you! You hope it was something worse. Well, I never in my born days heard of anything."

But Dick Grubb didn't return home that week or the week after.

"It must've been something serious," Mother explained. "Complications set in."

"Ha!" I snorted. "Appendicitis? I don't think so."

"What're you talking about?" snapped Mother. "You think you know everything, don't you."

I went with my parents and sister and one of our woman neighbors to the hospital in High Point that weekend.

Mother had baked cookies as a gift. When she had asked me to make them, I told her: "He doesn't need cookies. I'm not making him anything."

"And after him being so nice to you!"

Nice to me? I looked at her and thought: what a stupid bitch you are? You don't know nothing about anything. But I kept quiet and decided that I'd like to see this monster all weak and sick in a hospital bed.

I remember entering his hospital room.

Dick Grubb lay pale and haggard on the bed.

He greeted us, along with Chrissie, his wife, and several of his co-workers from the factory. They all looked like rednecks, I thought, including the patient. The women chomped on gum. The men, with bellies plopping over the belts beneath their flannel shirts sipped coffee.

Chrissie was white-faced and looked like a pig about to be slaughtered. No make-up marred that pulpy, pale face. Her thick lips were gray and ragged where she had chewed on them. Her hair was again in metal curlers.

Her jaws moved up and down on her pink wad of Juicy-Fruit.

"It's real nice of you folks to come by," she said wetly. In a mournful voice, she explained solemnly that an infection had set in and that it had spread. But the doctors were confident it could be treated.

"I ain't used to just laying on my butt and not doing anything," the pale patient grinned to his visitors. "I'm used to doing stuff. Lifting weights. Eating anything I want."

When he grinned, that missing tooth made his gaunt face resemble a skull.

He looked over at me as I stood by the door.

"Well, here's little Jason, too, to cheer me up."

I said nothing. I looked at him and wondered what I had ever seen ravishing about this animal? He had lost weight. That rich copper tan was washed out.

Eyes had sunk into his head and dark circles formed beneath his eyes. He looked nothing like the dazzling Adonis who had viciously tricked me that hot afternoon. Instead of smug conceit, his brown eyes glinted with an expression of fear.

I glanced down at his lap. A white sheet covered the lower body while pale green pajamas covered the upper torso.

"You reading anything good?" he oozed to me.

"Yeah, I am. It's about a guy who fought in a war and he got blown up by an enemy bomb. He wasn't a man anymore."

"Huh?" grunted Dick. "Wasn't a man anymore?"

"What kind of book did you read?" demanded Mama.

"What'cha mean, 'wasn't a man anymore?'" asked Chrissie sharply.

"He couldn't make babies anymore," I giggled "You might have heard of the book. *A Farewell to Arms.*"

"Lord have mercy!" wailed my mother. "I don't know what this freak reads anymore. If it's printed, he reads it."

"I think he needs a shrink!" snarled Chrissie. Her mouth hung loose, like she had swallowed something sour and pasty.

"Look at you!" I said and shrugged. "You could sure use one, too, ma'm."

I slipped away as an akward silence fell over the room. Chrissie had gulped and Dick blinked his eyes uneasily.

When the patient returned home a week later, several neighbors, including my parents, visited him and presented him and his wife with the customary casseroles and desserts.

I had watched him hobble into his ugly, green house.

Not long after that, a pickup truck parked in their front yard. All the Grubb's possessions were loaded into the back.

Dick Grubb and his wife came by our house that afternoon. They wanted to tell us they were moving back to Hogansville, Georgia. They had kinfolk there and he had a job waiting for him—selling Bibles.

My parents were all sympathetic and wished him good luck.

He had lost even more weight and his skin had the hue of old candle wax. His wife had bloated up into a shapeless turnip. Chomping gum, she said little and wore a grieving expression on her white lard face.

For once, I didn't see her hair in curlers. It hung in a thick, greasy mane on either side of her face. A small bow of yellow silk curled above her right eye, fastened by a bobby pin.

She made me think of a St. Bernard dog with her blubbery features peering out.

Dick Grubb looked down at me. He held out his hand.

"Well, Jason. I'll miss showing you how to use the barbells and weights. Ha, ha!"

I ignored his hand.

"I sure hope they have a good crop of tomatoes in Hogansville. Oink. Oink."

I turned around and walked for a long time along the old railroad tracks near our house. My mother asked me later what did I mean and how could I be so rude to the wonderful Dick Grubb and his wife.

Four months later, she got a brief note from Chrissie Grubb.

Her wonderful husband, Dick, had passed away and she just wanted us to know and to thank us for our thoughts.

When Mother told me and Daddy that I burst out laughing.

"That's just like you!" screeched my mother. "Crazy and nutty as a fruitcake! He tried so hard to be nice to you."

I enjoyed taunting her and now I sneered: "Gee, Mama, maybe there is something to that idea about Karma. We reap what we sow. I hope he's got lots of tomatoes wherever he went."

Mother looked at my father.

"What are going to do with him? He gets crazier all the time! Maybe we should send him to the mental hospital."

"I'll pack up my things tonight then," I grinned. "When they ask me how I got this way, boy, will I give them an earful! Get on the phone, Mama!"

She blinked her eyes and gasped out: "Oh, Lord, Lord, what's going to become of him! What did I do to deserve this?"

In later years, I heard that Dick Grubb had lost both testicles and blood poisoning had set in.

The house where he and his wife lived briefly still exists on Main Street. Countless tenants have come and gone over the decades. The present one has fixed it up nicely with white paint and dark green trim.

The window where I peered into that one night in 1956 now has a heavy screen and thick draperies.

Sometimes I wonder what would have happened if I had taken that BB gun and first shot my mother, and then my next door neighbor.

But then I didn't want to spend my life behind steel bars. I hoped to find a new life in college and meet new men.

I had no idea I would find my first husband.

PART II
College Days
✦
1960–65

○ ○
"Will you still love me, Tomorrow?..."

—*The Shirelles*

Chapter Three
The Husband

I knew he was a new kind of man when I first saw him that night outside the student canteen at Brevard Junior College.

Unlike the other guys back then, he wore a beaten-up black leather jacket. All the other college males in the year 1960 sported James Dean windbreakers or Pea Coats that you brought at Sears or Pennys.

I glimpsed this stranger's snug jeans cuffed above leather boots.

Thick, black hair was swept from his face. He wasn't freshly scrubbed and fair-skinned. A hint of rose touched his flesh and a five-o'clock stubble shadowed his square chin.

He had propped a foot up on a low wall outside the building and smoked a cigarette.

This pose emphasized a shapely rear-end and his cigarette and long hair also made him stand out.

All the boys at college that year of 1960 sported crew cuts and hair worn with a neat part on the side. Contact lenses were still in the planning stages. Big, box-like glasses set on the noses of many students.

This was also years before the hippy revolution changed forever the way men and women looked.

Another attention-grabbing feature of this handsome stranger was the guitar case at his feet.

Only two other guys at this small, mountain college played guitars. But they merely plucked at the strings and sang a couple of pop songs. Or worse, they tried to act like the current pop king, Elvis.

That night in early January was freezing and dark. I had just finished dancing with some of my female friends in the canteen.

The Shirelles were popular then with their hit, "Will You Still Love Me Tomorrow?" Johnny Mathis was king of the ballads with "Chances Are?" My favorite dance tunes were the Drifters singing, "Ruby, Baby," and "Steam Boat."

I had worked out cute little routines with a few of the girl students. They liked to dance with me because you rarely saw other Southern boys kicking up their heels. This was considered sissy.

I had been at Brevard for half a year and was for once, fearless.

Many students appreciated my wit, my sharp style of dressing, my artistic abilities. Except for the usual bunch of smart-ass fraternity boys, who begged me for blowjobs and flipped their wrists at me, most of the young guys were polite. Although I certainly acted and looked like a sissy—no one had proof that I might be that horrific creature known as a "homo…fag…cocksucker."

Several boys had already propositioned me. With much reluctance, I turned them down with a quiet, "Sorry, I don't do that." Like my small town, I knew that if I should ever "go down," word would spread fast over that campus. I had already heard that just the year before, two boys were expelled because they were believed to be queer.

No one could prove it. But the Dean of Admissions had kicked them out because rumors had the unlucky duo as being more than "buddies."

But this was a way of life for me. I was conditioned to always think of myself as an undesirable person who could only hope to be tolerated by others. I was to never ever consider myself to be as morally acceptable as the straight guys and gals. I could never ever have sex with a man. By doing that, I would become a horrible thing, despised by my classmates and probably expelled.

I wanted to, so very badly! No matter how hard I tried to push my sexual desires aside, I lusted after nearly every male I saw. I wanted to do it with hundreds and thousands of men!

Still, my being able to mix with the other students in this mountain school, was a sea change from how I was treated in my hometown. My mother made sure everyone in that small whistlestop knew of her disapproval of me. Now, she was 300 miles away. I had started fresh here and discovered the world wasn't as hostile as I had been conditioned to think of it.

Now, this handsome oddball attracted my attention. I pulled the collar of my new car coat closer to my ears. Nights in this mountain air were frigid.

As I approached him, I nodded and said hello.

He puffed on his cigarette and nodded at me.

"Hi! I'm Jason Fury. I haven't seen you."

"I'm Billy Dragon. I just got in this week. I'm a second semester student."

I was intrigued with everything about this man.

We made small talk but as the temperatures continued to drop, I shivered and said I had to go.

I told Billy I'd love to hear him play his songs sometimes.

"Why not now? It's only nine o'clock. We can go to my room."

My room.

The way he said it made my interest quicken. None of the boys at college had said that to me. Most were wary of being seen alone with me. If I was with a group of my gal pals, they'd come and chat.

Or, if I was in the hallway of the classroom building, they might pause briefly and we'd talk about the course and the teacher. None, though, had ever encountered anyone as flamboyant as me and who didn't cringe and try to hide in the shadows. My poor roommate was a schmuck from a small mountain town who was demoralized that he had to room with the campus weirdo. He blushed every time I said anything to him. He was terrified I might want to grab his goodies.

He even changed his clothes behind his closet door. He was hysterical that I might try to make a move on him. I heard that he constantly asked to be transferred to another room.

This lumpy looking clod with huge black-framed glasses had nothing to worry about. He was one of the few males I had not even a trace of desire for.

With Billy, I instantly felt secure. For one thing, he was bigger and more rugged than the other guys. His broad shoulders filled out his jacket.

An aura of maturity emanated from him. In no way did he resemble the fresh-faced, innocent young college kid.

So I said yes. I'd "just love" to go his room and listen to him sing.

He had a room on the top floor of the dormitory and he had already made friends with some of the older guys on his hallway. The roommate he was supposed to share with had abruptly dropped out of school because of money problems.

So he lived alone.

His few buddies were a more mature bunch, having served in the military or worked before signing up for school.

Three of them joined me as we listened to dark, bitter songs that Billy had written.

He didn't sing either pop or country music. As he strummed the strings of his instrument, he sung about hitchhiking on wintry nights, watching the sky from the window of a small trailer, or wanting to be a famous man one day.

His voice was deep, simple, with no vibrato. Sometimes he simply spoke the words.

I was enthralled. He fascinated me in everything he did. I glanced around his room. It was bare, except for his bed that was covered by a cheap flannel blanket, a calendar from a funeral home in Salisbury, North Carolina.

The doorway of his closet gaped open. A single pair of dress-up pants hung there along with a sports coat.

He had taken off his jacket and boots and sat on his bed like a Buddha. His plain white undershirt bulged with a powerful chest, shoulders and arms.

Yet, he wasn't like that monstrosity, Dick Grubbs. The more I thought about him, the more repulsive he became. Dick looked like the kind of man who spends hours building up his torso—to be admired, drooled over because he had nothing else going for him.

Billy resembled a mature man who did manual labor and who had acquired his stunning physique by nature.

When I left him, he was alone and I said I hoped to see him again. He winked, smiled strangely and closed the door.

We met again during the next few weeks: in the cafeteria, in the hallways, and often I visited him in his room.

He didn't like light. He kept his room in dramatic shadows by burning candles and a single lamp. He always wore only his jeans. I was certain he wore no underwear.

He no longer wore an undershirt. It was like he wanted me to see his upper torso in all its splendor. A light dusting of hair shadowed his chest. His pectorals were round and heavy and capped with large nipples.

Since he was half Indian, his flesh was the tawny hue of peach and apple.

He was beautiful in a natural way. When near him, his body heat was extraordinary. You didn't need a radiator to keep warm with Billy close by.

His face was strikingly proportioned with a boyish nose, deeply set eyes of dark brown and thick lashes. Amidst all that macho splendor, he did sport one feminine feature: a perfect cupid's bow of a mouth.

Red, perfectly shaped, it was an incongruous but sensual attraction. His lips were always moist.

He tantalized me by saying very little about his life. He had served four years in the Marine Corps. His father lived alone in a house on the outskirts of Charlotte, North Carolina.

When Billy finally arrived at Brevard, he was already twenty-two. He was on a scholarship. His older buddies liked and admired him. I could see that. He had a bitter way of laughing, of smirking but he had a gift for listening and drawing one out. Several of the freshmen boys often went to him with their problems.

Some of the smart-ass fraternity guys on his hallway teased me about my visits to Billy's room.

"Wooo, Jason's gonna have some hot fun with Billy tonight!"

"Jealous?" I joked back.

Or:

"We hear Billy singing you those love songs, Jason! You must be treating him good!"

"Wouldn't you like to know?"

Billy heard the joking and he just rolled his eyes or snorted.

One night, I knocked on Billy's door and he opened it, wearing just his jeans. At that moment, a group of the frat guys walked by.

"Oh, boy, Jason's got a hot date tonight!"

"Okay, you guys!" Billy said quietly. "I told you I don't like you joking with my friend here."

One of the guys, a loud-mouthed bigot from New Jersey actually blushed.

"Hey, we didn't mean anything. We did it in good nature."

"Well, I for one don't like, so cut it out."

"Sure, sure!"

He shut the door and I sat down on the other bed. I had adopted the habit of smoking, enjoying the sensation of doing something my parents had strictly forbidden me to do. Besides, I thought it made me look more dashing. I lit up a Salem. Billy always chain-smoked Lucky Strikes.

"Those guys never give up," I sighed. "They're just like the ones back in my hometown."

Billy lay down on the other bed and struck a match to his Lucky Strike.

"They gave you a hard time?"

"Oh, God, did they? They were always joking about whether or not I was boy or girl. Some of them were okay. But the majority were the pits. So, that's why I'm not surprised to hear the same old shit here."

"So? Let'em talk. If I wanted to ball with you, I'd do it. Wouldn't matter a shit to me. Because I know you want to ball with me. Right?"

Everything became still. I studied the gleaming dot of fire at the end of my cigarette. Instantly, images of Dick Grubb and that horrible afternoon when I stooped down before him, flashed into my mind. With it came that sense of danger and doom. I trembled.

"God," I stammered. "I don't know what to say—."

"I know you would. I've been around. Wanna do it now?"

Again, I was stunned at how fast—and easy—he made it. Outside his dorm door, other men shuffled up and down the corridor. He got up and locked the door.

As if he had done this before, he lit a red candle that sat on the lid of an old peanut butter jar. His strong fingers clicked off the lamp.

My breathing increased so fast my shaking worsened. I had fantasized about doing it with this sensual, handsome hunk, but I had resigned this vision into the realm of dreams. It would never happen.

But now, I was being offered a chance to ball with a man—someone I lusted after and who I sensed would never give anything away.

"Come on over here," he muttered and I joined him on his bed.

"I'm scared," I gasped. "I'm afraid to. I've had some bad experiences, Billy."

He still sat with his back propped against the wall.

"Feel me up," he said quietly. "Put your hand in my lap. Feel it? You want it?"

I couldn't speak. I nodded my head. My fingers undid the top of his jeans. He slid them off and dropped them to the floor.

And there he was at last—naked, beautiful and aroused.

He leaned over and began to kiss me. Gently at first, around my face, my eyes and then my mouth. Somehow, I got out of my clothes and we lay down together.

No one had ever kissed me before, or held me like that, nor had I tasted a man's flesh like his. Except for Dale.

From his lips to his nipples, my mouth traveled, and then over his stomach. His phallus had swollen up impressively and with both hands grasping it, I finally did what I hadn't done since those minutes alone with my teenage satyr.

In the next few hours, I used this magnificent body to slake my desires that had simmered over the past twelve years. He said nothing but occasionally groaned as my mouth and my hands used him as a lust object.

Occasionally, I would glance up and see his eyes closed, his mouth parted, and low words of exhilaration: "Ahhhh! That's it! That's it! Don't stop now! Keep doing it, don't stop!"

Even more, after he completed orgasm, he urged me to not slack, to resume my worship of his body. His phallus was a thing of wonder. Dark, flushed, never soft, I was certain it had received steady usage in its time.

Billy didn't want a gentle, timid homage paid to his maleness. He wanted an energetic reaction with much tugging and stroking and I fulfilled these requirements.

When he climaxed again, he now turned to me and used his mouth to arouse and explore. He was as passionate as I and tongued and nibbled and sucked and threw himself into the whole act as if this was his first time.

He turned over so I could worship this side of his body. So smooth, so warm and I became lost in his buttocks and in between.

I had never felt so secure and so exhilarated. I fantasized that this was Dale and Dick beneath me. I might lose all of this overnight, I thought. Enjoy it now. Something horrible will happen. It always does.

I made certain that no portion of his body wasn't tasted by me. Before I left, I lay in his arms and my hands continued to massage and pull at his manly wonder. He smoked a cigarette and enjoyed my fascination with his erection.

"That thing has traveled in a lot of trenches in its time," he muttered. "I started using it when I was nine. My Mama left me and my old man before I could remember her. Daddy and I slept together, naked as jaybirds, and he taught me a hell of a lot."

"Your own Daddy did it with you?"

"Sure. Why not? He started sucking me when I was eight and he did this every night until I went into the Marines. He'd bring his buddies from the pool hall in Charlotte and they'd suck me. He charged 'em five dollars each. He made money off my cock. So you see, my beautiful little sissy, I'm used to getting it all the time."

How much was true and fantasy? I later learned that he and his father did live in a small wood house on the outskirts of Charlotte. I also discovered his father had served time in prison and Billy may have been behind bars himself.

I left him very reluctantly a few hours later right before dawn. I met no one as I returned to my room. I couldn't sleep because I had experienced a revolutionary point in my life.

I relieved every moment of that incredible encounter.

I played visions of his nudity and his arousal feverishly in my mind.

I imagined the sensation of those moist lips of his on my mouth, on my body.

His sensual scent, the taste and feel of his warm flesh—all that pulsated in my memory all that morning and through the day.

I saw him again the next night and this was a repeat of my sexual initiation. Before I left, he whispered:

"Why don't you move in here? You'd get all the cock you'd want. Anytime of the day. You love it. So do I. Let's pretend you'd be my wife. I'd be your husband. We could be a married couple."

I was thrilled the way he portrayed this arrangement. I had dreamed of being a wife with a straight, handsome husband. I had told him that. And now, he was making this off-the-wall dream actually happen.

"Stop pretending you're this pretty little sissy who doesn't want cock," he muttered. "You're being a hypocrite. You're trying to be like all these other little redneck jerks and you're nothing like them. Be yourself! If you want to swish and wear make-up and flirt with the guys, do it. They're convinced you're queer anyway, so why pretend otherwise?"

That little speech electrified me.

I was still trying to be what my mother and all the rednecks in my hometown demanded of me. This was the way I had been brain washed. If I dared be my real self, they had warned, I'd end up in the nuthouse and taken out on a lonely dirt road, be gangbanged and thrown aside like road kill.

Who was I trying to please anyway? And what did I owe them? I'd turned down lots of guys on campus already who'd asked me to ball with them.

Although they offered me their cocks in a smart-assy, joking manner, I knew they were serious.

My answer had always been no and an expression of hurt, as if I were thinking, "Why, how could you think of me doing something like this?"

Yet, I wanted to do it with them in the worst way, especially a group of cute, hunky guys who went around together.

They were always saying, "Anytime you're ready, we are!"

Now, I packed up my things and before I left, I told my roomie: "Okay. Now, you don't have to apologize to anybody or explain that you're not a homo like me. Enjoy yourself."

And so I moved into the room of my husband that freezing weekend in January, 1960.

On our first night together as roommates, Billy insisted that we should make our love official and marry.

"What a fantastic idea!" I gasped. "How will we do it?"

"Nothing to it. Let's get naked."

We undressed. Billy lit one of our strawberry candles and placed it on the desk. We put two pillows on the floor.

He and I knelt on them. Before us he had placed on the edge of the desk a white sheet of paper.

On it, he had neatly written in thick, black ink the following words:

Billy: *"I, Billy Dragon, do take this boy/girl to be my lawfully wedded wife. I will love and protect this person. I will fuck and allow myself to be sucked by this person forever. Through sickness and in health.*

Jason: *"I, Jason Fury, do take this handsome, sexy man, Billy Dragon, to be my lawful wedded husband. I will orally and anally make myself available to his desires at all time.*

Billy: *I will play the husband role at all times. Whenever my spouse wants me to make love, I will do it completely to the best of my abilities. I accept thee, Jason Fury, from here on in, as my wife.*

Jason: *And I, Jason Fury, will respect and treat my husband like the macho, virile man that he is. I will see that he is always satisfied, both in body and in spirits. I accept Billy Dragon as my husband.*

We filled up our old coffee mugs with cheap wine that we chilled on our windowsill. He slipped the golden paper ring from a cigar on my third finger.

We kissed hungrily and it was several hours, just an hour before dawn that we finally slept.

I'm married, I thought before closing my eyes. Right next to me is my husband. How many women or men could say that on any college in America tonight?

His warm breath kissed my neck. Billy's strong, warm body was pressed firmly against me. Like a powerful wand, his manhood bulged against my rump. With his arms wrapped around me, I could see, by the rays of the moon, his strong, young hands.

They were those of a worker, of a man who has done manual labor. Beautifully shaped, they looked like this extraordinary creature I had married. Earthy, simple, strong and quiet.

I had never felt so peaceful or happy before.

◆   ◆   ◆

The men on the floor were open mouthed when they realized I now lived down the hall from them.

While the usual slobs joked and giggled and whooped, they were careful not to do it around Billy. He had already made it clear that he didn't like to listen to fag jokes.

When we closed and locked the door that first night, I symbolically locked away my old self. Never again would I try to be a hypocrite. With Billy as my husband and protector, I would never go back into the closet again.

◆   ◆   ◆

The campus was all-atwitter about us.

Brevard College was like a small town. With only six hundred students, it was only slightly larger than my hometown.

I stopped going to the canteen to dance. I wanted to spend every second with my handsome, swarthy husband. In classes, I was barely aware of what was being taught. I was busy sketching pictures in my notebooks of a naked, rampant Billy.

In our room, we both studied until about nine. Then Billy would stand up, close his books and say:

"That's that. I'm hitting the shower."

When he returned, he locked our door, dropped his towel and slid into bed next to me. He felt so warm and juicy from the shower and I can remember even tonight the way he tasted and smelt and kissed.

We said little during our strenuous lovemaking. Rarely did his phallus become limber. Even on soft, it hung heavy and thick over his hip. After I had used my mouth to bring him to his first orgasm, he got over me, pulled my legs around his waist and entered me.

He did this repeatedly each night and he whispered into my ear: "Jesus, you're better than any woman!"

A candle flickered, casting shadows to ripple on the walls. An aroma of strawberry perfumed the air, along with our cigarettes.

We took breaks and smoked and sipped from coffee mugs the cheap wine we cooled on our windowsill. My face lay on his shoulder, touching his chin and I'd look up and study his swarthy face.

He acted like a man who had done this before, to other men or women. His arm felt powerful, he appeared used to someone rubbing his big pectorals and sucking on his nipples.

My greedy fingers massaged his sexual power and that area between his scrotum and buttocks. Nothing jolted him. I loved to lick him all over—from the thick hairline, down his face, over his upper torso and then his back, between his legs where he smelt so virile and sexy.

He gave me only hints of his past—one in which he was always being pursued by men. If he hitchhiked, the driver would park on the side of the road and do him.

If he picked apples for a summer, then the farmer had Billy to come in and become his Sex Master. In the Marines, he couldn't take a leak at a movie theater or a park without the guys lined up to do him.

I know now that he fed me fantasies that I wanted to hear. I wanted my boyfriend to be a full-blooded sex machine and so he became one.

By day, we went into our normal poses. We were students who went to classes and ate meals in the cafeteria. But as the shadows grew, and night approached, I felt a tingle of intense anticipation.

I knew that within a few hours, my daytime self would vanish and I would be in the arms of the most desired and virile man on campus.

I knew my enemies gossiped about us. The frat jerks kidded me before but now that I vanished into my room at dark and didn't come out, they lobbed out bawdy suggestions:

"Wooo, Jason, you keeping your lover boy satisfied? Can we come in and make it a threesome?"

If Jimmy heard them, he ignored them. He said this was to be expected from immature rubes from the boondocks. Behind their bantering, though, I sensed that many of the guys were serious.

When I discussed this with Jimmy one night, he startled me by saying:

"Why don't you find out? Take them up on it. I'll bet you'd be amazed at how fast they'd drop their drawers."

Well! Now that I had evolved into a sexual creature, I tingled all the time. Wouldn't it be fun if I tried out another guy—and compared him to Jimmy?

"Go ahead," shrugged my husband.

There were two types of jokers. The mean, redneck type who really were trying to get under my skin. The other type was guys who I was friendly with. My sissiness didn't bother them.

One of my most persistent jokers belonged to the second group. Emerson was a lusty, beefy hunk from New Jersey. He was also an outrageous exhibitionist.

He never wore clothes around the dorm.

Whenever we encountered each other in the hallways, he would grab his privates and squeeze them hard, miming masturbation.

"Wooo, this is what you do to me, Jason? Look! You got me all hard."

And indeed, he would sport a semi-hardon and the other guys howled. When he and his buddies had a circle-jerk, sitting around naked in a circle and beating off, Emerson was the first one to ejaculate.

He did it not once but several times for his buddies. He thrilled to showing off his naked body and his equipment.

He lived four doors down the hall from Jimmy and myself. After I moved in, Emerson took to throwing his arms around me in the hallway and pulling me hard against his naked body.

"Man, I just wanna fuck you like crazy!"

One afternoon, I passed Emerson's room. His door was open and he sat at his desk, wearing nothing but his gleaming flesh. He looked up and grinned.

"Hey, Jason, I'm holding something hot for you! Looka what I got for you!"

He came up to me and held out his manhood.

"See?" he muttered. "I can't stand it. I'm hard all the time. Feel of it."

This time, instead of pushing him away, I grasped it.

"You've got one hell of a nice looking hose, Emerson."

To my surprise, he didn't recoil in disgust, or snarl: "Hey, I was just joking."

No, this hunk gasped. "Come on and play with it."

He pulled me into his room, locked his door lay on his bed and held his arousal out for me.

"It's yours! Come on! Get some of it!"

I obeyed with little prompting and as Billy had predicted, Emerson was thrilled to have me ball with him. As I had suspected—and had heard—this New Jersey guy was an oversexed young bull.

He proved his resiliency just in an hour. Once was not enough.

"I jerk off at night just thinking of you," he muttered as he plunged up into me again. "Everybody knows you're sucking dry your roomie every night."

"Everybody doesn't know," I protested. "We're just good friends."

"Shi-yat!" he bellowed. "Don't tell me you just sit there, listening to his guitar music. We hear you guys carrying on."

"Liar. You don't hear anything."

"Wanna bet? One night, we heard you say: 'Billy, you're hurting me! Take it out!'"

I was startled because I really had said that the first time Billy entered me. I had never taken it up the ass before. But after my roomie had conditioned me to it, I loved it.

Emerson was a frisky, high-spirited young bull who knew nothing about inhibitions. He was obsessed with sex. The other guys on our floor thought it just an outrageously "boy" thing. They even thought it a hoot that Emerson always won the circle jerks.

They admired him for his sexual stamina and outrageousness. None suspected that he was bisexual.

Emerson's roommate, Tommy, was away for the weekend but when he returned, Emerson arranged for me to get with the young lad.

He did it by having Tommy drop by my room one afternoon. Billy was working out with his older buddies in the gym. I had zero interest in this activity and Billy approved. His "wife" shouldn't want to be tough and muscular.

Tommy cracked open my door. He wore only a towel. He was slender, boyish and instantly I knew what was going to happen.

"Emerson says you can give a good massage, Jason. Could you maybe give me one? I'm really stressed out from football practice."

Tommy clearly expected more than just a massage and he got it. He was a quieter version of Emerson but he was thrilled with what happened. And when I later saw a naked Emerson in the hallway, he leered: "My roomie says you made him feel soooo good! It must've been one hell of a massage."

"He was stiff all over!" I joked. "I soon took care of that."

Emerson howled and when I told Billy of my two conquests, he grinned.

"See? You just need to give out the right signals, and you'll have the guys lined up!"

I was amazed at how my life was evolving. From being a repressed sissy from a cow town, I was suddenly creating an eager gallery of young hunks that any campus nymphomaniac would envy.

While I couldn't believe my luck in finally achieving sexual fulfillment, I was painfully aware that such activities could quickly terminate my college career.

A homosexual had no place at this Bible school.

Either male or female, one whisper could terminate your stay here. I had no illusions that my name was being discussed all over campus.

They gossiped during bull sessions, in the showers, over beers at the hamburger hangout.

Lucky for me, the dorm manager was an easy going man, Vernon, who was always pleasant to me. I made him laugh with my comments about some of the faculty members. A dorm manager was the one who could get the ball rolling for expelling a student.

Now that I look back, I wonder if Billy wasn't really urging me to self-destruct. I had discovered by this time that out of bed, my lover boy was a complicated, moody, often prickly loner. I should have known this beforehand. This was what had attracted me to him: his dramatic aura of mystery.

When we took a break from our sex sessions, I lay in his arms, both of us smoking, and one night he said:

"You know what I've always been. A body. That's it. A hot, lean body that people like to use."

"Oh, come off that, Billy. You've got to have a brain behind your body."

"When I start losing my looks, I'll be nothing. Like my old man. He hustled until he was almost forty. Still a good looking guy. But who wants to ball with a forty year old man?"

"Huh? Lots of people."

I couldn't budge him from his dark moods, though. I learned to be quiet and to leave him alone. Billy and his body. I thought about that a lot. It would one day emerge as my most popular short story only I named it, "Eric's Body."

I learned another valuable lesson from my complicated partner. He had nothing but contempt for peer opinion and being popular.

I was basically the same way although I was still too brainwashed to completely drop my hatred for peer approval. Remnants of my old self still floated around my psyche. I still wanted to be liked.

However, With Billy's encouragement to "be myself" I became bolder.

One Saturday, he and I walked uptown to see a French horror movie, "Blood and Roses." Afterwards, we passed a drugstore and paused to look at the make-up display in the window.

Lipstick, liquid make-up, mascara, eyebrow pencils.

"I'm buying some of that," I announced.

"You're kidding?" Billy grinned. "You mean you'll wear it?"

"Of course. If all the guys are convinced I'm a fag, I might as well be one. Why disappoint them?"

And so I began using light color—a little brown pencil, some liquid make-up, a faint touch of rose lipstick.

Boys began to study my face intently. I laughed when I watched them scrunch up their eyes as I passed them and scanned my face.

Even this modest application was instantly noticed by some of the guys. Especially, Emerson, who came up to me in the dorm corridor one day: "Oh, man, you look like a beautiful slut. You're making me harder all the time."

Billy was delighted. I used heavier make-up at night when we were in bed. When he pulled me close, he often muttered: "It's like having a real pussy in bed with me."

What was ironic was that none of the students could conceive of the butch, macho Billy Dragon as doing anything "queer." They thought that he just liked having me around. In my case, nearly everyone who thought about such things was certain I could definitely be doing "homo" stuff.

Yet, I was careful to watch myself when outside the dorm. People could gossip but they had no proof. And Emerson and his roomie were not stupid enough to accuse me of being a pervert when they were having just as much fun in bed as myself.

An old Marine buddy of Billy was passing through town one weekend. His name was Winters.

"I can hardly wait to see him," I gurgled. "Will he fuck me as good as you do?"

"Don't mess with him," Billy said sternly. "He doesn't know about us."

"You act ashamed," I snapped. "And you said there wasn't anything to be ashamed of."

"Well, this is different. He's super straight. He digs the chicks."

"And I dig the dicks."

I was stung but intrigued. Billy had mentioned his military chum a few times—about how they'd find whores in the military and fuck them and how they'd get rip-roaring drunk.

I suspected they had other kinds of fun, too—like getting sucked off by other guys. An oversexed stud like my roommate would never turn down a hot mouth or ass, I thought. He was a lot like my satyr friend, Emerson.

Billy spent most of that freezing, wet Saturday squiring his old drinking buddy around the small town of Brevard. There wasn't that much to see and so I wasn't surprised when they both joined me in the dorm room around five that afternoon.

Both were covered with snow because outside we were being hit with a major blizzard.

"Jason, this is my friend, Winters. I told you about him. We were in the Marines together."

Winters was a rugged, well-built guy with thinning dark hair. He wore a leather jacket and jeans, like Jimmy. He looked too mature to be a college kid.

I could see him driving a truck or wrestling before a TV camera.

He smiled and lit up a cigarette. Both had been drinking a little but not much.

I wore a favorite terrycloth bathrobe of navy blue.

I was planning on visiting Emerson and Tommy that night. They had both informed me that they'd both be in—and waiting for me.

But I was very attracted to this mature, very virile visitor with a handsome face and big shoulders.

We talked for a while about the college and then I listened to them remember some of their escapades in the Marines.

Both had stripped off their jackets and boots. In just white tee-shirts and jeans, they nipped steadily from the paper sack of beer.

I hated beer—then, so I didn't drink anything.

Around ten, I yawned.

"You two guys keep on talking," I said. "Don't let me bother you. I need some shut eye."

"I'd better get on back to the motel," Winters said.

"It's pretty late, man," Billy put in. "You can crash here. I'll put you a blanket on the floor. It's really rough out there."

Snow had turned to sleet that froze on our single window. The motel Winters was staying in was about a mile away.

"Don't make our guest sleep on the floor, Billy. You and me can double up for one night. I don't bite. Winters can have your bed."

"I couldn't do that," said Winters.

"Jason's right. You take my bed and I'll double up with my roomie. He's smaller than us."

"If you insist…"

I had lost any desire to sleep. Something was going on—something sexual and exciting.

Billy and his buddy casually stripped naked with Winters putting his clothes in the corner. He was a big, boxer type of a guy with fair skin and a blue tattoo on his right bicep.

He pulled casually at his equipment and slid into Cochise' bed.

My boyfriend got in beside me and I instinctively nestled close to him. He was hard. He moved his erection over my back, down between my buttocks.

Although we had turned out the lights, a candle still flickered on the desk.

Billy rubbed his hardness up against me and then into. I must have gasped softly.

Winters said in a low voice:

"Hey, Billy, don't you know you're suppose to share with your guest?"

He had pushed his blanket aside. He lay there, fully naked and massaging his privates.

"Go on over," whispered Billy. "I told him you'd make him feel good."

I was dazzled by this arrangement.

"May I join you over there, Winters? You look a little lonely."

"I'm real lonely. Don't let Billy there hog everything."

I slid in beside our visitor and it was like being enveloped by a powerful, young bear.

He kissed me passionately while pressing his hardness against me. Although he was big, he was wonderfully sensitive. He moved carefully up into me and got over me.

He continued kissing me and licking my nipples.

It was then I noticed Billy standing close by and he lowered his hips to my face so that I could love him up. While I took him with my mouth, Winters was deep inside me.

Through that wild night, they changed places, with Billy entering me and Winters pushing his lap close to my mouth. Then I watched as the two buddies coupled passionately on the floor.

Dawn finally broke the spell. Ice and snow had fallen and Winters sat up, with me still in his arms and muttered:

"Well, guess I'd better get a move on! Morning and I gotta catch that eight o'clock bus."

"We'll see you to the bus!" I said.

"You wanna come? Shit, yeah, the more the merrier!"

We all threw on our clothes, our overcoats and boots. We hurried out of the building, pushed our way through the snow, laughing and joking.

I jumped on Winter's back and he carried me for a few blocks. Then I climbed on Billy and he did the same.

We had time for hot coffee and cigarettes in the tiny lunchroom before Winters climbed aboard the Greyhound.

"Nice meeting up with you Jason Fury!" he winked.

"Hurry back to these here parts!"

Back in bed, Billy and I hugged and he told me Winters demanded that we be introduced—after my boyfriend hinted at the good times we had in bed.

"If you liked Winters, you'd love my old man."

"I've got to meet him."

"Come with me to Charlotte next time I go and he'll give you a welcoming you won't forget."

◆   ◆   ◆

I became the most controversial person on campus.

While I remained friends with my gal pals, the males couldn't figure me out.

Gossip whirled around me. Much of it justified. I had come completely out of the closet by this time. My light make-up caused my enemies to become even more vocal.

Yet, I was extremely careful, too. I heard whispers that two of the girl students were called before the dean and questioned about their alleged lesbian tendencies.

One girl student was supposed to have become so suspicious of these two young women that the accuser climbed out on a second story roof and peeped into the window of one of the accused.

She later admitted she saw nothing but damage to the two friends had been done. One of them dropped out. The other one remained a student under a cloud of rumor.

A group of smart-ass fraternity guys, though, made it crystal clear they didn't like me one bit and they wanted me to know it. There were six of them and their leader was a loud-mouthed Neanderthal, Larry, from Winston-Salem.

They thought they were hot shit in their fashionable sweater and slack sets and expensive jackets and by the fact they each dated the campus beauties. A few of this group escorted the Home Coming beauties or were named this and that in the college yearbook.

They'd jeer at me in the hallways, on the campus, flip their wrists, lisp greetings like, "My, isn't she bee-out-ti-full today, guys?" When Billy wasn't around, they'd try to knock my food off my tray in the cafeteria, or empty sugar or salt containers into my plate.

Ironically, each of them had approached me privately over the months and asked me to give them a blowjob.

"I hear you're one hell of a sucker!" jeered Larry the leader one afternoon in the dorm hallway. "Come on inside my room and I might let you have some fun with it."

"Go fuck yourself, you loser!" I retorted. "I wouldn't touch your diseased cock for a thousand bucks. Stick it in your girlfriend's pussy—if you know how to use it!"

Needless to say, they stepped up their campaign of harassment. Of course, they didn't do this with Billy around. They were good at discovering when I would be alone on the campus.

But on the other hand, I also had a group of close friends who weren't bothered by my controversial image.

One of them was a heavy, vivacious girl named Mamie. Possessed with a powerful singing voice, she adored gay men. In fact, she was engaged to one back in her hometown of Greensboro.

To the tiny group of closeted homosexual men on campus, she eagerly acted as a "beard", a woman they could go around with, dance with, to protect them from rumors. Today, she'd be referred to affectionately as a fag hag.

I told her everything and she playfully raised one eyebrow: "My, but aren't we being wicked. If your Mama could see you now!"

She introduced me to her circle of gay boys—nearly all of them music majors. They went around together and were ignored by the regular male students. They were also regarded as automatically "homo" since they majored in music. But they played down their effeminacy and could hide it, thus giving the bigots no ammunition.

I found them boring and pathetic. While they spilled their guts to me about how much they wished they could have some fun with a few of the handsome jocks, I knew that it would never get out of the wishing stage.

"Do it!" I'd exhort them. "Don't just wish it. Go up and ask them."

"Like you?" sneered Kendall, a red-haired queen who was a master on the organ. "We don't want to be talked about like you are."

"Let them talk," I shrugged, "but I'm having my fun. And you never will."

Another closeted male was Osgood, a pale, bland guy who wore huge glasses and whose male equipment was nothing to sneeze at.

Mamie had also introduced us and from that first moment, he was determined that we were to have sex.

"You know everyone's convinced that you and your handsome stud, Billy, are having wild sex," he smiled wickedly. "I'll bet he's fantastic."

"Really?" I smiled back. "Why don't you try and find out?"

"He's gorgeous," groaned Osgood. "He's got the sexiest walk. But you're the one I want."

"I'm afraid I'm already spoken for," I teased while batting my eyes.

"I'm sure you are," whooped Osgood. "About a dozen guys have spoken for you."

One night I sat at the back of an empty auditorium while the drama majors rehearsed "Arsenic and Old Lace."

I had worked on the sets and costumes. In the dark, a figure slipped quietly beside me on my right.

"At last," groaned Osgood with an impish grin. "We're alone."

"Not so fast," said another voice. I looked up to see my steady boy toy, Emerson who plopped down on my opposite side.

Saying nothing, he quickly unbuttoned his britches, pulled his impressive length of virility out and handed it to me.

Osgood saw this and without a word, he did the same thing. Had they planned this or had they both recognized in each other a fellow sensualist? I squeezed both of them in the warm darkness and prayed no one would see us.

We were alone, though, and Osgood had thoughtfully brought along a hand-kerchief which we had to use quickly. Emerson used his empty Dixie Cup.

Neither one had said anything all during this time.

Emerson gave me a wink. Osgood pretended to glare at me.

"We've got to stop meeting like this."

When I told Mamie, she howled.

"You're so wicked! While all us girls climb the walls for a date, you're doing two guys at once."

My list of bed partners grew. I was very careful with who I had my fun with. I didn't want a blabbermouth or an enemy who was testing me.

In the year 1960, "nice" girls simply didn't put out. Some of them might do it with a steady boyfriend. In the meantime, most of the guys were climbing the walls for sexual release.

That was what made it so easy for me to have fun with so many men. They had heard the rumors. That first planted the idea of sex into their minds. More importantly, I joked and laughed with them because I could imitate some hated faculty member with brutal precision.

That put them at ease. So when the situation was right and we were alone, nature took its course.

Among those joining Billy as a second semester student was a charismatic male beauty I'll call Kelly.

Of medium height, his dark copper hair was worn in a page boy style. His deeply set eyes glimmered like brandy and his full lips were kept moist by his passing his tongue over them.

Swishy, voluptuous, he was as brazen as I, in not trying to hide who he was from the masses.

In his case, he terrified nearly all the males because of the intensity in his eyes and face. When he looked at a handsome male, it was like he was going to gobble them whole right there.

There was nothing light or amusing in his expression. He telegraphed his desires like an old-fashioned vamp from the silent screen.

We became intimate—not physical—buddies. Billy hated to be around him.

"You know that sex is all that goes on in his mind," complained my husband. "At least you look like you think of other things—"

"What? Besides cock?" I joked.

He was right, though. I tried to keep my relationships with my sex buddies light and playful. I didn't groan and writhe and pant for them.

Kelly had a hilarious sense of humor that was much like mine. We kept each other in hysterics. With Mamie joining us, we became even more outrageous. We walked uptown together, we hung around the canteen and smoked and danced. We three loved to talk about the new foreign films we'd read about that were opening in New York—films like *Hiroshima, Mon Amour, Last Year at Marienbad, Wild Strawberries.*

Kelly's sense of cutting edge fashion was nearly as sharp as mine. He plucked his brows and used light pencil on them.

He was also a brilliant pianist. He never mentioned his piano studies at the school. One morning, for our weekly assembly, I was startled to hear his name called out as the featured musician.

We students were spellbound by his performance. He threw his whole passion into it. When he finished it, we all gave him a standing ovation. Yet, he shrugged off the applause.

Rarely did anyone ever find Kelly without his pack of Marlboro Cigarettes. He chain-smoked them relentlessly. I was envious over his small vials of perfume, his wardrobe, and his fur-collared jacket.

He had worked a half-year as a waiter in Asheville and splurged every penny he could on these luxuries.

"I'd do anything to sleep with your roomie," Kelly sighed nearly everyday.

His feelings were identical to the closeted homosexuals who were a little awed by Billy Dragon. He certainly didn't fit the image of your average college guy.

He was sexy, mature, quiet and he didn't pal around with any group. Billy cared nothing for fashion, for public opinion, and enjoyed smoking.

He didn't flirt with the girls or join in any extracurricular activities. Although he enjoyed lifting weights with some of the men, he refused to join the college's Weight Lifting Society.

He had no interest in joining bull sessions or joining others to study.

The very few buddies he did talk to were the older, mature types who lived with their wives off campus. Or the two or three on our floor.

Even Mamie said many of the girls thought my roommate was soooo cute! They wondered how he was in bed.

I told Billy this: "Hey, can you believe it? You've got all the gay guys in a sweat. Now Mamie says some of the girls who'd love to get you in bed."

He glanced up from his biology book. With a typical sneer, he snorted: "Tell them all to go fuck. I don't like being a sex stud."

◆   ◆   ◆

Our Glee Club left campus in early December to give its annual performances in different towns.

I wasn't a singer but I had joined the group just for the fun. Mamie encouraged me to jump in and give it a try. Also, I liked many of the people in the group and it would be fun to get away from campus for a week.

When I left Billy that December morning, we hugged and kissed.

"I'll be back in three days," I said. "Now, I don't want anybody else swinging on your lucky charm."

He closed his eyes briefly. "It'll be here all nice and warm and hard—waiting to give you an arousing welcome back."

I shared my bed with Emerson and Tommy. They both sang a good bass but at night, they really came to life. Rarely did they want to sleep. Emerson said his tool was "a-buzzing and it needs to be used."

All the closeted gay boys were along for the tour—but not one of them dared indulge in any sexual hanky panky. When I suggested that Emerson and Tommy would be delighted to give them a whirl in bed, they acted shocked.

None of them were attracted to each other. They all fantasized about macho hunks like my own lover boy, Billy. Yet, even if he had gone up to them and told them point blank that he was available, they would still have refused.

They were terrified of what the others might think.

Although my friend, Kelly, was along, neither Emerson nor Tommy wanted to get near him.

"He's scary!" Emerson complained. "I'm afraid he'd swallow me whole."

I had to agree. When Kelly was near any of the good-looking guys, he'd run his tongue along his lips, half-lower his eyes and stare at the object of desire in what he thought was a hypnotic expression of sexual fever.

I missed Billy, though, and as soon as the bus arrived back on campus, I hurried with my suitcase and took the elevator to my floor.

When I entered my beloved "love chamber," I knew something was very wrong.

Billy's bed was naked of sheets and blanket.

His side of our desk was empty of pencils and pads.

His few clothes and his guitar were missing.

An old cardboard box overflowed with correspondence, most of it from his father. All his books and term papers had been thrown into this box. I hadn't had time to shut the door.

One of the men on my floor passed by just then and paused.

I didn't know him well. Bennie was a sullen, tight-faced guy from Florida. He didn't mingle. He was a religious fanatic who majored in religion and who didn't think women should wear make-up or provocative clothes.

"You looking for Billy? He left."

"Yeah," I lied. "I know he was going home for the weekend."

"No, I don't mean just for a break. He's left for good. He had to. They caught him breaking into the Dean's Office because he wanted to steal answers to midterm exams."

"I don't believe it. He wouldn't do something so stupid."

A smirk spread over Bennie's weasel looking face.

"I heard it from somebody in administration. Your roomie was a thief."

His expression was triumphant. Bennie had made it clear he didn't like having me on this floor for he had told someone that I was "a disgrace." He had lectured Billy about having me as a roommate until my boyfriend had threatened to deck him.

I glared at him.

"You sleazy jerk-off. It was probably you who broke into the Dean's Office."

Bennie's face paled, like I had struck him.

"You don't say those kind of things to me. You're just mad because your boyfriend's not here. They should kick you off the campus, too."

"If I go, I'll drag you with me. I've heard some things about you, too, Bennie! Didn't they catch you with your ear to my door one night? You were looking for some cheap thrills?"

He opened his mouth for a moment and then closed it.

"I'm not going to argue," he muttered. "But I'm going to bring this up at our dorm meeting. You made false statements against me."

"And so have you. I know you gossiped about Billy and me to anybody who would listen. You defamed me and slandered me. I'll bring up those charges, too."

He worked his mouth but left.

I remained still for a long time.

Billy was really gone. Gone forever.

That hot, funky vibe he created was completely missing.

He had cleared out in a hurry. The floor was covered with old term papers, reams of poetry and music he had written and personal letters.

These were few but I grabbed them up and locked them away. That night, I lie in bed and read the letters from the father of Billy to his son.

What I read amazed me. Billy had written to him in graphic detail about what he and I were doing in bed. On cheap, notebook paper, his ex-con father penned his reply:

"Ha! You sure are one lucky dude. You're getting free head and a man can give you better head than any woman. I'm getting fired up thinking of you fucking your burr-head homo. I'd sure like to join in for some of that hot loving. You're one lucky sumbitch 'cause you get it all the time. Bring'em home with you so's I can gets me some of that boy ass fun."

Bennie had spoken the truth about Billy's break in.

I knew Billy agonized over failing the mid-term exam. His scholarship depended on him passing it. I knew he was flunking algebra and government.

"I can't go home a broken down student," he had told me. "I've got to pass this exam."

I couldn't imagine him becoming frantic with worry or acting so stupidly that he would actually try and break into the Dean's office to steal exam answers.

From what I picked up in the days that followed was this: a security guard had discovered Billy trying to break into a window of the dean's office one night. When interrogated, he didn't try to hide his motive.

They told him he could leave and not face charges or he could stay and there'd be a hearing. Billy reportedly told them all to go to hell. Then he cleared out.

I could imagine him facing his accusers, studying them from beneath his long lashes, ready to spit in their eyes.

To this day, I still don't know the real reasons behind the sudden departure of my first husband.

I didn't try hard to discover the real reason. He was gone now and I knew that I would never see him again.

Over the decades, I had contacted the alumni bureau at the college to see if they had an address for this strange, beautiful man. Ten years ago, they told me they did have one.

I jotted it down. I was amazed. It was the identical address that Billy had used in college. After nearly half a century, he still lived in the home of his youth.

I kept that address and last year I finally decided to see it for myself. I was visiting friends in North Carolina for the Christmas holidays when I got into my rental car and started driving.

The day was cold and slate colored. I entered the outskirts of Charlotte and after directions from several service stations, finally found the right street. It wandered miles away from downtown.

The house was small and sat alone at the end of a nearly deserted street. White paint covered its exterior. Green shutters framed all the windows. White curtains covered them all. Smoke trailed up from the small red brick chimney.

A dusty, black pickup truck was parked in the driveway.

On either side of the dwelling, a large field of broom sedge rippled from the frigid wind. A sense of intense loneliness hit me. This was exactly the type of house Billy would live in.

Alone. Away from all others. Unpretentious and isolated.

Was Billy in there? Or could he have been married all those years and now grandkids visited him? I turned my car around and drove slowly by it again. A curtain parted slightly. Someone stood there, watching me.

Was it he?

I drove away. Reality had no place in my memory of Billy Dragon.

I never contacted him. We had both traveled our own paths. What we had in that magical little dorm room could never be recreated. The era, the vibes, the situation unique to that moment could never be evoked.

Wherever you are tonight, Billy Dragon, you're not forgotten.

Chapter Four
The Patient

✦

1962

Mountain Manor still looms high today in the mystical city of Asheville, North Carolina.

I drive up that twisty, narrow lane occasionally when I visit my home state. You can't see it from the road for it rears up against the sky on one of those marvelous tree-covered hills that abound within the city. At night, dozens of golden lights glow in the many windows of this castle like structure.

Today, it operates as a drug rehabilitation center where only the very rich can afford to go for treatment of alcohol and drug problems.

When I went to work there in 1962, it was a place for mental and drug patients.

My love affair with Billy still obsessed me. Even when I was shown my room at the top of the Tudor styled mansion, I thought relentlessly of my former obsession.

A favorite aunt of mine knew I needed money to continue college. Since Brevard College was only a two-year institution, I couldn't return there anyway.

I wanted to attend one of the big state universities and had sent in my applications to them all.

So my Aunt Tessie arranged me to get a job where she had worked all of her life. Mountain Manor. I could work as a nurse's aide for just the summer or as long as I wanted.

"Oh, you'll love it there," she told me. "The job is easy, you meet the most fascinating people, you've got great meals and you'll have your own room!"

Mountain Manor was an amazing architectural marvel that suddenly hit you in the eye when you turned a corner of that wounding road from the main boulevard of Asheville.

It resembled Manderly—the legendary Cornish estate made immortal in Daphne du Maurer's classic, *Rebecca*. In the movie, Laurence Olivier, who portrays the brooding hero, guides his car around that corner of the five mile drive and shouts out to his new wife:

"Look!" There's Manderly!"

Mountain Manor still stuns a first time visitor as he guides his car along a wounding little lane of asphalt that continues upward until one turns a corner and paw—there it is.

It's an enormous complex covered with numerous mullioned windows, brown trim, huge portico, chimneys and countless doorways.

The place was made for drama. My function was mostly to baby sit some of the one hundred male patients. The pay was lousy but you received free lodging and food.

A powerful sense of timeless drama and age saturated the walls. A cloak of oldness, of past eras thickened the air. Décor and furnishings were from the past. Ornate frames for huge mirrors and paintings of British royalty filled up the walls.

I continued to be thrilled by my new home: Marble floors and wood-paneled rooms and velvet drapes and enormous fireplaces in the library and the lobby that always crackled with flames.

It proved to be a self-contained little world that had nothing to do with reality. Staff lived on the topmost floor. My room was a snug cocoon with a large bed, a writing desk tucked into a window nook that overlooked miles of the famed Pisgah Forest.

Some old-time workers rarely left the building, except for an occasional bus trip into downtown Asheville.

Everything they needed to live was right there. We had three free meals a day in the sumptuous dining room.

We had barbershop and hairdressing services, a small post office, a canteen to buy snacks and stamps. A beautifully furnished theater was used for dances nearly every night. Crimson curtains of thick velvet could be parted, too, to reveal amateur theatricals staged by staff and patients.

A large bus traveled each week with patients and staff to scenic spots where a lavish picnic spread was provided. A city bus stopped at the bottom of the drive and you could get off right in the center of the city at Pack Square.

Asheville's own literary giant, Thomas Wolfe, had written much about Pack Square and the city, one, which had always fascinated me.

Most of the male attendants were pleasant guys—either working there until other employment plans worked out and a few who had no ambition to do anything else.

I felt none of the negative vibes that I experienced wherever I went. I guess they had seen it all among the weird and colorful patients who passed through those portals.

We gave out trays for each meal to room bound tenants. We helped admit new patients; we assisted the nurses in restraining inmates who were too violent. We took them to painting and handicraft classes, played tennis or softball and at the nightly socials, we were expected to dance and entertain.

I was never any good at sports but then neither was most of the patients or workers. The medical staff just wanted everyone to jump around a lot to get their daily exercise.

I loved all this. The patients were usually harmless and often brilliant. Men, women, young people, they had experienced breakdowns of some kind. A few were allowed to go into Asheville and enjoy star appearances of concert piano artists, symphony orchestras, or a movie. This also included dinner in some restaurant and then a cab ride back to Mountain Manor.

I felt completely content for the first time in my life.

I was no different from many of the patients there. My flamboyance was no problem for most of the staff—with the exception of one big, hairy lesbian, Miss Tyson, who supervised us attendants.

Since she was cross-eyed, and had a dark moustache that gained her the nickname of 'Miss Clark Gable,' she resembled a clumsy elephant. Big, shapeless and barely literate, her persistence paid off over the years as she evolved from a lowly attendant to head of the attendant staff.

This neurotic, shapeless creature would prove to be my enemy throughout the six months I was to eventually stay at Mountain Manor. From the first moment we met, pure hate flashed back and forth between us.

But this was an irritating fly in the ointment compared to the hostility I had endured at college. After that, everything was routine.

During the third week of my stay, my enjoyable summer was transformed into an experience even more magical: the arrival of Eric.

He had been admitted the night before and when I reported to duty on the third floor's nurses station, Miss Holiday, the chief nurse, said to me: "Jason, you've impressed me with your work and attitude and so I'm giving you a special assignment today. We're supposed to use a registered nurse for something like

this. But we don't have one. So, we're giving you a chance. You'll get higher pay. I want you to be in charge of a new patient."

"Is he the man-killing kind?"

She laughed. "No. He's a beautiful person but his mother has had him committed here because he's become suicidal."

Two years before, he was forced to undergo a lobotomy—ordered by his mother. In other words, an operation had resulted in the removal of a tiny area of brain cells.

These cells monitored the person's emotions. Eric would never become angry or hostile anymore. Because of the lobotomy, he had become a person who never grew angry or belligerent.

The operation had not, however, killed his desire to harm himself.

Miss Holiday gave me a brief lecture on do's and don'ts:

I was to take care of him as if he were my brother or child. I was to see that he got cleaned and dressed up in the morning. I was to make certain he took his medication and that he participate in therapeutic classes.

His parents were more than just wealthy. The father was a direct heir of a giant pharmaceutical corporation, whose products we use even today.

I could take Eric into town for entertainments but they wanted me to stick as close to the facility as possible—in case anything unusual happened.

"And most importantly—don't get emotionally involved. It's easy to do. But you must keep a certain distance. And don't fall in love! That'll really get you kicked out of here."

"But what if they fall in love with me? How can I help that? Is it my fault I'm so damned beautiful?"

I had discovered in Miss Holiday a kindred spirit. I felt immediately comfortable with her and didn't try to pretend anything.

She laughed again. "You're toooo much. Ready? Let's go."

She escorted me to Room 400.

Knocking on the door, she opened it.

A beam of early morning light filtered through the barred window. Lying naked beneath a thin sheet rested my patient.

"Eric, this is Jason Fury. He'll be your special duty nurse."

"Hi Eric! I'm so glad to meet you."

I hardly knew what I was saying. He lay completely nude beneath a sheet that barely covered his hips.

He was as beautifully shaped and proportioned as the cover boy for a muscle magazine. In fact, he looked like he was posing. His hands were clasped behind his handsome head.

Thick hair, the color of coal, was swept back from his square face, but a lock dangled provocatively over his right brow. Long, dark lashes rested on his cheek.

My eyes drank in this dazzling sight: he wasn't a collection of grotesque weight-lifting muscles. His pectorals were big and heavy and rose naturally, each crowned with large nipples. His flat stomach sank in and out, as if he were asleep.

And I had thought Billy Dragon was one hot looking Apollo!

An impressive bulge pushed the thin sheet up over his hips.

"Eric?" repeated Miss Holiday.

His eyelids fluttered. He looked at us puzzled and I was dazzled even more by the stormy emerald of his eyes.

"Huh? Oh, yeah. I'm here at the new place? How long have I been here?"

He sat up suddenly while the sheet slipped down to his knees. Now, I was able to see everything. This Adonis would never have trouble attracting either men or women.

Miss Holiday pulled the sheet back over his lap.

"You were admitted last night, Eric," smiled Mrs. Holiday. "The doctors gave you medication for sleep."

"They did? Oh, yeah, yeah, it's coming back to me. I was in Pennsylvania yesterday—and now I'm here."

He seemed completely unaware of his dazzling nudity with his manhood hanging heavily and impressively between his thighs.

"Here is the nurse's aide we told you about. This is Jason Fury. Now, he's going to be your friend, your companion and he'll see that you receive anything you need."

Miss Holiday left us alone.

"Eric, how about us getting you all cleaned up and shaven and then I'll show you around this joint."

His strange eyes stared at me. He squinted slightly as one hand rubbed his right nipple.

"You'll be with me all the time? Okay. I like you. I can tell that you and I will like each other." An impish grin formed on his full lips. "When I do potty, will you wipe me, too?"

"Of course. If you want me to."

"If I wanted you to—"

He made a masturbatory gesture with his right hand. I felt faint with desire. But—I knew I had to watch myself carefully.

"Well, now, I don't know about that—"

"Look!" he giggled and held his phallus in his right hand. "See? I've been told it's big and smooth. Wanna feel of it? You'd like it. I can tell."

The temptation was so powerful I felt dizzy.

Yet, I also knew the door could fly open at anytime by some of the staff and if they saw what was happening, that'd be the end of me.

"Now, now, Eric, let's behave ourselves. Come on. Let's get cleaned up."

He studied my face, which had become flushed.

He laughed softly. "Oh, ho, ho, I can tell you'd like that. But—I guess you're right. *Herr Doctor* wouldn't approve of that, would he?"

He slid out of bed and stretched. This is one sight I still see in my mind like it happened just minutes ago.

Eric stood at six feet four and despite his mental problems he had kept himself in magnificent shape. Somehow he had acquired an all-over tan. His skin gleamed like soft amber and muted gold. How could someone be so perfectly proportioned?

And his manhood dangling loosely between his powerful thighs was merely the main jewel in his crown of physical wonders.

"You look like a Roman Gladiator!" I blurted.

He went into classic muscleman poses. Then he grabbed his privates and shook them at me.

"I'll bet none of those muscle guys have got a set of jewels like me!"

He said this with such a sweet, innocent smile that he resembled a small boy whose always been told he's the most handsome of the bunch.

I pretended to swoon, which made him laugh. In less than two minutes, he had told me he knew what I was all about and he didn't care.

◆   ◆   ◆

When he got dressed, I whistled.

"Hey. You're going to have all the women crawling all over you!"

His wealthy parents had provided him with a stunning wardrobe of cutting edge fashion, circa 1962. A starched white shirt gleamed beneath a black v-neck sweater. Gray, silk slacks hung over gleaming black shoes.

His dark curls still glistened from shower water. No one would ever mistake this magnificent young Adonis as a mental patient.

I came to his shoulder and I loved having to look up into his handsome face.

"You've got a spec of shaving cream right here on your chin," I said and wiped it off with my finger. He made comical faces and I laughed and he laughed, showing beautiful white teeth.

"Wait!" I smiled. "You forgot your aftershave!"

"Will you put it on me?" he asked.

I spilled some drops of Royal-Lime Aftershave into my palms and patted his face with it. He made more childish faces and laughed with me. His own, woodsy scent intermingled with the lotion to create a subtle, but exhilarating scent.

I took him down to our sumptuous dining room for breakfast. In the elevator he had casually grabbed my hand and I left it there. He felt so warm and strong. When the doors opened, though, I withdrew my fingers.

The place was half-filled with other staff members and patients. They all looked and did double takes when they saw my gorgeous charge and me.

One of those staring was a gay attendant who I loathed. Eddie was a flamboyant queen, with a receding hairline and crooked front teeth. You never saw him without a cigarette. His plucked brows arched above flat, sullen eyes.

When he first saw me in the nurse's station, he snorted and muttered to Miss Tyson, who sat with him. I had already noticed how close they were. I was also to discover that these two had vehemently fought the plan to have me be Eric's special nurse. Eddie thought that he was the one to do it.

As we passed his table, Eddie muttered loud enough for me to hear: "Why, look what the dogs dragged in."

I studied him briefly and sneered: "Yeah, you do look pretty dirty, Eddie. Better get cleaned up!"

He popped his eyes and dropped his mouth and the butch Miss Tyson glared at me.

I ignored them and went with Eric to the lavish breakfast buffet.

We filled our platters with food and a red-jacketed waiter came by our table to pour us coffee. We sat before a large window that overlooked mountain peaks and forests.

"If you look hard, Jason," Eric said very seriously, "you'll see some flying saucers out there. They stay hidden behind the clouds. But they're out there. I took a trip on one."

He said this so sweetly and seriously I wanted to cry. So this was part of his problem!

"Wow! I'd love to travel on one. Where'd you go?"

"Different places. You're beautiful. Has anybody told you that? You're a boy but you make me think of a girl. You've got blonde curls and a kissable mouth. I hope I can fuck you real soon."

He said this so casually, while eating scrambled eggs, I was a little startled—but thrilled, too.

"We have to be careful, Eric. We're being watched by the medical staff. If we do anything crazy, I'll be taken off special duty with you."

"I wouldn't like that," he said quietly. "I want you to stay with me always. I want you to always be my friend."

"I certainly hope so, too."

"I can hear them, Jason. The flying saucers. They're talking to me. Listen."

He cocked his head and stared out of the corner of his eyes at the window. My heart sank. In that one moment, I knew he would never be sane, or live out in the real world. This abrupt glint of insanity chilled me.

His incredible body was only a human shell that moved like any other human shell. It housed that poor brain of his which had already been tampered with and partially destroyed.

I didn't know the full ramifications of what a lobotomy could do at that time. I only understood all of this later on. At that moment, I didn't want to know the results. I was later to discover that Eric was an exception. His eyes and face were vibrant and animated.

Even after he had closely shaved with a safety razor, his five o'clock stubble shadowed his square jaw. When he flashed a lop-sided grin, revealing those perfectly shaped teeth, the effect was dynamite.

A lock of black, glossy hair had a habit of falling over his left brow. It matched those jet brows and long, dark lashes that looked almost artificial.

He looked like the fabulous young scion of a vast fortune—which he was. I began to worry why his mother had committed him. Could it have been suicide or was it something more ominous on her part—as Eric believed.

He was convinced she had ruined his brain so she could get all of the enormous fortune he was entitled to.

I showed him the outstanding gardens there, the tennis court, the Olympic sized swimming pool in the basement, the therapy rooms where we found other patients weaving baskets, painting china and canvases.

Twenty or more patients dabbed watercolor paint on canvases. Some wove baskets out of strands of straw. A few whirled brushes over the surface of vases and bowls and coffee mugs.

From there, we went to the outside area that was transformed into a softball field and a volleyball court.

Eric said little. None of this really interested him. Instead, he kept his head cocked at a slight angle, as if he were listening to an invisible friend. I caught him occasionally nodding his head and smiling.

It was the same type of smile one saw in that final image of Tony Perkins in the movie, *Psycho.* You knew instantly that it wasn't a normal facial movement.

"Wouldn't you like to play some volleyball, Eric?" I asked. Numerous patients filled the court. Few had any athletic coordination. They jumped around and waved their hands in the air.

I felt completely at home.

"Yeah, I guess so."

He stripped off his sweater and joined the fun. His body in motion was a magical sight. Some of the other nurses joined me. I liked them. They were older, mature gals who had seen it all.

"Woo, he's gorgeous!" muttered Cynthia. She was a bleached blonde woman who had worked at the facility for years. "He could be a movie star."

"He looks like Clark Gable without the moustache," noted Rhonda. She was a sweet, mountain woman who was working special duty with a stubborn little man, Mr. Phipps. "You're so lucky, Jason."

"You should've seen him naked this morning," I joked. "What a sight!"

"Now, now!" teased Cynthia. "Don't get emotionally involved. If the doctors see you are, they'll take you off the case."

"Your aunt went to bat for you, Jason," noted Rhonda. "She urged them to let you do special duty. Usually, only a veteran nurse can do it."

"I have a way with men," I joked.

"I'll bet you do!" whooped Cynthia. "Just don't let the doctors know that."

It was then that they told me how my two enemies, Eddie and Miss Tyson, had both vehemently fought to keep me from getting this special assignment.

But both my aunt and Miss Holiday had argued just as vehemently to the doctors why they thought I would be outstanding.

"Eddie and Butch Tyson are not your friends," Cynthia whispered. "Watch out for them. They work together. I've seen them squeeze out several really sharp attendants. That's why we have such third-raters here."

After the volleyball game, I guided Eric down to the shower and massage rooms. He stripped naked with the other men and stood against the wall as another attendant sprayed them lightly with a hose.

As he danced around in the water, he laughed and waved at me. He was stunning. Some of the other patients studied him in amazement. An inmate as magnificent looking as this guy was a rarity.

Because of the heavy medication they took, nearly all the men were flabby and out-of-shape. All they wanted to do was to sleep or sit and watch television.

Eric even playfully grasped his package with both hands and flapped it childishly.

Then Eric got up on a table for his rubdown. Several of the other male attendants usually did this. Eric, though, said aloud: "I want Jason to rub me down. I know he'll do a good job."

The other attendants, with the exception of Eddie, were nice, friendly guys who weren't bothered by me. They even joked about how "we'd better watch our backs when you're around."

I was thrilled to have this magnificent looking Hercules literally beneath my hands. It was like all the other times in the dorm when some of the most handsome guys on campus came by my room "for a rubdown."

I splashed alcohol over Eric's gleaming body. A smile of contentment settled over his handsome face. My hands smoothed the wetness over his hard skin. My fingers ran over his buttocks and down between his thighs.

He grunted pleasantly. He spread his legs slightly and I saw his obvious arousal forming. Uh oh. There were too many others around. Poor Eric just didn't realize the dangers he created for me.

When he turned over, his privates were visibly at half-staff. I moved the towel over them, but one of the other attendants, Tommy, laughed.

"You must be doing something right, Jason!"

"Shhhh. Not so loud. I don't want to get in trouble."

"Aw, nobody's gonna say anything."

I grabbed the towel and moved it over over Eric's skin and I couldn't resist squeezing his hardness with the terrycloth. Eric responded by grinning and saying aloud: "Ahhhhh!"

The other guys giggled. They'd seen it all. Masturbating men was a routine sight. To see yet another guy with a half-hardon was nothing. Seeing men trying to have sex with another guy in public was also commonplace. Yet, if these guys were patients, there wasn't much of an alarm. But if an attendant did this…?

I was relieved to get him back into his clothes.

Thus ended my first day with one of the most beautiful men I've ever encountered anywhere.

Eric. I whisper that name even tonight.

◆   ◆   ◆

Through a stroke of great luck, I realized that I had been put into a place that was perfectly attuned to me.

I was fascinated with all the patients I met there, even those on the violent ward. These men were strapped down and locked away because of their extreme homicidal tendencies.

But most of all, I had a job that placed me with a stunning, handsome man who wasn't from the South. Eric was a new breed of male for me. He resembled one of those Hollywood figures you see on the screen who are just too good to be true.

He came from a background of staggering wealth. His mother had provided him with an eye-popping wardrobe of tailored clothes from British and Italian geniuses.

His closet was stocked with V-neck cashmere sweaters of dazzling hues—pink, powder blue, canary yellow, black, white, and tangerine. A magnificent trench coat of soft leather, the color of charcoal, would ward off the mountain chill.

Hats of all shapes were also part of his wardrobe: biker caps, French berets, ski hats lined with fur.

Handmade shoes of soft, Italian leather. Robes of linen and terrycloth in black, navy blue and salt white were matched with slippers of the same hue.

When he was in session with his doctor, I slipped into his room and explored it. I was enchanted with everything about him. I pressed my face against his moist bath towel, his bathrobe, and his skivvies from yesterday.

All of them smelt of Eric. On his dresser were specially made brush and comb set, trimmed in ivory, with backs of gleaming copper.

His toothbrush was a transparent wand that contained plastic sea horses and fish and gleaming specks of scarlet, jade and gold sand. His emerald green bottle of Royal Lime emanated a haunting scent that clung to him throughout the day.

When he returned from his daily session with his doctor, we played cards with other patients. We joined groups in long walks around the buildings. The doctor wanted him to interact more with other patients.

I saw to it that he joined in the ball games, checkers, dancing.

What he loved above all was to swim.

When I took him down to the Olympic sized pool, Karl, our swim instructor greeted us and took Eric to the locker room to change into his swimming attire.

When he emerged, he made a stunning sight.

He was naked, except for a pair of black briefs. His bulge was visible. Thin nylon covered his rump like jet paint. It was a sight to behold.

His body rippled with natural beauty. Powerful shoulders, chest and arms tapered to a narrow waist, flared out slightly at the hips and merged into strong thighs.

He swam laps and dived and resembled an aqua marine creature. Since several men were being treated for their homosexuality, they stared hungrily at this shimmering morsel of beefcake.

When Eric finally emerged from the water, he gleamed like the statue of a Roman gladiator come to life. I watched old Joey rub down the naked torso of my Dream God.

Oil and alcohol glistened on the perfect skin.

"You're one fine looking gentleman, sir," croaked Joey, "yes you are, sir, a fine looking figure of a man."

Eric's daily swim sessions attracted not only the gay patients but the women as well. They were not that mentally impaired as to not appreciate such a beautiful sight as a nearly naked Apollo performing for them in the water.

Eric often took my hand and squeezed it when nobody was around. I smiled. If we were walking along an empty hallway or outside, he would bend down and give me a kiss on the cheek.

"Eric! We have to be careful!"

He rolled his eyes and grimaced.

"Why? I want to do this."

In his strange world, nothing was forbidden or censored. He couldn't understand why he should have to obey stupid, man-made rules. To make it even more difficult for him, he had grown up in staggering splendor. He had shown me pictures of the various houses his parents owned: penthouses in Manhattan and L.A.

Deluxe mansions on the French Riviera, in Estoril, Portugal, in Venice, Italy. Enormous estates on Long Island, Connecticut, in North Carolina.

Dramatic, meandering trails encircled Mountain Manor. Some of them twisted down to the main boulevard that led to downtown Asheville.

On one such hiking trip, Eric and I composed a group of around fifteen. Johnny, another attendant, was in charge. Our group of patients was not considered risks. They were people suffering from mild mental breakdowns or who had recovered from their bouts with alcohol or drugs.

Eric and I made up the rear guard. On this afternoon, he wore a beautiful jacket of black leather. A scarf of crimson wool wound around his neck. A biker cap covered his dark curls.

I had thrown on my weathered old green trench coat.

His hand reached over and took mine.

No one saw us. No one cared. We were alone here. It was growing dark. Soon, it would be time for supper.

He pulled my hand up to his mouth and kissed it. Then he brought it down to his hips and pressed it against his lap.

"Can you feel how hard I am?" he whispered.

"You feel wonderful."

Quickly, he pulled me behind a large tree. Everyone was far ahead. He pulled his hat off and pressed his mouth against mine. My hands ran over him. I couldn't resist him any longer. But I had to. We were running a terrible risk out here.

"We'll get together soon, Eric," I whispered. "I promise."

"Will we really get together?" he muttered. "Can I trust you?"

"I'll find us a place where we can be alone," I swore. "I want us to get together, too."

His mouth was like a potent drug that made me dizzy. Moist, soft, sweet and passionate. I gasped when we pulled apart. I held onto the tree to keep from falling.

Billy had been a blunt, animal like kisser that certainly sizzled. Eric's was beyond description. Where had he learned to smooch like this?

While Eric continued kissing me, his hand unbuttoned his slacks and he drew my hand to the fully aroused instrument of his extraordinary virility. My hand squeezed and massaged it. I felt it pulse and luckily had a handkerchief in my coat pocket.

"I want more than that," he muttered hoarsely. "If you don't, I'll find somebody else."

"No, no, Eric, depend on me. Tomorrow! I'll find us a place."

The sanatorium had a huge ballroom with a stage for small entertainments. Although we used the place each night for dancing, the stage remained curtained. I had explored it one morning out of curiosity.

Furniture was piled on top of each other in the corners. Beds, chairs, tables, all used for plays. No one ever ventured back there. Even with the nightly dances, the stage remained unused.

The following morning, I escorted Eric to his daily psychiatric session with Dr. Steele. He was the aloof, frosty psychiatrist who operated the sanitarium along with his two brothers.

I had met him in the corridors several times. His idea of a greeting was to barely nod his head. His hard, gray eyes made one feel like an insect ready for dissection in a biology course.

From Dr. Steele's office, Eric and I went to his psychodrama gathering with other patients.

We had lunch and then we were finally free for the afternoon.

All this time, Eric knew I had something planned. He gave me curious, sweet glances and I smiled back.

"Come with me," I said quietly. Behind the ballroom ran an unused little corridor that casts or musicians utilized for entering upon the stage.

It was dusty and airless. I took the hand of my beautiful patient. We opened a door and entered the old stage.

Above us were several narrow windows that let in a faint light. I had prepared us a large sofa, covered with a fresh sheet from my room.

Eric pulled me quickly against him and we kissed intensely. He tasted so sweet and boyish and wonderful. I felt dizzy from finally savoring his mouth. My hands explored him and he quickly stripped off his clothes. I did the same.

On that sofa, he pulled me down with him. It was an incredible sensation—to finally be in the arms of this shimmering young giant.

I sensed he was starved for physical affection and after a few minutes, I moved my face down his spectacular torso, kissing the nipples and the navel and then I grasped his impressive arousal.

He made no sound except a faint gasp. His beautiful body squirmed and tightened itself, as I loved him with my mouth. He was as incandescent as I had fantasized him to be.

His torso was slightly bronze in color, hard and warm and it possessed that intangible aroma that he emanated.

With his thighs on either side of my face, I felt transcendent, for this was the identical position I had first discovered this hidden part of life with Dale.

I imagined it was Dale who now enwrapped me with his powerful legs. Eric grunted softly and he released his sexual energy in startling abundance. Then he pulled me up to him and we embraced passionately. He moved on top of me, while supporting himself with his arms and knees so that I wasn't crushed by his weight.

Skillfully, he moved into me, very carefully at first.

He watched my expression, whispering, "Okay? Did that hurt? Here's more...and more...just a little bit more..."

I had allowed only a few of the guys at college to do this because the first time had been one of sharp, searing pain. I discovered there were men, though, who had the knack for doing it in a way that created shivers of delight, instead of ripples of agony.

Billy and then Emerson had both proven adept at this skill. Now Eric joined this rare class of men—for he continued kissing my face, my ears, as he gradually completed his entry.

A lock of hair fail over his brow and his face scrunched up in intense activity. His mouth parted as he kissed me hard again. His shimmering white rump moved in steady motion behind him. My hands moved over them, into the cleft and this thrilled him more.

When he finished, he moved slightly away and now used his mouth to explore me. He was hungry and curious and after his journey, I took one final trip over his gleaming body.

He was rampant again and as he became used to me, he made certain I enjoyed this time around more than the first.

We heard noises out in the ballroom. Workmen had come to set up the folding chairs for a concert that night. Swiftly and silently, Eric and I dressed and after I checked the narrow little corridor behind the stage, we both left our "passion pit," as Eric called it, and entered the cool air of September.

No one had seen us. We went out to the walk that corkscrewed around the hillside to the main road. Lighting up cigarettes, we said little.

A powerful bond was created back there on the dark, dusty stage. Perhaps it was similar to the wedding night of two virgins. I had now had sex many times over. But except for Dale and Billy at Brevard College, they were merely casual sex drop-ins.

With Eric, a powerful rapport had sprung up. Maybe because of his lobotomy, his sense of mental telepathy was more acute than in others. But I could glance at him, smile, and he smiled back.

I knew now that I had to be ever more vigilant in hiding my affair with this dazzling patient. My enemies wanted to destroy this relationship. The doctors certainly guessed I had no interest in balling with women.

This may have been a relief. At least they had no worry of my impregnating a female patient. Yet, I heard from my nurse buddies that both Eddie and the butch Miss Tyson were determined to remove me from special duty with Eric—they wanted me out of Mountain Manor completely.

I confided in Eric my problems with these two misfits, he grew as angry as possible.

"I'll go out there and cuss them out," he said quietly. "They aren't treating you like this."

I grabbed his arm. "No, Eric. Don't even let anyone know I've complained to you. Don't you see? If the doctors heard this, they'd be enraged. I'm the one who's supposed to be looking out for you, not the other way around."

If Dr. Steele had any doubts about me, he didn't show it. In fact, he gave us permission to take a cab into downtown Asheville that night for dinner and a movie.

I dressed up in a favorite outfit of black corduroy slacks and a crimson sweater of angora. My old trench coat would protect me from the frigid temperatures. It got cold up in that mountain city.

Eric dazzled everyone at the nurse's station when he met me. He looked so Hollywood handsome in his overcoat of moss green, worn over a white sweater and black slacks.

A purple scarf at his neck gave him the touch of high fashion panache that made him so extraordinary looking.

Eddie sat in the corner, glaring at us, chain-smoking his Camels.

Eric and I dined at Tingle's Restaurant, a classic fixture of Asheville form the 1920s. We feasted on Southern gourmet dishes—soft, white rolls and fried chicken and candied yams.

Then we walked a few blocks to the Paramount Theater where *The Music Man* was playing.

In the darkness of the theater, we sat against the wall. I remember little about the movie. My left hand busily massaged Eric's private possessions. I had brought along several handkerchiefs. I used them all up by the end of the movie.

When the cab dropped us off at Mountain Manor around ten that night, we had him stop far away so we could walk the rest of the way. In the thickness of the Evergreen bushes, we kissed passionately. I got on my knees to complete our night of passion.

We had to be careful not to betray any unusual emotion. I was careful to wipe the pine needles from my knees and when we arrived back at the nurse's station, we were full of our night on the town.

Nurse Holiday beamed at the glowing radiance of her favorite patient. She had told me how much she loved to see Eric and me together. "You're two such beautiful men!"

When I saw him back to his room, I gave him his capsules, watched him swallow them.

"It was a wonderful, wonderful night, Eric."

"Without you, it would have been nothing," he smiled. "We'll have to do it again and again."

My joy was short lived.

The next morning, I was called before Dr. Steele and informed that I was fired.

◆   ◆   ◆

When I entered his large, carpeted office, the head of Mountain Manor sat stiff and somber behind his desk.

Facing him sat my two worst enemies: the mustachioed Miss Tyson and the chain-smoking, brow-plucked Eddie. Both glanced at me with a smirk.

"Have a seat, Mr. Fury. I've—"

"I prefer to stand."

"Well, stand then. I've heard some serious charges against you, Jason, about your relationship with Eric Bronfman."

"Have you? Like what? And if the charges have come from Eddie Kerns and Miss Tyson here, I can easily imagine what the charges are."

"These two employees claim that you've become more than a nurse's aide to the patient. That you've been having sex with him. Is that true, Mr. Fury? Because if it is, I'll have you instantly dismissed."

So. There it was at last. Both the charge I had feared and that my two foes had finally struck. I faced them.

"First of all, Dr. Steele, I gather that you've gotten an earful from this two-faced attendant, Eddie Kerns, and from this two-faced head of attendants, Miss Tyson. Neither one of them like me very much. Both have threatened to get me out of here, no matter how they do it."

"That's a lie!" snarled Eddie. His face had become a bright pink, so that his eyes bulged out more than ever. "You lie all the time. I should be doing special duty with Eric Bronfman, not you. I've been here longer. You think you're so much better than anybody else. You go swishing around—"

He flapped his wrists and rolled his eyes.

"That's enough," Dr. Steele interrupted. "I—"

"We don't have to threaten anything," seethed Miss Tyson. Her eyes rolled crazily around in their sockets. "The facts speak for themselves. Jason is always, always alone with this patient. People have seen them holding hands."

"Who are these people?" I demanded. "I've seen you holding the hands of female patients, too, Miss Barnes. I've seen you hug them and kiss their cheeks—"

"They're female patients!" she snapped. "Men don't do that—"

"Wait a damned minute!" I countered. "We're discussing patients here. I've heard rumors about you, too, Miss Tyson. How you much prefer the company of women over men. Especially if they're young and easily dominated. I'm working with a patient—not your man on the street. These patients need acts of friendship and caring and holding their hands is one form of that. Eric needs reassurance that people care about him and—"

"Oh, brother, care about him!" whooped Eddie. "Yeah, you care about him alright. You can't take your eyes or your hands off Eric."

"Oh, really, Eddie? Seems like you're always there at the swimming pool when Eric dives in. And when he comes out, all wet and nearly naked, you're right there, drooling over him. I've seen you roll your eyes and wiggle your tongue. When's the last time you've beaten up one of the patients? Are you still putting a bar of soap in a towel and slugging the shit out of them?"

Several of the nurses had told me about this—that Eddie derived sadistic delight in beating up on helpless male patients. And his favorite weapon was the old soap-in-a towel trick.

"You little bitch!" screeched Eddie. "Don't you dare—?"

Dr. Steele had remained silent as he watched and studied us. As I hoped, both my enemies revealed themselves for the liars they were.

"The bottom line, Dr. Steele," I cut into Eddie's scream, "is the mental condition of Eric. I think that your staff would all agree he's in a hell of a better condition than he was when he first came here. He's become more outgoing, he's relating to people on a friendly basis. Why not ask him?"

"That's what I'm going to do."

He picked up a phone and said something in it. Eric had been waiting in another room. He entered his doctor's office and smiled when he saw me.

"Hey, Jason!"

"Hi there, Eric."

"Oh, brother," muttered Eddie.

Eric's expression changed as he studied the expressions of my two accusers.

"Is something wrong, Jason?"

"Eric," asked Dr. Steele, "I want you to be frank with us and tell us how you feel about having Jason as your special duty nurse? Would you like somebody else—like Eddie here?"

Eric resembled an angel at that moment. His face was freshly shaven. His eyes sparkled and his navy blue sweater and gray slacks made him resemble a college hero.

"Eddie?" Eric repeated. "I don't like Eddie. He's mean. I've seen him slap the men around."

"That's a goddamned lie!" howled Eddie. "You've got this jerk telling you what to say. I—"

"I want Jason. He makes me laugh."

I held my breath, fearful that he might blurt out more of what we did.

"Do you and Jason have sex, Eric?" blurted Eddie. "Come on. Tell us. We know what goes on!"

"That's enough, Eddie!" ordered Dr. Steele. "I'll not have you intimidating our patients here."

"You can get these patients to say anything," Miss Tyson griped.

"Do you really think so, Miss Tyson?" I asked. "Maybe we should bring in Harriet Snyder—that young, woman patient you're always hanging around with. You always sit with her at all the meals. I've seen you walking alone with her out into the woods. I've heard you write her love notes."

"Don't you dare suggest that I'm doing something nasty like that?" barked Miss Tyson.

"Well, you and your good buddy, Eddie here don't hesitate to come in here and try to get me fired. You can't have it both ways."

"Jason," smiled Eric, "are we going on the picnic this afternoon? I like picnics. Will we go see *The Music Man* again? That was a great movie."

"I hope we can, Eric. We'll have to wait for Dr. Steele to decide that."

We all watched those metallic gray eyes of the executive physician study the patient. Then he glanced up at me:

"Jason, go ahead and take Eric along with you. You can stay as you are. I'd like to say a few words to Miss Tyson and to Eddie here."

"They're going to try and get revenge for what I've said, Dr. Steele. Remember that. I know these two people. They have ways. They're going to do everything they can to get me out of here."

"Go along now," Dr. Steele said. I took a last look at my accusers. If facial expressions could kill, I would have been a mass of tortured flesh right there in that office.

As Eric and I went out into the frosty, crisp air of morning, I felt triumphant—and nervous. Did Dr. Steele know just how treacherous my two enemies could be?

But when I got my mail later that day, I forgot about them and momentarily even Eric: I had received a letter from the Office of Admissions at East Carolina University.

I was accepted for the winter quarter that began in just a month. As I waited for the elevator, my buddy, Nurse Holiday, came up to me.

"You don't have anything to worry about, Jason," she smiled. "You can stay on here. I just saw Dr. Steele. But you'd better be forewarned that Eddie and Miss Tyson are not your friends here. They were royally chewed out."

"They should be fired. Why does this place keep deadbeats like that on here?"

"They can't go anywhere else. Nobody would hire them. They get paid zilch here and they're miserable people, so they want everybody else to be as wretched as they are."

◆　　　◆　　　◆

I've often wondered how life would have continued that winter had I not decided to resume my college career at East Carolina University?

Maybe it was all for the best. I couldn't have spent the rest of my life as Eric's special nurse. Even in 1963, I heard rumors that Mountain Manor had been sold to a New York City corporation that had a chain of super-exclusive drug and alcoholism rehab clinics.

Within a year of my departure, this is in fact what happened. Nearly all the staff was discharged. Most of them were deadwood anyway. Only a few RN nurses were rehired.

Miss Tyson, Eddie and the others were kicked out. New personnel were brought in and the mental patients were transferred to other facilities. Even Eric.

I found that out years later because after my appearance before Dr. Steele, I felt victorious.

Eric and I sat across each other in the dining room as we enjoyed our breakfast.

"That was so close, Eric!" I gasped. "Those jerk offs nearly got me kicked out of here."

"I'll take care of them!" he said simply. "I don't want them to ever separate us, Jason. And if they try to hurt you, I'll hurt them really bad."

I wanted to hug and kiss him right there. He was so sweet and handsome and in his own vulnerable way, brave.

I had four weeks left. I planned to take a train directly from the picturesque little Biltmore station just blocks away from Mountain Manor. From there, I'd travel to Greenville, North Carolina.

I had no idea where it was—or what kind of place East Carolina University was. It was a big school, though. Also, I loved the word "East." I felt it symbolized something wonderful and mystical.

How little did I know when I only nineteen.

In my spare time, I had to buy new clothes, new bedclothes for my dorm room.

Eric and I became even closer. We could sit quietly at meals, or watch television or the others playing ball and I imagined this must be what a newly wed couple felt about each other.

An extraordinary stream of energy connected us and I could glance at him and he would look at me and we smiled. When no one was around, he covered my hand with his and held it to his mouth to kiss it.

His body heat was phenomenal. Billy Dragon had been unusually warm but Eric was amazing. If the day was chilly and we were outside, I instinctively moved closer to him.

He smiled, as if understanding why I did so.

I didn't let him know I would be going away soon. I hoped we could arrange something so I would see him now and then.

We very carefully kept up our rendezvous on the unused stage. Both Eddie and Miss Tyson kept out of my way. When I did see them, I didn't even nod at them.

Eddie puckered up his face like he was ready to puke.

I crossed my eyes and stuck out my tongue. Miss Tyson lurched past me with her eyes rolling all over the place.

Gradually, I let Eric know that I would be leaving Mountain Manor. I didn't want us to lose communication with each other.

"You're not coming back?" he asked like a small boy.

"Not to work," I said. "Maybe we can arrange to meet somewhere in Asheville."

"I can get us a hotel room," he smiled. "A really nice one. I'll be out by then. I'll make my Mama take me out of here."

He sounded so child like in his simplicity. He had no conception of how the outside world worked. One afternoon, when Miss Holiday left the nurse's station for a bathroom break, I was alone and for the first time, I sneaked a peek into

Eric's record. No one but the head of staff, the head doctors and the head nurse were supposed to see this.

Although I was his special duty nurse, I still wasn't allowed to see his intimate chart. Before I heard Miss Holiday returning, I glanced at the top of the chart. Age: 34.

Thirty-four! I had thought he was 18 or a little older. But of course, the lobotomy prevented him from worrying about the things we usually do. With no worries, he had no stress.

I wanted to see more but had to quickly slip the file back into place.

◆　　　◆　　　◆

My coworkers, with two notable exceptions, were sad about my departure but encouraging that I planned to finish college.

"You don't want to end up here as an attendant the rest of your life," said Nurse Holiday. "The guys they've got now are deadbeats. Oh, maybe Bobby and James are okay. They'll move on. But the rest—"

The day before I was to leave, Dr. Steele gave permission for me to take Eric into town that night. The movie, *West Side Story*, had just opened.

We dressed up in our best and took a taxi to Pack Square. Eric was ravishing as usual in black wool slacks and an emerald green sweater that brought out the jade of his eyes.

I had splurged on a new winter overcoat—cocoa brown tweed with a fur collar. It matched perfectly my bronze-hued turtleneck of wool with matching tweed slacks and boots.

We ate once more—for the final time—at Tingle's Restaurant. From there, we walked the few blocks to the theater.

We sat against the wall again, in the dark, and at the back where no one was around. When we were sure no one was watching, my hands slid into his pants.

We kissed briefly. Oh, how I wished we could have our own private hotel room. This was too dangerous to carry out. I had no money for such a plan and Eric was given only enough for supper and a movie for two.

We smooched passionately, he used up three handkerchiefs and when we left the theater around ten, I floated into the taxi. Eric pulled me close to him and I guess the driver thought I was a woman: my new beret was pulled low over my eyes.

At the nurse's station, Nurse Holiday was waiting for us.

"Here's Eric's medicine for the last time," she said between tears. He and I went to his room.

He pulled me hard against him and kissed me.

"Don't leave me, Jason," he wept, "don't leave me. You'll never come back."

"Yes, I will, I will."

I watched him strip off his clothes and slide between the sheets of his bed. Tears still sparkled on his cheeks.

I bent down and kissed him one last time. He had turned his back to me and lay, curled up, like a child. His shoulders trembled as he wept.

I ran my hand lightly over his head, his torso, to remember him.

When I left his room, I passed Nurse Holiday. She hugged me.

"Oh, we're gonna miss you so much, honey! You get that degree and knock'em dead!"

◆　　　◆　　　◆

Snow had fallen overnight.

When my taxi let me out at the little jewel box of a train station in Biltmore, it resembled a Christmas card. The tiny station was located at the bottom of the hill where I could still see the tall chimneys of Mountain Manor.

A fireplace crackled with huge logs and coal in the snug waiting room. White tiles gleamed and the walls were decorated with oil paintings, dark with age and dust. Miss Holiday and several other nurses had all chipped in to buy me a beautiful white angora sweater.

Behind the grilled window of the ticket master, the small clerk sipped coffee from a huge mug.

"You've got ten minutes before the train's due," he said. "It should be a beautiful trip in the snow, over the mountains."

A few minutes later, I watched the toy-like train creep into the station when a blast of cold air hit me from the main entrance.

I looked around.

"Hi," he smiled. "I had to come and say goodbye."

"Eric! Oh, my God, how wonderful. How did you manage to get away?"

"I ran away," he said sweetly. "I didn't tell anybody. I fooled that old woman who's with me. She was asleep in her chair and I just walked away."

Even now, I can see that beautiful face of his—those eyes, opened wide and excited, his square face and that tuft of dark hair that hung over his brow.

His long coat of black cashmere, the red muffler around his neck, the dark beret over his jet curls, made him look like a movie star.

He put his arms around me and held me close to him.

"You won't leave me, will you? I'm all-alone here. I want to go with you. Let's go to New York. I've got some money. You wouldn't have to work anywhere. I own buildings there. We could live in one of them."

We had moved to a corner of the deserted room. Over his shoulder I could glimpse the top tier of Mountain Manor, way up there against the dark clouds.

A dot of gold light gleamed there. How I wished I were back there! Behind it raced those charcoal layers of clouds. A snowstorm was on its way. Wind blew the pine trees furiously.

His cologne, Royal Lime, clung like a sensuous dream to his neck.

"I wish you could come with me, Eric," I smiled. "I really wish it. But, you've got to stay here for the time being. I'll visit you."

"They're mean to me," he frowned. "They don't make me feel good like you did. I don't laugh like I used to."

He had opened his coat and unzipped his pants. "Make me feel good right now?"

"Hey, we can't do that here, handsome!" Lord, how I was tempted but the wizened old ticket clerk had noticed us.

Through one of the small windows that overlooked the main drag, a familiar van turned into the driveway.

Two of my former attendants in their white jackets slipped out.

"I think they've found you, Eric. But it was so wonderful of you to come and see me off!"

His eyes glanced upwards.

"I'll bet they're up there right now, Jason. The flying saucers. I want to be the first aboard. Will you come with me?"

"Oh, Eric, please. No flying saucers now."

He pulled me close to him and kissed me right there in the waiting room. I sank into his beautiful body again—for the last time.

My old buddy, Donald, came up to us and shook his head sadly.

"Eric, you've got to come with us," he ordered. "You shouldn't have run away like that. You've got the whole hospital in an uproar."

"I had to come and see Jason go away. He's not coming back."

Donald wrapped a big arm around Eric and held him close, like an older brother taking control of an unruly young sibling.

Smoke from the train billowed into the air. It no longer exists but at that time, the train was the replica of the kind you may still see climbing the Alps in Austria. Cars were painted a gleaming, rich red, with black trim.

I hurried out and stepped aboard. I found a window seat and stared out at a man I knew I would never see again.

Eric and Don waved at me. Eric had become excited and Don smiled down at him but held his arm firmly around his shoulder.

Like an old Warner Brothers movie from the forties, I looked out of my window, weeping, as the train rounded a bend and I lost sight of Eric.

Years later, I heard he was tricked by one of the nurses into marrying her. I knew her and was aware that the others considered her a slut. She slept with anybody and everybody who could help her out.

The marriage ended quickly because Eric was not the kind of lover you married for the long term. Yet, the nurse ended up a wealthy divorcee. That was her plot all along. To get her hands on some of that huge fortune.

Fate, however, hadn't finished with my black-haired boyfriend and me.

Twenty-five years after leaving Mountain Manor, I had stopped in Asheville on my way back to Montgomery, Alabama where I was then working as a reporter for the daily newspaper.

I stood at the corner of the main thoroughfare where the city's art deco library and old Rialto Theater once stood.

I was saddened by all the changes I found in this mystical city. Mountain Manor was now strictly a drug and alcohol rehabilitation spa. The little train station was no more. Tingle's Restaurant had become a junk shop.

The Biltmore area was now a scruffy neon jungle of ugly fast food joints and used car lots and relentless traffic jams. Wendy's, McDonalds, Army's all squashed each other out for space along that once beautiful boulevard.

As I stood on the corner, waiting to cross the street, someone called out my name:

"Jason?"

To my right stood Eric.

He smiled at me, shyly, as if we were both back at Mountain Manor.

"Eric! Oh, my God!"

We hugged but it was like being pressed to a mannequin.

All was gone.

"They're up there!" he grinned and looked upward at the gray, charcoal sky.

His eyes were dull and distant. He looked around us. A jacket of black leather perfectly outlined his broad shoulders and narrow waist.

His hair was still thick, but silver had crept into it. A glassy expression now replaced that warm glimmer in his eyes. Now, it was like he was not aware of either me or his surroundings.

That unforgettable sparkle and aura of vitality were gone.

Staring heavenward, he smiled.

"They're still up there, Jason! Flying saucers are coming to earth soon."

"Eric, I've thought and thought about you! What are you doing now? Are you still at Mountain Manor?"

"I live across town," he nodded and studied the cracked pavement. "I have a live-in nurse now. I can go out by myself. Do you know I saw a flying saucer last night?"

"Did you?"

He studied the sidewalk and clenched his jaw. His expression had gone from flatness to grimness.

I still grasped his arm. I wanted him to embrace me, to hug me or show me some affection. His mind had disintegrated, though, into a chaotic jumble.

"I told the space men I would join them soon."

A bus roared to a stop. Workingwomen with bundles and crumpled paper bags climbed aboard. A construction worker with his metal lunch pail mounted the steps.

Smiling at me, Eric joined them.

"I'm going up there real soon," he called out and looked up at the sky.

"I love you, Eric!"

He smiled and nodded.

"That's nice of you. We'll fly up there together one day."

The bus rattled off. Eric was staring at the sky through the window.

Where he went and what became his fate remains a mystery.

I don't believe in visiting the dead. Let their memories remain intact.

Chapter Five
James

✦

1963–65

His face was one of those cute-ugly mugs.

You've seen the type on professional wrestlers, hunky construction workers, electricians and plumbers.

Coffee-hued eyes slanted slightly, suggesting a touch of the Oriental.

When he grinned, you wanted to grin with him. It was one of these loose, ballsy expressions, touched with innocent boyishness.

He could pass for the family goofball—impish, macho, endearing.

What made him stand out was his powerful torso that supported this bewitching face. James was rugged, powerful, with a boxer's build. He moved like a star athlete, with a menacing swagger—yet, he detested sports as much as I did.

I watched him one night take on three thugs and he creamed them all with minimal effort. I was waiting for him to come out of the library when the trio of psychos had started baiting me and threatening to break my queer, cock-sucking, homo neck.

I told him he should consider becoming a cop or a trooper and he just snorted.

"Shi-yat, that warn't nothing."

He was so butch looking and acting that I was amazed when it was he who came up to me and propositioned me. That's what always thrilled me about James. He hated game playing and building up to a proposition.

James was one of the very few nice things to happen to me while I was a student at East Carolina University.

Coming there was the major mistake in my life. Maybe nearly every campus back in 1963 was just as bigoted and redneck and homophobic but this one had become a nightmare.

While the small population of Brevard had become use to me and had come to know me, the 23,000 students at this Southern party school were appalled and dumbfounded at the sudden appearance of this swishy, girly, flamboyant guy.

I made no pretext of being anything other than myself. I had become used to acting my real self at Brevard College but I had forgotten that it was small enough where you got to eventually know nearly everyone.

Not at East Carolina University.

It was enormous. Picture this large tract of flat land, located in an ugly tobacco producing area where the summers were hellish and the winters were beyond freezing.

Yet, it was small enough that word spread like lightning of this blonde-haired, flaming homo who made absolutely no attempt to tone himself down.

After two months in the gigantic dorm on top a small hill, I was forced to move out. It had become too dangerous.

Boys by the dozens met me in the hallways or in the bathrooms and loudly demanded blowjobs.

In groups, they studied me in the corridors and called out: "Hey, ain't she pretty? You wanna give us all some head? Come by Room 8-B at eight tonight. We'll all be waiting."

Beneath the smirking contempt, I sensed sincerity. Yeah, they might want me to come by and give them all head, but they more than likely would have a very unpleasant surprise waiting for me.

The boys at Brevard now seemed wonderfully sweet and innocent and fun. These guys were dangerous and repulsive. Occasionally, one would sidle up to me when no one was around and say something like, "Anytime you wanna suck cock, I'll be there."

But I suspected this was all a set-up by the gang leaders who were testing me out.

On the weekends, after getting roaring drunk at the bars, they returned to pound on my door and demanded I "suck me off, you fucker! Open up the fuckin' door! I wanna plow that faggy ass of yours!"

Several times, they set fire to my door when I wouldn't open it. The floor proctor did nothing. He was among those drunken bigots who wanted "to get sucked off!"

When notices went on dorm bulletin boards to vote for the Home Coming Queen, someone doctored a picture of me—drawing on long curls, extra long lashes—and the words, "Vote for Jason Fury as Home Coming Queen."

There was nothing fun, impish or good-natured about these taunts. These boys were encouraged by their cohorts to see to it that I was run off the campus. They might screw everything that moved, impregnate girls by the dozens each year, total their cars and drain their parent's bank accounts. But I was the blot and the sinner who had to be removed.

So I moved out of the dorm into a room in a large, rambling Victorian house near Main Street. My small studio was in the rear and had its own private entrance, which I loved.

Yet, my reputation as a debaucher of anything in pants grew to mythic proportions.

In the hallways of class buildings, groups of students nudged each other and stared at me with unblinking gaze when I came into view.

"There he—I mean It—is!...come're...look! Oh, My God! Look at the way he moves!...that is definitely a fag!...Definitely!...See how he swishes along and look at his eyes!...I'll bet he's wearing make-up!...Look at that coat!....It's a woman's coat!...Guys don't wear long coats with fur on them!...Oh, My, God, I've got to write my buddies back home about this!...They will not believe this!..."

I heard the giggles and guffaws. The more brazen rednecks sang out: "There it is! Miss Fag America!" Fraternity jerks were especially vociferous. They knocked books and papers out of my hands, tried to trip me on stairs, flipped over my food tray in the cafeteria.

If I sat down at a table in the crowded cafeteria, everyone stood up and moved elsewhere. As word spread that there was an out-and-out fag on campus, fraternity brats passed the word to other fraternity Neanderthals.

"We've got to get rid of this animal! It's our duty!"

Their main form of strategy was for the jerks to cluster along the sidewalks and corridors that I had to traverse on my way to classes.

If I tried to diverge from my pattern, they quickly found out and regrouped. One of the most obscene of my enemies was an acne-scarred ape named Gene Schmidt.

"Here it comes!" he regularly sang out. "What is it, guys? Is this a man or a woman—or could it be a fuckin' cocksuckin' homo!"

I remember him especially because of his pustule-laden face, the shapeless, blubbery body and a big, purple mouth that stretched from ear to ear, revealing yellowing teeth. Pizza and hamburger crumbs always clung to his chin.

In the hallways, I was often pushed, spit on and tripped. Passing faculty members did nothing. They thought it was just good, ole fashioned hijinks performed by over-spirited campus brats.

I found a little security in a small group of literary types, headed by a marvelous earth-mother type, Patricia. She and her hunky husband, Tolson, offered us understanding and nurturing.

We worked on the campus newspaper and magazine. Often we had coffee and burgers together and now and then, Pat and Tolson had us over for wine and cheese at their roomy old Victorian residence. But they could hardly expect to be with me all the time.

I also discovered a tiny cluster of gay students there but like at Brevard, these kids were also terrified of being singled out as "homo." I felt no kinship with them. They were smug and superficial and camped it up only when we were all alone.

They talked much about making it with some aloof jock star but this is all they did: dream. The only sex they had was with each other—and they complained about these trysts.

In public, they were like the other same, boring, bland students. Their hair was parted neatly on the sides. They wore conventional pea coats and slacks and loafers.

I enjoyed getting together with a few gay guys who were not students. They held regular jobs through the week and then I'd go with them to Raleigh, a city that had several bars that attracted the gay people from nearby campuses: Duke, Wake Forest, University of North Carolina, North Carolina State and East Carolina University.

In the smoky darkness of these bars, I didn't stand out. And if I did, older, macho men noticed and liked. I met several out-of-towners this way.

But on campus, my lot was a grim one.

Since I now lived a block from the commercial district, I met a group of sexy, impish hustlers. They never finished high school, most had probably been in reformatory school, but they fascinated me.

They used their bodies to advance their fortunes. With me, it was all free because they liked me and I liked them.

Each had their specialty. Arnie was so well hung and so resilient, his nickname was The Hammer. Derrick was a handsome cutie-pie whose ass was spectacular. Loren was an all-round sex machine who proved to be a master of soul kissing.

They described in graphic detail their encounters and what all had happened in cars. On one freezing night, I invited them to spend the night in my room.

We all pitched in and got a supply of beer and wine and chips. None of us were aware of the blizzard that broke all records. When you share a bed with that many people, you tend to ignore such trivial matters as a screaming snowstorm.

I had met them all at Willie's Newsstand, right on the edge of the campus. It was in this plain, crowded little hole-in-the-wall that straight men made contact with me.

Everyone had heard of me and recognized me. It was here that they could communicate with me without being gossiped about. Small, endearing little Willie loved watching me and the others get together. He resembled a white mouse behind the counter.

When any of us regulars needed a loan, he handed over a handful of dollars.

With his glasses perched on the end of his nose, a cigarette always hung from his mouth.

The cops liked him, too, so they turned their eyes away from the busy, silent scene of males making contact with other males.

This is where fate thrust my Demon Lover and me together.

He had instantly intrigued me from the beginning. Occasionally, he dropped in to browse through the sports magazines.

"He comes in now and then," said Willie. "I don't know how he swings. He's one hot looking hunk but he does look pretty tough, though. Be careful. Look at his toolbox. He's carrying a heavy load."

"Looka those arms and shoulders! He's a boxer!"

Was he one of the campus jocks? A star football player? A star wrestler? He certainly looked like one handsome bruiser.

I was looking through the muscle magazines one day when I noticed this macho dream just a few feet away. He wore loose jeans, a white tee shirt and work boots. Thick, sandy hair was combed away from a square face.

His slightly slanting eyes suggested he had Oriental blood. His full lips hinted that he might even have some Negro ancestry in there as well. Although he certainly had the muscles and the build to be a boxer, he didn't preen or strut his stuff.

We were in the last row of magazines, tucked away in a corner of the store. No one else was around. My pulse beat faster because I sensed he was back there just because I was.

Willie had set aside one section For Adults Only. You found the usual girlie magazines there, like *Playboy* and *Oui*. But daringly, he also displayed male model magazines.

These publications showcased handsome exhibitionists completely naked—except for white posing straps. This was another example of how the cops turned a blind eye to Willie. In the rest of the South in those days, the store would have been padlocked.

You could display girlie mags but you couldn't feature boy entertainment. That was considered pornographic.

I inched closer and reached for *Male Model*. A rippling, bare-assed hunk grinned from the cover.

"You like that?" murmured the studly stranger. Suddenly, I wondered if he could be vice? And if I said yes, he could lock me up.

"Maybe," I replied cautiously. "I hope it was warm when he posed."

"I posed for one of those mags one time," Mr. Muscleboy smiled. No one else was around.

He had moved up beside me and I looked up at his face.

His eyes were opened wide, like he were constantly surprised, and he stared at the bulging physique model on the cover. I ran a finger over the cover god's gleaming torso.

"You did? What kind of pose?"

The stranger bunched up his biceps and looked over my head.

"Like that."

"Were you naked?"

"Ha. I wore just a G-string. Like this guy has on."

"Whew. Weren't you bashful?"

He looked at me and laughed. "Shit, no. I like showing off my bod. It was just a fun kick. I was passing through L.A. and met some guys and we all posed. We got twenty-five dollars. We all got drunk with it."

"And you had to wear that little posing strap! What a waste. I'll bet you had plenty to show off."

The stranger beamed sweetly.

"You want to see it?"

I decided to trust him.

"Of course. My room's just a block away."

Little Willie raised his brows when he saw me and my new acquaintance leave. Willie pretended to fan himself.

Although delighted, I was also on guard. I had balled with several guys at ECU during my three months there so I had grown to be careful. I had heard of several cases of fag bashing by redneck fraternity guys.

We walked the two blocks to my rooming house and ascended the private entrance.

James followed me into my room. He looked so big and brawny in his casual attire.

"Nice place," he said.

"I'm a little nervous," I blurted. "You're a pretty big guy."

"So?"

"I don't bring that many men here you know—"

"Hey, cut it out. I'm not rough trade. I'm not gonna bother you. Now you wanna see my prize winning bod or not?"

He stripped off his tee-shirt. He did indeed resemble a boxer. He performed some mock physique poses.

His chest was broad and strong with a dusting of hair. Muscles danced across his shoulders, his arms. His stomach was flat and hard.

Then he kicked off his boots and slipped out of his jeans.

"Don't stop there!" I laughed.

"I might be bashful," he joked.

"Bashful, my ass. Come on. Let me see it all."

He turned around and made a joke of shimmying out of his BVDs. His ass was beyond cute. It was tight, round and boyish.

Then he turned around and covered his jewels with his hands.

"You wanna see the rest."

"Lemme see, lemme see!"

He took his hands away. This guy had nothing to be ashamed of. I had thrown my clothes into the corner of the small room and lay naked on my red bedspread.

James joined me on bed and was eager for me to make him feel good. I had grown proficient at practicing this talent by now. I enjoyed a man just laying there, letting me groove on his body and who enjoyed my enjoying him.

James was a perfect partner. With his hands behind his head, he watched my head move steadily over his nude torso. From his nipples my mouth traveled, down to the flat stomach and down to his treasure.

He grunted in pleasure as I increased his arousal. Now and then I glanced up to see him with an arm thrown across his eyes and his mouth opened slightly. Gradually, he writhed and muttered about how hard he was and then his hips arched slightly.

I held his phallus in both my fists and watched it erupt. Then I tackled it again and after a few minutes he repeated the process. After he caught his breath, he pulled me up against him and kissed me.

James was a wonderful kisser. His lips touched my face lightly at first, just brushing my skin, and then his full lips pressed harder until he covered my mouth.

From there, he licked and mouthed my nipples and to my amazement, he covered my own arousal with his mouth. He displayed all the signs of having done this before. His tongue knew exactly how to tease and caress.

When I achieved my relief, I lay in his arms again. We lit up cigarettes and he studied my face.

"You're better than I expected. I've seen you in the newsstand. I've seen you on campus. You could have any guy you want."

"You think so? It's too dangerous. Many see me as an animal."

"You're ahead of your time. One day, guys like you won't have to be afraid of anything. You'll be accepted."

"I'm not holding my breath. I'll be dead and buried."

He laughed and glanced at his watch.

"Uh oh. Gotta get on home. To Kay."

"Whose Kay?"

"My wife."

He said all this like I should have known. I raised myself up and stared down at that boyish face. His thick, sensual lips sucked on a cigarette.

"You're married? God, you're so young looking. And daring."

"Yeah. I got two kids."

"I can't believe this. That is so very strange."

"I'm a strange dude."

He got up and pulled on his clothes. He stooped down to see his face in my mirror and used both hands to sweep his thick hair back from his temples.

"Thanks," he said quietly. "I liked that. I like you."

"I'll see you again, I hope."

"Yeah. But let's don't get too hung up on when or where. When I can get away again, I'll find you."

And so started my strange relationship with James McCrorey. It was to last even to this day.

I didn't see him as much as I wanted to for the rest of my three years at East Carolina. I didn't know what he did all those months when he seemed to vanish

into thin air. But occasionally, I'd glimpse that handsome, square head bobbing around in the crowd of students in the hallways.

He was always alone. All the major men in my life were loners. Maybe that's what attracted me to them. I sensed that they had no interest in being part of the mob.

Or the mob didn't want them as a member.

These men were all independent—like myself—and they had zero interest in peer opinion or pressure. This is why I was forever amazed when they got married to a real woman.

Now and then I'd find James smoking a cigarette alone in front of the cafeteria and we'd talk.

"I miss seeing you Jim. I miss sucking your cock and licking your body and just having you there with me."

His face crinkled up into that cute, bull-dog grin. I could talk bluntly and sexually with him and it didn't faze him.

"I miss seeing you, too. I've got to study hard to keep my scholarship. My wife keeps her eye on me."

"She should. She doesn't know what a prize bull she's got."

Jim laughed. "You appreciate me a lot more than she does."

"How many others do you have?"

"Others? Oh, how many other guys and girls do I ball with? I don't."

"Oh, sure. I believe that. I'll bet you've got lots of guys and girls just waiting for you and climbing the walls for you."

He laughed again, saying nothing, and I was to never know about his other life. He did show me a picture of him and his family. It was a strange grouping. A plain, sweet looking woman sat on a bench, holding a little boy. A small girl stood beside her.

James sat unsmiling beside her. He wore his uniform, even for this family picture: faded jeans, work boots, a white tee shirt. He did not resemble a happily married father and husband.

When I finished school at this hell campus in 1965, I had put James away into my memory box. It had been fun but I had finally lost sight and contact with him.

In 1967, I moved into a large apartment complex in Charlotte in 1967. I hated it because of its impersonality. My home was one of two hundred identical townhouses. The only difference was the apartment number on the front door.

I had lucked into a career in journalism. After two years working for a daily newspaper in Wilmington, N.C., I had snared an even better job in Charlotte with the Associated Press.

I hated everything about my new position there. Unlike the colorful, off-the-wall friends I had made in Wilmington, the Associated Press was a small, crowded little bunch of older men. They had no interest in me because all of them had families and grandchildren.

Since I worked from three to midnight, I had zero chance of meeting handsome men. In this apartment complex, everyone stayed to themselves. They were all married, with kids, and had no interest in sissy single guys.

Two months after living there, I was walking to my car when someone called out my name:

"Jason Fury."

I looked behind me.

James stood there.

He was naked, except for a pair of brief, green trunks. He looked even more like a rugged boxer, a Marine, a professional wrestler.

His beard and moustache were thicker. His hair now touched his broad shoulders.

I ran up to him and embraced him. He laughed and held me close. He lived there, too, with his wife and little girl. No, it wasn't the same wife. This was a new one.

"My first one was too possessive. She didn't want me to get out of her sight. I couldn't take it."

"I understand how she felt, Jim," I smiled. "If you were my husband, I'd be worse than possessive."

He grinned that big, boyish grin.

"You ain't changed any. I can see that. I've missed you."

He didn't work anywhere. He kept the apartment clean and looked after his little daughter while his wife held an important job at a local hospital.

His profession was astrology.

He showed me his astrology chart he used and he got customers by advertising in the local newspaper.

We went back to my apartment and he looked around.

"You're doing pretty good, Miss Jason Fury," he smiled. "I always thought you would."

He pulled me close and kissed me. We looked at each other.

"Have you thought," I murmured, "that fate must have something in mind for us both? Of all the gin joints in the world, you chose this one and I chose it, too. Strange."

"I've always felt we were connected somehow."

"Forever," I smiled.

He kissed me and answered: "Yes, forever."

He pushed his shorts off and stood there naked in all his splendor. In my bed, he was ardent, passionate and stayed with me for several hours. I had fixed up my bedroom in crimson, gold and black.

A small lamp with crystal beads glowed beneath its scarlet shade. From the mouth of a small, gold dragon, incense perfumed the air with a suggestion of sandalwood and strawberry.

James had become bigger and more powerful. On weekends, he boxed and wrestled in amateur competitions around Charlotte. Sometimes he moonlighted as a bouncer in single bars. He also worked occasionally as a bodyguard for visiting celebrities.

I squeezed his hard muscles.

"Do you provide other services to our celebrities as well?"

"Nope. I don't do that. I'm a married guy."

"But we're having fun, James."

"You're different. I don't feel this way about any other guy. Although you aren't really a regular guy. You're the best of both worlds. Half woman, half man. That excites me."

This initial reunion was the closest we would get, however.

For six months I lived there but James was as elusive as he had been at school. Although he lived only a row of houses away, I rarely saw him. Our unspoken rule was that neither of us would visit the other without warning.

He never gave me his phone number, nor did he ask for mine.

A serious problem arose during my fourth month at the apartment complex. A hulking, black janitor, Rufus, visited me one day to repair a stopped up bathtub drain.

After he unstopped it, he turned to me and lowered his jeans.

"Wanna have some fun?"

"Sorry. Not interested."

I was unnerved by both his proposition and by his tone. It was like: okay, Fag Boy, here's you some fun stuff.

"Oh, come on. We all know you're a homo. We've seen you swishing around the complex."

"Have you finished with the drain, Rufus? Thanks for your help."

"Hey, just a minute."

He came closer. He reeked of Jade East Cologne. His old sweat stunk even more. Flab drooped over his waist and his hands still grasped his dark privates.

"You can have it for free. I won't charge you anything. Other homo's out here like what I got. I only charge'em ten dollars."

"Listen, will you please get out of here? I'm not interested."

His blubbery features hardened.

"Fuckin' fag. You'll be sorry."

What if I reported him? The manager was a sneaky looking man who I heard from James hated homosexuals.

I began to receive threatening phone calls. "I know where you are," rasped the voice. "You'll be sorry, fuckin' pervert!"

I came home one night around midnight and the minute I entered my apartment, I knew someone had been there.

A dirty glass sat in the sink. My comforter had splotches of gooey, sticky stuff. It looked like someone had either spit or ejaculated on it. And I smelt that nausea inducing Jade East Cologne.

The next day, I saw James. He wore just bathing shorts and had a green bandana tied around his dark locks.

I told him what had happened.

"Don't worry," he said. "I'll fix him. I've seen that tub of black lard skulking around here and I've heard bad things about him."

He doubled up his fist and spit on it.

"He won't bother you anymore."

I don't know what James did but the calls and the intrusions stopped after that. When I spotted Rufus, he headed the other way.

From Charlotte, I moved to Fargo, North Dakota, in late 1968, where I worked in the Associated Press bureau there. I had wanted a change and boy, oh, boy was this ever a change.

I was amazed at how easy it was to pick up straight men and have fun with them.

They were everywhere. In bars, in cars, at grocery stores and car repair shops. We'd begin to chitchat, and then I'd mention how lonely it was for me in that snow-buried city and they'd mention they might come by for a beer and bingo. They would and they stayed.

The two bigots I worked with in the Associated Press office were something else. They were shell shocked when I waltzed in one October day in 1968 as the new reporter.

They never got over their astonishment. They did everything they could to squeeze me out and hire someone more conventional and more macho. The sandy-haired retard, especially, needed someone who could become as alcoholic as he was.

The blubbery one resembled a boar with a small, upturned nose, a thin mouth and thick glasses. He fancied himself a great reporter.

I had found a snug studio apartment in the basement of a building near Main Street.

My windows revealed little except the snow-covered ground. Yet, I had my own private entrance and plenty of privacy. Since I got off work at three in the afternoon, I had plenty of time to visit one of the many bars along Main Street and usually met a single, lonely guy.

One freezing Saturday afternoon, when everything was buried beneath our latest blizzard, a knock at my door surprised me.

No one visited me unless they phoned me first. I knew it couldn't be the two village idiots at work. They made it clear they wanted no contact with me on any level.

When I opened the door, my macho, unpredictable Demon Lover stood there.

He wore his cowboy hat, leather jacket, jeans and boots. A guitar was strapped to his chest and he carried a duffel bag.

"James!' I squealed. Like a big, scrumptious bear, he held me close and kissed me.

His beard and moustache made him look like Grizzly Adams. He smelt like ice and snow and trucks and cigarettes.

I ran my hands up under his black turtleneck and felt those wonderful pecs and arms.

"You are one fuckin' hard-to-find weirdo!" he complained. "Of all the shit holes to end up in, you chose the worse! Fargo!"

"Hey, it's not bad at all! It's different. And the men! Woooo, I love these North Dakota hunks!"

"You're making me jealous."

"None can ever compare to you, my handsome stud!"

I fixed us a big, old-fashioned steak supper. We guzzled beer and then we went to bed.

It was like the old Demon Boy of college days. He was passionate and resilient and he had kept his body hard and in good boxer condition. He had lost some of his bulk but not his muscles.

He said nothing of his past three years. Except that he had now left wife number two (that I knew of) and was wandering the road. He had just read Jack Kerouac's intense road bible, *On the Road*, and he had adopted it as his road map of life.

That was a magical weekend. Since my basement apartment was tiny, my bed was the largest piece of furniture and so we spent most of our time there.

He asked me questions about my life and what I had been doing and enjoyed listening to my male experiences here.

"Believe me, it's a hell of a lot better than staying there in Charlotte! I never met anybody!"

After a few days, I caught him gulping amphetamines. I noticed he babbled a lot, nonstop and his eyes contained a strange glimmer. I said nothing except: "Oh, I didn't know. Whatever gets you through, whatever gets you through."

Other than that, James was fascinated by this snow-encrusted world of Fargo.

I showed him the great little malls, the Main Street and the hotel where I had first stayed, The Donaldson. In the bars, we met numerous lonely men and we all returned to my place.

I was surprised to see a new side of James as he became the active partner in our mini-orgies. He gulped and gagged and licked and kissed passionately.

My miserable professional life there was made much more bearable with this hunk to return to at night. In his brawny arms and beneath his kisses, he made the nights glide by fast and passionately.

He stayed for a month and then suddenly left after we'd argued. He had developed a sadistic trait of playing "mind fuck" games and I refused to join in. He liked to point out my weak points and dwell on them but when I returned the favor, he became furious.

He became vicious and mean. I found signs of other people in my place that he had brought home. Wadded clumps of toilet paper, semen stains on my sheets, a lipstick smudge on a glass.

He finally bragged about the pussy he was bringing there, along with old railroad bums who wanted to blow him.

Sex became taboo. He couldn't get aroused and expressed zero interest in getting it on. The rare times he permitted me to caress him, he remained soft. Nothing could get it up.

He banged away at his guitar while I tried to write. When I asked him to please lower the volume, he flew into rages.

He became demonic in the ways he tried to belittle my life and my writing.

"You'll never amount to anything because all you do is copy other writers! There's not an original word in all your stories!"

I ordered him to leave.

And so he did one bitterly snowy day in March of 1969. He told me to go "fuck yourself. You'll never be a fucking writer of any kind. All you do is talk about it. You'll never do it because you're just a sleazy fag like all the other fags. All you want is a cock to suck on."

"At least I can find a cock that's hard which is more than you can say."

From Fargo, I moved to Montgomery, Alabama where I was hired for a top job on the newspaper there. This time my apartment in mid-town was on the ninth floor of a swanky building, Capitol Towers.

One year after I settled in there, on a rare day where it actually snowed in Montgomery, Jim suddenly appeared again out of nowhere. He never told me how he found me but all our past spats were forgotten.

I picked him up at the Greyhound Bus Station, just a block from my apartment building.

We hugged and he picked me up and kissed me and I felt of his chest and crotch.

Constant wandering resulted in him losing much weight. No longer did he have that swaggering bear-like torso. Now, he was slender and pale looking.

I didn't want to think about drugs. I was just glad to have my Demon Lover back with me.

I had acquired many boyfriends by this time. In my work, I met countless men every week—from politicians, detectives, ex-cons, visiting celebrities and yes, even hot-eyed evangelists.

Some were jealous of my new boyfriend and others were fascinated. For James was now determined to be a famous folk singer. He had brought his guitar and sang for us. I wrote him up as a feature for the newspaper and others wanted to meet him.

With his dark curls and beard, he looked the perfect image of a hippie folk singer. While he had accused me of being a hypocrite in trying to ape being a writer, he was trying to cast himself in the mode of singers Bob Dylan and James Taylor.

To my dismay, he quickly dropped his façade of loving, caring friend.

He became surly and moody and hostile. When he began babbling incessantly again my heart sank. Speed had taken control.

Our lovemaking was nowhere as intense as it had been. He seemed to force himself to do it with me. His old problem of non-arousal was obvious.

Then he began to taunt me for my desire of him.

One night, he began that horrible, sadistic mind-fuck game.

"All you see in me is a cock. Ain't that right? A cock, cock, cock. You don't see me as a person. You act like all the fags I've met. You're like a breed apart. Don't you guys think of anything else?"

"Yeah, Jim, I think of other things. Like, why are you still roaming around in your early thirties with one pair of jeans to your name and why do you keep getting married and popping out babies and then leaving them behind? At least fags don't make babies."

I was astonished when he suddenly broke down and wept. He heaved and shook and cried silently.

"Stop it, James. Cut it out. You have to admit you asked for it."

"Jesus, you're a vicious bitch!" he wailed.

"Why did you start it? Why do you play these mind games? Let me make it clear. From now on, no more game playing. The game's over."

He continued to weep as he sat Buddha like on the floor of my den. I became concerned and called up his mother who I had talked to over the years. She was a sweet, country woman who naturally doted on the black sheep of her large family.

Everyone in the family was fond of Baby James but all were worried about him. He didn't act rationally and he took so many risks. We agreed that I would put him on a bus to his hometown in North Carolina.

She and his older brothers would meet him and take care of him.

I brought his bus ticket at the nearby Greyhound Bus Station. With his guitar and beaten up old suitcase, he took a seat in the rear of the bus. He tilted his cowboy hat over his forehead.

The last I saw of him, he resembled an old man.

A month before I left Montgomery for New York City in spring of 1978, he wrote me a letter.

It was a horrible letter that dripped with terrible hatred and darkness. He accused me of destroying his life. He said I was a nothing talent who would never amount to anything. I, according to him, was a predatory, sleazy fag homo who would spend my life looking for cock.

"I wish you the worst the world has to offer. I hope you die a violent and endless death because you're a deadbeat and a coward and a pervert who should be locked up forever."

I tore up the letter. Our relationship had ceased to exist.

The morning I was to leave my apartment forever, I checked my mailbox and was surprised to find another letter from James.

"Why haven't you written me, you beautiful slut? Is this any way to treat a man who truly loves you? I hope my last letter didn't upset you. I wrote it as a joke. You know my quirky moods and me. Tell me you forgive me. You and I are forever connected. Fate threw us together. You're the only one who can tolerate me. I'm a bastard. You know that. Please say you've forgiven me. I'm holding my breath.

"Love, your old pal, Sweet Baby James."

Once again, I ripped the apology into shreds.

Pieces fluttered away over the parking lot and into the sultry, Magnolia scented air of Montgomery, Alabama.

With a sigh of relief, I headed my little red Chevette away from that apartment building for the last time.

Even tonight, though, I half expect someone to knock quietly at my door.

And when I open it, my Demon Lover will be standing there.

His first words, as always will be:

"Hey, what's up?"

And I'll probably squeal: "James!"

PART III
The Working Freak
◆
1965

Chapter Six
The Master

He was an ugly sonofabitch.

He was childish, demanding and spoiled rotten.

Scotty was my first newspaper editor. I hated to think of what my future ones would be. I prayed he would die the worst death of all.

From the minute I joined his news team at the *Wilmington Star-News,* in 1965, he made my life hell.

I realize now the shock that must have knocked him for a loop. In no way, did I resemble anyone in his intimate, incestuous newsroom of twenty reporters and editors.

The cubs groveled at his feet and laughed too loud at his jokes. They scurried downstairs to buy him coffee in the sandwich shop and listened raptly to him spin yarns of his glory days as a cub reporter in Chicago.

In that newsroom in 1965, you beheld a perfect case of rabid hero worship. Like a great charismatic coach or teacher, Scotty had that magical combination of shimmering male beauty, a brilliant creative mind and the uncanny insight as to what buttons to push to elicit a reaction from his worshippers.

The experienced veterans saw through his blatant manipulative genius, his childish tantrums and studied emotional outbursts.

They were also aware that if Scotty sensed even the slightest spark of criticism, of disgust against him, then you were dead meat.

He tolerated no one in his charmed circle that sneered at his hyper displays of virility and brilliance. I learned quickly that he reveled in his reputation as a super Tom Cat.

He flirted with every female, no matter what the age, like the stereotypical Italian stud. I'd spot him in the corridor talking to one of the girl reporters.

He would be in full bedroom mode: eyes half-closed, staring intently into the eyes of his victim, his attention fixated on her mouth, a little boy quality of innocence when he fluttered his eyes, as she—standing just an inch or two away.

His pelvis jutted forward, just an inch from rubbing up against the quivering object.

And his quarry: spellbound by those sparkling, sex-inflamed eyes and a tongue that occasionally moistened those thick lips.

Even his rare critics, though, had to admit that his leadership methods were worth it—at a price. With him at the helm, the newspaper regularly won state journalism awards for outstanding reporting, writing and criticism.

He babied and coddled and flirted outrageously with his favorites—both male and female—to the point of imbecility. They forgot their requests for raises or promotions and concentrated on making the newspaper proud.

What Scotty hoped no one would realize was that his newsroom also had a notoriously high turnover. Reporters who butted heads with him were quickly squeezed out.

An outstanding reporter who covered City Government and who dared to argue with his lord and master would suddenly find himself doing "desk work"—the lowest level of them all. You were forced to write up obituaries, do the weather reports, and handle in-coming calls.

A brilliant girl reporter suddenly saw her stories buried at the back of the newspaper. No byline heralded her work. And this was a newspaper where even a minor traffic accident story was automatically preceded with the reporter's name.

Her offense? She had objected to Scotty demanding she have dinner with him, and then breakfast and then lunch. Her husband objected.

. If you lasted six months in Scotty's world, then you were considered lucky.

What rankled him was that I had been brought in over his head. He never had a chance of grilling me or feeling me out. Luckily for me, his boss, managing editor Harold Holmes, spent much of his time touring the South in search of recruits for his newspaper.

Before I finally graduated from the hellish two years at East Carolina, I had sent out a flurry of resumes to all the newspapers in North Carolina.

Somehow, one of my resumes ended up at the Wilmington Star-News, which badly needed a reporter.

So the managing editor, Harold Holmes, phoned me, interviewed me and that was how I was brought in over the head of Scotty. No one had even seen me! They had no idea I was a sissy to end all sissies. That my voice was described as soft and sexy and that I had my own sense of style and that with just one glance, it was obvious that sports and outdoorsy things was not my cup of tea at all.

When I walked nervously into the old, dark newsroom on Main Street that October evening in 1965, the whole staff was busy at work.

The six o'clock deadline for all stories was fast approaching. This was exactly the way I had always thought a newspaper would be like.

Nearly everyone had cigarettes aglow, coffee cups forgotten, as their fingers danced over their typewriter keyboards.

I had met with the managing editor, Harold Holmes, before my entrance. I liked him immediately. He was a soft-spoken, weathered looking man who smiled often.

I felt no tension with him and I was relieved not to see that sudden expression of shock, of amazement, that I had come to know only too well from past experiences.

For the occasion, I had sunk all my money into a plain, navy suit, a white shirt, a dark tie and black shoes. This would be my uniform until I received my first paycheck. It never occurred to me to ask my parents for help.

Quickly, a strange silence fell over everyone as the managing editor escorted me up to the big copy desk and I was introduced to Scotty.

He sat in the center, like a king, and I was told that he was the heart of the newspaper. I was thrilled. Again, he could have walked out of Hollywood movie about newspapers.

His shirt was unbuttoned halfway down a tanned chest. A thick crew cut crowned a square head.

His face was pockmarked with scars of an old Acne attack. Instead of reducing his handsome image, this enhanced his reddish flush, as if he were in the throes of sexual longing.

The eyes are what you always noticed about this strange creature: green and aqua, they reflected perfectly his emotional state. Thick lips hid large, white teeth. When he grinned, it was like someone had sliced his face in half.

He greeted me politely, barely looking at me with no smile and assigned one of his reporters to find me a desk and get me started. Those around him saw that expression and I saw one of them roll their eyes.

Uh oh. They knew. Scotty was highly pissed and now he would start the game of terminating the new hire. What he didn't realize was that by this time, I had become an old pro at playing the game of survival. My mother had been my first enemy and I discovered that I could hold my own with her.

From her, the brutes in college were more primitive and relentless but I honed my survival skills.

I didn't crumble and I didn't cry. By now, I was conditioned to encountering hostility, brute hatred and lethal barbs I was aware that from some strange source

or gene, a flame of invincibility glowed. Contempt made me resilient. No red-neck was going to make me grovel.

In other words: I liked myself. I might not fit in anywhere but I had nothing to be ashamed of. I thought I was good-looking in a feminine way. That I had talent, there was no denying that. Those who got to know me liked me. I had a quirky sense of humor that made them howl.

From the corner of my eye, I noticed how the other reporters were glancing at each other and nudging one another.

Nearly thirty minutes later, Scotty suddenly stood up and stalked out into the hallway and slammed the door behind him.

I knew it was about me.

His words left no doubt to anyone for everyone heard him scream:

"…A fucking faggot! Goddamn Harold!Not on my team…"

I experienced zero surprise at his reaction. I had seen his type before in the fraternity Neanderthals and Scotty struck me as a former frat retardate who missed those days and nights of drinking and fucking and smoking.

And so I was witness to a brilliant commander who is determined to destroy an enemy: me.

If it were raining outside, he'd have me to go outside and get him a cup of coffee. He didn't want the coffee from the hamburger shop in the lobby. His coffee had to come from The White Castle, hole-in-the-wall down the block.

He'd have me work until midnight, then demand I report to work the next morning at six.

Instinct warned me to keep my mouth shut and do anything he asked. This man held my future in his big, oversized hands. This was my first professional job, my entry into journalism. If I could just put six months, hopefully a year on my resume of steady newspaper experience, I could find other work.

I had to admit that despite his strange face and head, and his nothing body, his animal heat was startling. Thin beads of sweat gleamed on his forehead and face.

Rarely did he look at me in the eyes. He barked out his orders while pretending to edit a story. But I could glance up suddenly and see his eyes fastened on me. He quickly looked away.

He made a big production of announcing that he was having a party at his house to watch the football games. He verbally invited individually the entire staff but I was somehow overlooked.

And the next day, he continued his production of joking and laughing with the other reporters about who got drunk at his party and how great that chili was that someone had brought along.

I ignored him. While he brayed over my head to one of the male reporters about who passed out, I continued working on my rewrites. This was one of my assignments: to rewrite stories from the smaller, weekly newspapers.

After his bragging had continued on and on, I suddenly had enough.

"Oh, you guys don't know what you missed when Bette Davis was on television last night!" I trilled with a big grin and much batting of my eyes. "Oh, she was fabulous! *Dark Victory* was the movie. Ever heard of it. I simply cried and cried."

Scotty had frozen, with his mouth half open while I carried on. Some of the reporters became hysterical at Scotty's expression. By now, everyone had my number. They knew what I was doing. Scotty didn't.

He just blinked his eyes, shook his head in bafflement and stomped back to his desk.

While I hated him, I enjoyed the company of the other reporters. Unlike Scotty, they were a motley crew of young liberals and burgeoning hippies. Someone as weird as me fitted in perfectly with this crowd.

They reminded me of that vibrant little group at East Carolina University that I enjoyed being with. We were proud of not being part of the mainstream. In this tiny little enclave, we could be as eccentric, as sissy as we wished.

Sammy, the photographer, quickly made it clear that he was attracted to me. He was a dashing, sexy young genius whose whole life revolved around the camera. And smoking pot.

How this guy could work was a mystery since he was enveloped in a perpetual cloud of marijuana.

He smoked in the dark room, in his car, in private, outside the building. He hid his joints in regular cigarette boxes so no one could figure out what was in those strange smelling sticks of tobacco.

Although straight, he enjoyed fooling around with all genders to satisfy his powerful sex drive. His charming smile, his easy laughter attracted everyone. We quickly began a torrid relationship that lasted during my whole stay at the newspaper.

He also gave me the real lowdown on what kind of newsroom I had landed in.

For instance, although Scotty was a notorious homophobe, he was fascinated by several of the sharp lesbian gals who worked in the newsroom.

He saw absolutely nothing contradictory in this attitude. He pursued one of them, Vera, with such determination that it had become a running joke.

It was as if he thought that if he could have the dazzling Vera succumb to his charms, then he would have hit the jackpot. It didn't faze him that she lived openly and naturally with a female cop.

Fortunately for me, Vera and I became instant friends. She was neat, slender, freckle-faced and resembled a basketball coach from the mid-west. She playfully flirted with Scotty, too, but always kept it very light. She admitted she was as fascinated with Scotty as the rest of us were.

But her heart definitely belonged to her femme roommate.

As I managed to cling to my job and weeks turned into months, I was able to buy my very first car—an undependable heap with an alarming tendency to stop dead at every stoplight. But with my car, I found a wonderful little apartment at nearby Wrightsville Beach.

Driftwood Apartments was a picturesque, rambling old wooden building that was nearly empty of tenants during fall and winter months. But the landlady was happy to rent me a room that faced directly the ocean. Her rugged husband, Jack, was even happier.

We hit it off instantly one day when he was fixing my faucet. From that day on, he saw to it that I had the best-maintained apartment on the beach. And I saw to it that he was one happily serviced landlord.

Before I entered my apartment late each night, I paused for a moment and closed my eyes: Good God, you've got your first car, your first apartment, your first set of friends, and your first job.

And you did it on your own! Never did I take any of these mundane assets for granted. From growing up under a cloud of notoriety and rejection, I was seeing a more positive side of life that I thought would never come my way.

I was amazed to realize each night that I really had my first close friends in my life. I didn't have to fear being beaten up or gang raped anymore if I held a newspaper job. But I was still in that delicate stage where I could be fired outright and lose everything.

With the urging of Vera and Sammy, I worked like a demon on a feature about a young rookie cop who patrolled the night beat. Morris was a handsome, over-sexed officer who lived briefly in my building at Wrightsville Beach. We were attracted instantly. He bluntly asked me one afternoon: "You wanna do me?"

He was plain, simple, down-to-earth, and good-natured—exactly like the young hustlers I had known at East Carolina University. If I wanted to ball, I merely knocked on his door and he, saying nothing, let me in.

When he wanted some fun, he'd do the same to me. This meant every night or afternoon he was free.

My photo buddy, Sammy, was fascinated by my relationship with the young cop. Morris happily posed nude for Sammy's camera and I got all the pictures. He was excited about being the subject of a big Sunday feature.

Sammy did an outstanding job taking the dramatic black and white photos of Morris on his beat at night.

So my portrait, "A Lonely Job for a Young Cop" was turned in—Scotty accepted it, but not before indifferently tossing it aside, as if I had delivered a bag of road kill.

He said nothing.

I heard later he had argued why he didn't want to run the feature. When he decided to, he wasn't going to give me a by-line.

But Vera argued just as persuasively why it was hardly fair to refuse me a by-line when Scotty gave his cronies a name beneath the headline on even the most routine of weather and traffic stories.

Later, she told me what she said to Scotty.

"Jason could use a by-line, Scotty! For God's sake, he's new and young and bright. Give him his chance! You do if for everybody else!"

The feature received overwhelming praise and the police department loved it. Morris became a celebrity and was featured on local television.

The Police Chief wrote a charming letter to the editor and this bolstered my stock. When I went to the 'Cop Shop' to see what was going on, the night crew was all bawdy, affectionate and fascinated.

I saw some of them flipping their wrists and batting their eyes, but most were real he-men who openly flirted with me. But—I knew I had to be careful. If Scotty heard any rumors of hanky-panky between me and the men in blue, he could fire me on the spot.

A week later, I turned in another story, about an old newspaper woman, Melanie, who had retired from the *Chicago Tribune* and was living her life as a recluse at a lonely end of the beach. I described her award-winning career as a star reporter, the great trials she had covered, and the underworld gangsters she had met.

Sammy took striking pictures of her walking along the beach and feeding the sea gulls. Her neighbors called her The Bird Woman of Wrightsville Beach.

Once more, Vera had to argue with Scotty why she thought the feature should run. She, herself, wrote the promos for it and made sure it was given a full-page in our Sunday edition.

The feature received strong reaction from readers. Scotty had to notice me. I spent my weekends now with Sammy and he and I worked up several more colorful, offbeat feature page articles.

I interviewed an activist young nun who worked with former prisoners and helped them find work and a place to live. I spent the weekend at a visiting circus and described the life of these colorful nomads and had meals with them.

I interviewed a former silent screen actress who had retired years before and who lived quietly in a lonely old mansion in the city. The story ran with pictures of her during her heyday as she posed with Mary Pickford, Valentino and Charlie Chaplin.

My cop buddy, who I had done a feature on, suggested I accompany him and some other policemen to a huge Ku Klux Klan rally outside the city. The cops were assigned there to make sure no trouble exploded.

They'd look after me. They could arrange it where I interviewed the big cheese, the Grand Dragon, Robert Shelton. Vera was thrilled at the idea of running a straight news story on what really happened at a Klan rally.

I was excited at the chance. With Sammy and Morris and the others with me, I felt no fear. These hard-faced Klansmen who watched me like I was an exotic bird of Paradise also fascinated me. Later, I heard that to them, homosexuality was a hideous abomination. And in me, they saw the perfect incarnation of a queer.

Although repelled by their beliefs, I was still fascinated by these weathered faced men. Occasionally I saw a familiar flicker of lust in those staring eyes. If we were alone, away from everyone, I could have had a quickie with them.

I worked hard to keep my personal feelings out of the story. The result was a chilling, striking account of a "Night at the Klan Rally".

Vera again promoted this spread. My fellow cohorts were thrilled that even though I was basically a cub reporter, I was turning in blockbuster after blockbuster on my own time.

After my Klan story ran, the newspaper was lauded for its courage to carry an article like this one without taking sides. Even an activist black group praised the story because of its insights into an "evil abomination."

With Vera's encouragement and those of other reporters, Scotty very, very grudgingly promoted me to his city staff as a general assignment reporter.

What I hadn't counted on was that this meant I would have to work alone with him on the "lobster" shift. From three until midnight. I would have to continue doing my Sunday features on my own time during the day.

I still loathed him and I had to work hard to keep my contempt and hatred hidden. Although I couldn't deny his simmering beauty, he was as transparent a hypocrite as all the others I had encountered in school.

For someone who made such a big deal of being woman crazy, I had no doubt that if he were drunk enough, he wouldn't care if it were male or female rolling around between the sheets with him.

My newsroom buddies had joked about this very image. We occasionally gathered at the Wit's End, a popular, darkly lit bar on Wrightsville Beach. Gays, straights, blacks, artists used this as their hangout.

"Get him drunk one night, Jason, and get a promotion the next day," urged Sammy one night when I was off work.

"Good God, what a nightmare. I think I'd throw up at those big, thick lips trying to kiss me."

"He wouldn't think of kissing somebody," joked Vera. "He'd want your mouth some place lower."

After eight o'clock, nobody was left in that dusty, cluttered old newsroom except he and I. Photographers dropped by as did men from the old composition room or sometimes a reporter who was covering a night meeting.

Nearly all were fascinated to see me—the newsroom freak—sitting just a few feet away, across that U-shaped worktable, from my worst enemy.

I knew that he was being teased about having a "homo…a fag…" on staff and one who worked just an arms length away.

How he reacted, I don't know, because he made a point of saying nothing to me except to bark an order: "Call up the police station about that robbery…check with the weather bureau about that storm warning…call up the sheriff's department about that arrest…"

I said nothing.

I obeyed my orders and did what I was told.

However, I always enjoyed camping it up with some of the cute photographers and rough and tumble guys from the composition room. They were the men who created the text that—back then—was composed from lead.

I liked being around them. They were big, burly, and bawdy and if you joked about anything to do with sex, they loved it.

These guys knew exactly who and what I was. It didn't bother them. They were so rugged and brawny anyway, they probably didn't see me as a threat.

They saw a golden-haired guy who was girlish and wore sharp looking clothes and had a quirky sense of humor.

One of them, Harrigan, was one of the key guys in the pressroom, and he was like a big bear. One night he brought the front-page proofs of the paper for Scotty and myself to proof.

While we worked, Harrigan and I discussed old movies. We both loved the same kind—old Universal horrors and Bette Davis.

Scotty listened to our discussions and said little but he appeared startled that although he didn't approve of me, other guys with more brawn did. Other men from the composition room made excuses to drop by and talk to the resident fag.

I made them laugh. I could shock them because they thought I was barely old enough to be out of high school. Occasionally, even Scotty couldn't hide his grin at some out of the outrageous banter.

The photographers who worked the night shift also found excuses to drop by and shoot the breeze with me.

Especially Sammy. Most of the staff was aware that he and I were more than work buddies. They didn't care. They liked him and they liked me. This was just another unconventional friendship that they enjoyed witnessing.

One night, Harrigan, the foreman, was waiting for Scotty to make a final edit on a story. As Scotty drew his pencil through sentences and paragraphs, Harrigan said:

"Hey, Jason, I heard that was a really wild party over at your place last weekend. Your buddy, Sammy, was telling me all about it."

Sammy had brought several of his straight buddies over and they were joined by several of my reporter chums. Although nothing really wild had happened, except nearly everyone got drunk, I knew when to lay it on thick.

"It was so wild I couldn't sit down for days afterwards. I told Sammy to please keep it in his pants."

I pretended to rub my ass.

Harrigan nearly fell off the desk laughing.

"Oh, Jesus, I can't believe I heard that. But that sounds like Sammy."

Scotty glanced up and for the first time, he actually flashed me one of his grins. He only grinned when with his buddies.

"I didn't know you gave orgies, Jason?"

"I believe in being a good hostess. If your guests want to have one, you should give the best orgy you can. And you do all you can to make sure your guests have a good time."

Harrigan left us, still gasping for breath, hurrying down to the composition room to spread this bawdy observation from the newsroom's freak.

That little exchange, however, opened the steel door between Scotty and me. This was exactly the key one used if one were considered a fag reporter to a presumably straight editor.

I nearly laughed aloud when I noticed how Scotty now created minor chit-chat. It was like he now preened because he was going to allow me to become a member of his golden circle.

Very, very gradually, he began making overtures of friendship.

One night, as we waited the final proofs of the next morning's paper, it was quiet in the newsroom.

I kept a stack of gothic romances to read during slow times. I was deeply engrossed in the new Victoria Holt thriller when my nemesis yawned:

"Bad weather coming up. You can't do any partying this weekend."

I had been expecting this. Scotty had drummed his fingers, chain-smoked, made several phone calls in a low whisper, gone over to the windows.

I sensed he was preparing to enter a new level in our relationship.

"Oh, I don't like going out in weather like this. People usually drop by anyway. They know I prefer to be visited than to visit."

He widened his eyes, as if surprised. "What if you get people you don't like?"

I rolled my eyes. "I've got buddies who can get rid of them. Remember that feature I did on the young cop? He comes by with another man in blue. They keep things in line if necessary. And if I don't want company, I just tell people I'm going to bed."

"You like having tough guys around, eh?"

I didn't trust Scotty and sensed that he could easily fire me if he knew for sure I balled with men.

"I like all kinds of people—men and women."

This last statement made him blush.

The always-handsome Sammy often came by my desk just then. He looked so cute in his black windbreaker and red scarf and dark wool hat. He had his photographic equipment slung over his shoulder.

He wasn't just a newspaper cameraman. He loved to work on his own during his free time.

"Ready to rumble?" he asked.

"We're going to my place, right?"

"Right on!"

We left together while Scotty said nothing when I called out: "See ya Monday!"

"What's his problem?" I asked Sammy.

"He's jealous. Can't you tell?"

"Of who? Me?"

"Scotty's used to being number one. I know him like a book. I've worked with him for ten years. He wants you to devote all your attention to him."

"He can go fuck. I have no interest in him as a friend."

Everyone commented how sullen and snappish Scotty was for the next few nights. His face was long and pale. He glared at me. I shrugged it off. My confidence in my work was growing.

I'd now gotten my first six months of journalism under my belt. From what I heard, this was all you really needed to start moving upwards elsewhere. A half-year was considered good for a job hunter because it meant you had your rough edges smoothed over.

And the bigger newspapers wanted someone who was still fairly fresh and talented. The longer you stayed at a newspaper, the more stuck-in-a-rut you appeared. At least I now had an old car that was paid in full. My nest egg would keep me floating for a few months until I found something else.

If I had to flip burgers, I would do it. I had no false sense of pride when it came down to surviving. I had discovered that if you worked anywhere, no one was likely to insult and threaten you with murder if they thought you were queer.

On one Saturday night, I shut my gothic romance, this one by Marilyn Ross, and put on my new tweed overcoat. I had splurged on it and a matching hat and a pair of black leather gloves.

Since my apartment was so cheap, I was able to both save a few pennies and to splurge on my passion: clothes. I ordered some of my wardrobe from Macy's in New York. Then I adored exploring the various men shops in the city and by driving the three hours to Raleigh.

Soon, I had the reputation of being the "Best Dressed Reporter" on the *Star-News*. I wore hats and gloves and boots when most men still clung to car coats and khaki slacks. Male cologne was not yet on the market. So I used a woman's perfume: Chanel 5.

The friends loved it.

Scotty had acted nervous and jumpy during our shift together. He drummed his fingers, he'd get up and walk around and light up a cigarette and lean back in his chair, his loafered feet propped up on the desk.

He had barely said five words to me in two weeks.

So, his mutter surprised me.

"What a fucked up night! I'll bet you won't do much partying this weekend."

"I just hope I can get home okay. Troopers said some of the roads are icing over."

"Where's your buddy, Sammy, tonight?"

My boss had pulled on his leather jacket and I pulled in the belt of my trench coat.

"He's at Myrtle Beach. So, I'm afraid I'll be all by my tiny little self this weekend."

He took a deep breath. His eyes flitted around the newsroom.

Uh oh, I thought. He's about to come up with something.

"You might slide off the road. Why don't you stay in town?"

His voice was husky and trembled slightly. He was not at all the egotistical, arrogant managing editor now.

"Where? A hotel? Can't afford to. No, I'll get home to the beach some way."

"If you're so determined to drive out there, I'll follow you."

"Follow me? You don't have to do that."

So here it was. His big surprise. He was so transparent I nearly laughed. This was what he had been fantasizing about. His plan to discover for himself if I was a queer who did all the things he had heard queers do in private.

This reputed satyr just couldn't say no to his cock.

But how was I supposed to handle this? I wished Vera were there. She was used to fending off his sexual moves without alienating him. A grin made him suddenly look halfway human—and attractive. He nodded toward the doorway:

"Come on. I'm going to the Wit's End anyway. I've got a buddy who wants me to join him and his girlfriend for a party."

Ah ha! Although straight people were by no means a rarity at the Wit's End, this watering hole was famous for its clientele of gays and eccentrics.

I hated myself when my pulse raced. Sammy and Vera and the others had filled me in on Scotty's amazing track record of bedroom athletics. Women were always chasing him—and vice versa.

"Well, thanks," I said. "But don't follow me out of concern. I'll be okay."

"No arguments," he mocked. "Let's go before it gets too bad."

He stayed close to me as I headed to my car in the new double-decked parking deck behind the *Star-News* building. When I nearly slipped at one time, his big hand grabbed my arm and balanced me.

He resembled the perfect image of the Big City Editor—in his leather jacket and fedora hat.

He followed me all the way to the beach, across the little drawbridge, and he stayed right on my bumper when I parked my car in the empty lot.

No one was there except me. My cop boyfriend, Morris, had moved closer into town. My rugged landlord, Jack, and his wife always spent the winters in Pensacola, Florida.

The wind ripped at my hat and coat. The Atlantic Ocean roared just a few hundred feet away.

I went over to Scotty's car. He had pulled the window down.

"Is everything okay now?" he asked.

"Yes. Thanks ever so much. It was real nice of you."

He didn't move. He shut off his car engine. Then he lit up a Camel.

"Eh, would you like to come in for a beer or some wine? I've got both."

"I was hoping you'd ask."

He followed me up the first flight of steps to the second level of the building where my apartment was located.

I unlocked the door.

"Welcome to the lair of a cub reporter," I mocked.

Scotty was so big he dwarfed everything in my cozy little cocoon.

"Hey, nice apartment. You've done a good job fixing it up."

Everyone said I had worked wonders in transforming a standard, beach studio into an exotic den of iniquity. I had put red wrapping paper and periwinkle purple curtains over the windows. From my window I beheld a spectacular view of the Atlanta Ocean, just a few hundred feet beyond.

My own original oil paintings, striking black and white photos by Sammy, and old movie posters covered the walls.

I lit strawberry candles and a stick of strawberry incense. It felt warm and toasty and in the next room, a large bed, covered with a vibrant patchwork quilt, occupied most of the space.

"Take off your jacket. You want beer or wine or a gin and tonic?"

"I'll take that gin any day."

I couldn't keep the smile off my face. If Sammy and the others could see me now! They'd be falling on the floor in hysteria. The newsroom fag now had the newsroom homophobe right here in this queer cocoon.

I nearly giggled. Was I finally going to discover what made Scotty such a wildly popular stud?

I brought him his drink. We sat beside each other on my sofa. His body heat was amazing. Wind and rain blew against the window. We could hear the sea pounding the shore close by.

"Don't you get scared out here?" he asked.

"I like it. Then I have some buddies who drop by all the time."

He had taken off his jacket. His shirt was unbuttoned halfway down which revealed much of his chest. Tiny bubbles of sweat gleamed on its tanned surface.

"Do you and your buddies have some, eh, fun?"

He smiled suggestively. Be careful, a voice warned me. Scotty can be treacherous.

I was cautious.

"Some of them drink too much," I said blandly. "I have to make a place for them to sleep on the floor or on the couch. Sometimes I've found them laying out there on the deck the next morning."

His strange eyes glimmered.

He ran a hand around his neck and the upper part of his chest.

"It's so warm in here. I'm taking my shirt off, if you don't mind?"

Good God but he was obvious! Not even Sammy had moved this fast. Scotty had already pulled the shirt out of his slacks and unbuttoned it. The powerful aura of sex whirled in the air.

He's done this many times before, I thought. He doesn't believe in playing sex games. Be very, very careful.

His exhibitionism, though, was a powerful turn on to me. Just an hour before, he was buttoned up and in the pose of city editor.

Now, he resembled a centerfold of an older, macho man.

I couldn't help but notice how thick his nipples were. He wasn't muscled. His torso resembled more that of a golfer, a tennis player than a weight lifter.

He moved his right thigh closer to me, providing me with an easy area to grope. I felt dizzy. It was finally happening. I had never been so physically close to him.

I could hear his breathing, see his stomach rise and fall slightly in excitement. And I certainly noticed a stiff ridge pushing against the fabric of his pants.

"You've got a beautiful face," he said hoarsely. His eyes scanned my face. "Like Marilyn Monroe. The same blonde hair. Full lips. You've got an ass like her's too. Did you know you've given all the guys and me in the newsrooms hard-ones—the way you swish around the room? See, I've gotten one now."

"Yes," I whispered. "I can see that."

"Hope you don't mind. I've simply got to get these pants off. Wanna help?"

Careful, be careful! Let him make the first move, I cautioned myself. If he later tries to claim that I seduced him, you can always say that literally he was the champ.

He raised his hips and unbuckled himself and pushed his slacks away. He wore no underwear. All of that incredible stuff was instantly revealed to me.

His phallus reared up now that it was free of its fabric confines.

The tip slapped against his stomach as he suddenly reached over and pulled me hard against him. I couldn't resist him any longer. He had made the first move and I responded. His mouth covered mine and he lowered me back on the sofa. This man was a smooth operator. Within a minute, he had stripped naked and had me out of my clothes.

This powerful transformation from city editor to a passionate, groaning lover was exhilarating. One part of me urged: don't forget this. It'll be over soon. Then: better enjoy it now. It might be the last time.

My fears and doubts evaporated instantly.

If he dared try to fire me now because I had sex with men, then I could honestly vow that Scotty certainly knew first hand the truth behind this charge.

Scotty proved to be a passionate, intense lover. He didn't just go through the expected motions of physical passion. He faked nothing. When he groaned and quivered and gasped, as my mouth traveled over his erect nipples and his stomach and then down to his privates, he was honestly thrilled.

Within seconds, I discovered that all those rumors of his lovemaking were not gossip. He exuded a wonderfully faint scent of a man—fleshy, slightly musky mixed with clean sweat.

It proved intoxicating, as I tasted his manhood. I was even more thrilled when he got over me, pulled my thighs up high around him and he gradually entered me.

Deeper he pushed himself and he whispered: "Hold on to me! I'll try to be careful!"

Reality vanished as I became lost in this intoxicating world of Scotty the lover. Scotty the Casanova. I clung to him and now and then drops of his sweat dripped down on me.

My large couch was the same as a bed. It witnessed the start of a torrid, hysterical affair that even today makes me shiver with joy.

What made Scotty so unforgettable was that most of my sex partners had been young guys—college boys and hustlers and youthful satyrs like Sammy.

Here was an experienced He Man who had practiced the art of seduction and sex for many years.

Between love making, we sipped wine, our cocktails, and confessed how shocked he was when I first waltzed into the newroom.

He had never seen anyone like me. Queers were things he had been taught to abhor and reject and degrade. Homo's were supposed to stay hidden from society and from guys like him.

And then suddenly, there I was, staring him straight in the face.

It was shocking!

"So," I muttered, "you discovered I wasn't a diseased, pouncing monster?"

He told me many things about himself, and his tears flowed easily, but then he was naturally an emotional man. Very sensitive. Very amorous and he loved beautiful things.

He thought I was beautiful—even though I was a male.

"I'm not a male," I explained quietly, as I had done to many men before. "I'm in between. Part male, part female. A merging of the two."

"Whatever it is, you've got me hooked."

When he left hours later, he was quiet but he pulled me close and kissed me for a long time.

"See ya at work."

And so we began a double relationship. I had dreaded that first day back in the newsroom after our night of exhilarating passion.

Would he be in denial, or suffer from acute guilt and now held me responsible for his lapse?

But it was no different than before except there was no hostility or tension or awkwardness. We worked quietly and intensely except we did talk now about ordinary things—the weather, books, movies, the job.

And then a few times each week, he came to my place and he slept next to me like he were my husband. In the morning, I fixed us a pot of coffee, buttered toast and scrambled eggs.

With me in my robe and him wearing nothing, I thought: this is how it must be to be married to him. This is what his wife sees most mornings when Scotty's not here.

While I was thrilled with his bedroom prowess, another part of me still loathed him.

I couldn't forget how he had tried relentlessly to destroy my budding newspaper career. He had done everything he could to get my faggy ass out of his newsroom. If I hadn't stuck it out, I would have been in desperate circumstances: broke, unemployed and with a blot on my resume.

I told him this and didn't spare him. He closed his eyes tight and nodded as he shook his head.

"I'm sorry. So sorry. You have a right to hate time. I wasn't really very nice to you. But I discovered you're tough. I could see that you wouldn't break."

"No thanks to you!"

"Can you ever forgive me?" he asked with tears brimming his eyes.

"No. Never. You did what you did and it'll always be there. But—let's put that into the past."

"Thank you," he whispered while kissing me. "Thank you for forgiving me."

I wondered what type of wife he had who endured these absences. And how about his two teenage kids? I didn't ask but from rumors in the newsroom, his wife and children worshipped him.

They thought he had to work all night at the newspaper. Or he was having some drinks and playing cards with his straight buddies. He brilliantly created separate lives and no one suspected anything.

Yet—a newsroom is where there's more gossip about fellow workers than any Main Street in Smalltown, USA.

I received knowing smiles, raised brows, and wise glances from my buddies when they asked me how things were going with Scotty.

Sammy certainly knew how things were because when he wanted to come by, I'd tell him I had a date "with an ape."

"Ha!" laughed Sammy, his dark eyes dancing and his white teeth flashing. "I think I know who the ape is."

"Do you? Well, ask me no questions and I'll tell you no lies."

"You still hate him?" asked Sammy.

"I've gotten over that."

"Yeah, I'm sure you have," he whooped.

"And what does that mean?"

"Ha! As if you think you're fooling me, kiddo! I've been around. So has Scotty. He always gets around. But I've never heard of him doing anything queer with another guy."

"Just because I'm faggy, doesn't make him faggy."

Sammy laughed. "Jason, you don't understand how you turn the guys on around here. You could have any of them. You've had me. Now, you've got Scotty. Just say the word—"

"You really think so?" I asked, suddenly interested. My relationship with Scotty had created a sense of arrogance. I had gotten the most sought after stud in town in my bed. I had no doubt that gossip was spreading through the bars that we reporters and photographers all enjoyed visiting and at the greasy spoons where we enjoyed a late bite.

"I'm going to think of a name or two. Maybe you could give them the word."

"Just try me."

I named a husky, macho reporter named Ron. He had never been hostile or friendly. He simply did his work and went home. But he was rugged and macho and one night, when my car wouldn't start, Ron had fixed it quickly.

"I owe you one, Ron."

He winked and grinned: "I'll make sure you keep your promise."

And next to him, I uttered the name of Julian. He drove one of the delivery trucks. We had chatted a few times when I left the newspaper building at midnight and I saw him loading up his truck with newspapers.

Julian resembled a wrestler and he did indeed tussle on the weekends in Amateur Wrestling bouts.

With thinning dark hair, a big, powerful body, I liked being around him.

Within two days, both men had made excuses to talk to me.

I was waiting in the lobby for the elevator to the third floor of our building where the newsroom was located. Ron joined me—as if he had been waiting for me.

Like me, he was bundled up in a heavy coat. He resembled a scrumptious bear with thick, dark curls above a square face.

"Whew, cold!" he shivered.

"Snow's expected tomorrow."

"Good weather to stay in," he said. Then he glanced at me: "I hear you're living all alone out there at Wrightsville in that old apartment building. You're not scared?"

"Not at all. Guys come by all the time so I'm not really alone."

"I might be out that way tomorrow. You'll be in? You mind if I visit?"

"I'd love to see you."

"Maybe in the afternoon, say, like around three o'clock?"

I told him how to get there—and he came. He didn't leave for several hours. Like Scotty, he was married with children but he believed that what he was doing had no relationship to his marriage.

It was just "fun." There was nothing emotional involved. Ron liked to kiss and embrace and his strong arms held me close.

Julian was even more blunt.

I was approaching the newspaper building one afternoon to begin my shift.

"Hey, Jason!"

Julian came toward me. Big, burly and all male, he threw the cigarette out of his mouth.

"Hey, Sammy says you've always got some beer at your place. Mind if I come by sometimes and swallow a few?"

"I'd just love to see you, Julian."

He lit another cigarette, gave me an impish wink and he also became a regular bed partner. In a strange way, the pattern was repeating itself: in college, word spread and the net was cast.

My net brought in some bastards but it brought in the goodies, too.

◆   ◆   ◆

Scotty had now promoted me to covering various city agencies. One of them was the U.S. Coast Guard, which was active in that old Port City.

When I entered the main office in an elaborate Victorian building facing the water, several handsome young men in white always greeted me.

We bantered and flirted and I told them how sexy they looked in their snug snappy uniforms.

"You like these tight pants," said Rocco, a swarthy Italian officer from New Jersey.

"Sure, I can tell your religion," I drawled. That always tickled them.

Rocco and two of his buddies visited me at my apartment one afternoon when I was off work. I had told them earlier there were still some beach bunnies around despite the cold weather.

When the beach bunnies never showed up, Rocco stayed behind and he proved that he had been around the block a few times.

Scotty sensed I was having fun with other men. Although our affair was private, he acted like a possessive lover.

One Saturday night, in the parking lot, we argued.

"I am going to see other guys," I retorted. "You're married. You've got all the sex you want. I love sex. A lot of guys want to have to fun."

"You're making me very angry," he said tersely. "I don't like sharing somebody."

"I didn't ask you to take over my life. You decided to do that on your own. I was going with other guys before you gave me the time of day and tried to make me quit!"

"You vicious little bitch!" he gasped. "Jesus Christ, but if you could just hear yourself! You're a slut!"

"And what are you? A hypocrite who got married just for the sake of getting married when you've had dozens of flings."

"You're gonna regret that," he fumed. "You shouldn't have said that."

At work, he acted like the pouting, moody reject. I ignored him, which was difficult to do since I had to turn in my stories to him.

When a big feature I had worked on regarding haunted houses in Wilmington finally ran, I was furious to see that it had been chopped in half and there was no by-line.

No longer was I in awe of this frustrating creature. I had also scrupulously squirreled away a small nest egg, so I was not as destitute as when I first started working here.

More importantly, I had been sending my best articles to *The Associated Press* in Charlotte. They often ran outstanding features from North Carolina newspapers over their wire to hundreds of member publications.

The bureau's chief, Carl Bell, was encouraging.

So I had actually gained some confidence in both my talents and my self. My old trap of a car was paid for, I had no bills and my savings would carry me along for several months until I found something else.

"Why?" I asked, flinging down the article in front of Scotty. "I worked my ass off on this story. You assigned it to me. You didn't give me a by-line. People who write stories about the weather get by-lines."

He didn't look up from the stack of copy he was editing.

"I didn't think it was that good. You could've done better."

I was so furious I swayed, as if he had slapped me. Since it was nearly deadline time, the newsroom was filled with all the reporters and editors. Although they pretended to work, I sensed all were keenly interested in this confrontation.

No one ever openly battled Scotty, the City Editor.

"Okay," I said. "If that's the way you want to play it. I'll go to our managing editor and ask him to transfer me to another department."

I had written a few articles for the Society Department, headed by a good friend of mine, Theresa. One of the features was on a perfume maker whose business thrived because he made scents from scratch.

Another featured heavily promoted by Theresa was on a woman who wrote popular mysteries under a pen name. Theresa wanted more articles like these. She was also in desperate need of a feature writer because her main one out on pregnancy leave.

I watched Scotty's face drain.

When he looked up at me, he was ugly and mean. His eyes bulged and the whiteness of his pallor exaggerated his acne scars.

"Do not visit the managing editor. We don't want to get him involved."

"No, I'm going to make an appointment today. When an article I know is damned good gets butchered and published without my name, then I think it's time for me to move on."

The whole newsroom now hung on to every word. Everyone knew by now that something was going on between this weird, flamboyant reporter and fire-snorting, macho editor.

"Come into my office," he said darkly.

I followed him out of the newsroom, across the hall into his corner office. He shut the door behind us, locked it and stood close to me.

"You're driving me crazy," he muttered. "I've never met anyone like you."

"You're letting our friendship affect our working relationship," I retorted. "You promised it wouldn't. You're not being reasonable."

He moved closer and quickly pulled me hard against him. His mouth found mine and I just couldn't resist. His right hand moved down to his belt. I heard the zipper being undone and then he thrust his hardness into my hand.

"That's always yours!" he gasped. "Nobody else touches it."

"Except your wife."

"No. Not even her. I don't go near her anymore."

I looked down and was amazed to see how big he had become. It perfectly personified Scotty: mean, swollen, and irresistible. It took little work on my part for it to suddenly pulsate and then guide it away from spattering us.

He continued kissing me and once more he swelled up and again, an impressive spurt of energy shot against the wall.

All this time, we heard people coming and going in the corridor. Through the gray glass wall, we saw forms of people passing by and I thought: if they could see us now, what a scandal that would be.

Our spat was over with. But I had made him realize that he didn't dominate me. I wanted to play around. And I made it clear that I didn't want our affair to affect my career fortunes.

Scotty's possessiveness, his moodiness left me on edge. My close buddies, Vera and Sammy, both urged me to aim for the *Associated Press*. This was the ultimate place to work for an ambitious journalist.

Your paychecks were big. You worked for an outfit that was famous around the world. The AP had international bureaus.

"You've got too much on the ball to be hidden away here," Vera said over coffee and a chicken salad one afternoon. We sat at the window of the White Tower Diner near the newspaper, as a cold wind whipped debris down Main Street.

"Why don't you leave?" I asked.

"Me and my gal pal have brought a house here," sighed Vera. "She teaches and we've got too much at stake. You haven't. Your stories are brilliant. You're a major talent, Jason. Don't settle into a rut at this stage in your life."

She also added something else: "If you're staying here just because of Scotty, don't. I've worked with him for ten years. He goes from favorite to favorite. Always women—except for you. They're left devastated. They leave and vanish off the radar screen."

"Not me," I vowed. "I'm going to be famous someday. Somehow."

She smiled that crinkled, cute-ugly way of hers.

"I'm sure you will."

I resumed sending copies of my best articles out to other newspapers and to the big, powerful *Associated Press*. Replies were always, "at the present, we have no openings. We'll keep your resume on file."

Six months later, I received a call, out of the blue, from the bureau chief of the *Associated Press* in Charlotte N.C.

Carl Bell sounded enthusiastic, warm and eager to talk to me.

Would I be interested in working there? Could I come up for an interview?

On my two days off, I took a Greyhound to Charlotte.

My interview was a success. Carl was a dream. He liked me instantly. I liked him. Like magic, my experience on the Wilmington newspaper had opened a coveted door in journalism.

I remember that freezing, December day when I typed out my resignation in the newsroom and left it in an envelope for Scotty. I quickly slipped away.

The newsroom was full and busy the next afternoon when I came to work.

Scotty breezed in an hour later, sipping coffee and smoking a cigarette. His eyes went directly to me.

"Hey, you!" he called out. "Come into my office."

The others had already heard the news. Two of my buddies looked at me. I muttered: "Uh oh. Here goes."

Scotty closed and locked his office door. He sat down at his desk.

"What does this mean?" he held up my typed resignation. "You can't do this. Not now. You're really starting to go places here. The sky's the limit. Call up the AP and tell them you've changed your mind."

He picked up his phone receiver and handed it to me.

"I'm going Scotty. It's a big chance for me. I want to get out and move around."

"Call 'em up!" he hissed. "Do it! I'm telling you to!"

"Sorry, Scotty. This is it. I've got to keep moving."

He pushed the receiver closer to me.

I shook my head. "I can't. It's final. I've already given my word to the AP."

"What about me?" he cried. "You're just suddenly leaving me? You cannot do this. You simply can't."

He got up and pulled me hard against him and kissed me and then he began to weep softly.

"Why are you leaving me?" he whispered. "You hate me."

He wasn't faking it now. I knew him well enough to know what an emotional guy he was. He cried easily, became enraged even faster and he didn't know the meaning of being rejected.

"I'll keep in contact! I swear I will."

"No, no, I want you to call up the AP and them you're turning them down! I'll make you a star here! You'll be my entertainment editor, my whiz bang reporter! I'll run your picture with all your stories—just like they do it on the big papers!"

I felt my resolve melting and so I backed away, unlocked the door and left him.

Before I closed the door, I watched him with his head resting on his arms as they pressed against the desktop. His shoulders shook. He made me think of a spoiled, beautiful little boy whose always been given everything he wanted.

The next week was torturous. Scotty was moody, mean and nasty to everyone. I avoided him until the last night, when I stood up and put on my coat.

I had already cleaned out my desk. I looked around me. Tears rimmed my eyes. How I was going to miss in many ways this beaten up, stuffy, smoke-filled newsroom. This is where my professional future was born. I didn't think of the grim, vicious first months of my beginning here, when one egomaniac held my future in his big hands.

Only a few people were in the newsroom. They came over to my desk and shook my hand and Vera hugged me.

"You tear'em up there in the AP," she grinned. "We hope to be hearing from you real soon. Okay, honey?"

Scotty stood up. He held out his hand. His face was the color of a sickly pink parchment. He had not visited me since the day I told him I was leaving. He had become distant, polite and cool in an exaggerated way.

"So long, guy. You can always come back here, anytime you want to."

"It's been great, Scotty."

He sat down and resumed work.

I left the building and never returned.

Six months later, I received a call at my desk at the AP bureau. Vera was on the line.

"I thought you'd better hear it from me. It's about Scotty."

"What's happened?"

"He had a fatal heart attack. Right before he came to work. It shocked the hell out of everybody."

"You mean, he's—he's dead."

"Yeah." I could hear her soft weeping. "He could be a mean son-of-a-bitch, but he was the real thing. A great editor."

"I—I can't believe it! Scotty was so alive! So passionate!"

"Right after you left," she murmured, "he just changed so much. He became so moody, so down. He began drinking too much. Smoking too much. He really took your leaving here hard."

"I didn't think he would. I thought he would snap out of it. He hated me so much when I first came there."

"Well, he certainly missed you, Jason. We'd hear him say, 'I wish Jason was here to write that story! If Jason was here, he'd know how to cover that trial.' You made your mark here, honey."

I remembered those intense, passionate nights at my small beach apartment, a big, emotional man holding me close. Smoking cigarettes, sipping cold wine, listening to the pounding of the waves and the wind outside.

Then, other reporters phoned or wrote me for the next year. They told me that Scotty had not died of a heart attack—but of an overdose of booze and sleeping pills.

I couldn't believe that it was just me that caused his breakdown. Yet, Vera and the others told me that his deterioration began just as I left his kingdom.

Sometimes I wish I had never left there. When the hard times came, I wished I stayed on and become one of those old newsroom hacks that never leave and end up hunched over, with thinning hair and grounding out headlines.

Yet, I would have been miserable, realizing I had never tested my wings elsewhere. I was to fly to many places before I finally reached my home in Manhattan.

Chapter Seven
The Convict

"Gimme your hand and then your money!"

—The Reverend Luther Landau
From *Lord Love the People* **TV Broadcast**
September 3, 1973

The naked man beside me in bed held me close as we watched him on television preach to his congregation.

Like an early Elvis Presley, he had electrifying animal beauty but even better than Elvis, the Reverend Luther Landau was big, powerful and as intoxicating as a triple Gin and Tonic.

"You look so hot, Luther!" I observed.

"Looka that gal there," he chuckled. "See, she's reaching for my balls. They're always reaching for my balls and cock."

"Well, that's because you've got such big ones."

He chuckled in that deep, rich baritone of his. He loved to talk dirty—and he loved even more watching reruns of his wildly popular *Love the Lord* show.

Like an oversexed teenage hunk, he got his real kicks from holding me in his arms, as my hands caressed him, and we both watched him cavorting on my TV screen.

One station in Montgomery during the early 70s ran a three-hour marathon each Sunday morning of *Love the Lord* meetings. These gatherings were huge and held in tents and auditoriums around Alabama. The star of the show could often be found between my satin sheets on Sunday mornings.

He'd tap on my door the night before, usually around midnight, we'd kiss, embrace and after dropping our clothes, we'd slide into my bed for a wild night of love-making.

Big, brawny, muscular and gorgeous, he exploited what Mother Nature had endowed him with and parlayed it into the moneymaking machine known as *Love the Lo*rd television show.

These programs followed a proven entertainment format. Music from the Love the Lord Choir, the appearance of the Heavenly Twins—a small pair of identical siblings who warbled tunes about Jesus—and then a rousing sermon from the star.

Each show concluded with a galvanizing, pull-out-all-the-stops climax where our sweating, stunning young giant held out his hands towards the camera and pled for money.

As the camera scanned over the thousands of hand-waving, eyes closed, swaying followers of the reverend, the preacher man was on stage, his full lips quivering, his eyes closed tight, as he pled for more and more money.

Sweat covered his beautifully sculpted face. It gleamed on his powerful chest that was halfway bared. He had this delightful habit of ripping off his tie and undoing the buttons on his shirt.

With his sport coat a limp mass in the corner, the soaked shirt clung to his incredible pectorals, arms and nipples. His thin slacks emphasized muscular thighs. He spread them as he fell to the stage and held up his hands upwards.

His voice quivered and sobbed as he asked the Lord to make his followers see the light and give, give, give more money to his cause.

As he wept and swayed and moaned, the organist began to play, "What a Friend We Have in Jesus." The choir softly sang the words and then the spellbinding evangelist gasped out the words.

"What....WHAT...a friend...we haveeeeee...in JE-sussssss!"

Around him on the floor glimmered splotches of sweat. He clasped his hands and held them upwards. His eyes brimmed with tears as he beseeched the Lord to look down and bless everyone watching him—and especially those who hesitated to give.

To close the show, the camera moved in steadily until his glowing face filled up the screens. The image froze then—with tears and full lips parted slightly to show his perfect white teeth.

The editing and the camera angles suggested a soft-porn flick. With Luther Landau, the hypnotic star.

"You look so hot, Luther," I murmured and stroked his chest and then grasped the electrical source of his virility. He gasped and shuddered for I had discovered that this hypocritical man of God was a sexual phenomenon: once was

never enough for him. Sometimes three to four times an hour he would prove why he was so vastly popular with women—and many men.

Like Scotty, my city editor from hell, and other Tom Cats I had known, the fake reverend had a magical way of putting his life into several compartments.

His most visible one was as the sensational young evangelist who thrilled—or repelled—thousands each Sunday morning on television. Many viewers shuddered at the sight of his money-grubbing white trash preacher boy demanding money and faith from his more feeble-minded followers.

He had another mental compartment for his dull, frowsy wife and his two buck-toothed teenage sons, who he regularly paraded on stage to give him legitimacy as a family man.

Other secret stashes that were never made public consisted of his countless female groupies. He liked to hint that he also had several wealthy widows on his list of sexual conquests.

And when I asked him how many other men did he have stashed away, he just laughed, winked and shrugged. It didn't bother him that one of the great sins he screamed about each Sunday was the horrors of homosexuality.

He referred to this aberration as "sexual degeneracy…sexual perversion…sexual horror…"

When I jumped on him about this hypocritical stance, he just shrugged those big shoulders: "That's what my followers want to hear, Jason."

"That's so fucking hypocritical, Luther! You and I have are doing the same Big Dirty that you scream about."

His confidence reigned supreme, though. Once again, a shrug and the vague explanation of: "I try to be all things to all people."

But I managed to ignore this glaring fault of his. Like him, I wanted our couplings to be harmonious and intense and I got a kick out of watching him on my black and white telly—while having him bare-assed and aroused right next to me.

As I ran my hands over his magnificent torso, grasped his even more magnificent package of manhood, and made him moan with delight, I whispered to him:

"What you've got, Luther, shouldn't be hidden away."

"You really think so, little Jason? Oh, man, I wish I could spend days and days in bed with you. But—I gotta get going. Have to have Sunday lunch with the family."

"Where do they think you are right now?"

"Oh, I've got all kinds of places, Jason. I could be at the TV station, looking over my tapes, or I could be with other preachers here in town."

"You are some kind of piece of work, Luther," I smiled.

"Why don't you write me up in your newspaper, Jason? The Most Popular Evangelist in the South!"

"And the one with the biggest cock!"

He laughed, delighted as always for his sexual prowess to be praised.

I had met him in the flesh a year before, right after I arrived in Montgomery to begin my assignment as a star reporter for the *Montgomery-Advertiser.*

I became aware of the evangelist when I flipped on my TV Sunday mornings and despite my repulsion, watched this electrifying creature galvanize his audience.

He and his big organization always needed more money for their Christian work and paying for Lord Love Sinners Amusement Park. This was an enormous enterprise being constructed several miles away from the cradle of the Confederacy.

I had become a well-known reporter for the *Montgomery Advertiser* newspaper. My nearly two years in the *Associated Press* was a miserable flop personally but it did help me professionally.

Charlotte proved to be one year of sheer boredom while six months in the Fargo, North Dakota AP Bureau was even worse—yet, in Fargo, I had bedded down with more men than even during my college days.

That city was so isolated because of its relentless blizzards, that the single men, and many married, were desperate for bedroom fun. I never lacked for bed partners.

However, to my sorrow, the two bigots I was to work with at the *Associated Press* Bureau in Fargo, reacted the identical way they had when I first entered the City Room o the *Wilmington Star-News.*

They never recovered from their shock and proceeded to do everything they could to get rid of me.

They needn't have tried so hard because I instantly tried everything I could to get out of there.

The power of the *Associated Press* was fortunately so great that from the first batch of resumes I sent out, nearly all of them asked me to immediately contact me.

Only the *Montgomery Advertiser* offered me more money and more power. I was uneasy about casting my net with this Deep South publication, but I eventually accepted.

I was relieved to turn in my notice to the AP Bureau in Fargo. After six months of grim working conditions, I was finally out of there. I never even said "Good bye" to my two Neanderthal co-workers.

If I thought my professional life would improve in Montgomery, I was right on one point: I was given a high profile niche on this Pulitzer Prize winning newspaper.

My picture appeared each Sunday on the popular movie column I took over. I was assigned to cover the court systems, the emerging mental health field, and the medical and prison systems.

I threw myself into doing a knockout job and I succeeded. Within three years, I was winning all the top journalism awards for outstanding writing. I was invited to all the top parties and civil rights events.

However, my relationship to most of the newsroom was chilly. The city editor was a hollow-eyed, white-faced recovering alcoholic.

Even more than the tragic Scotty, he didn't try to hide his revulsion to this colorful, flamboyant hire. He and his red-necked cohorts at the newspaper made a big deal of having nothing to do with me.

They barely said two words unless it pertained to business.

I was never invited to any of their weekend parties or was naturally ignored when they all went to their beer hangouts.

But I had seen it all before. A small group of writers and photographers did like me and we'd often go to the Quinn's Club, located literally beneath the streets of Montgomery.

And in the meantime, I was meeting so many handsome, sexy politicians, former convicts, Marines, military officials, evangelists, surgeons, priests, entertainers that my bedroom calendar was filled up nearly every week.

Rarely did I sleep alone for the eight years I lived there.

My job gave me the perfect excuse for meeting hundreds of men and enjoying a cocktail and wine.

My favorite partner was a jazz pianist who proved to be an amazing sexual partner. He never tired and stunned me with his acute sensuality. If I touched him on his arm, he gasped and rolled his eyes in delight.

We had met one night in the Quinn's Club when he'd come up to me and told me how much he enjoyed my articles.

Dressed in a leather jacket, with long, gleaming hair combed back from his face, he exuded raw sexual appeal.

He told me nothing about his personal life. Neither he nor I were interested in getting to know each other in that manner. He was an absolute sex machine. This is what fueled his existence. He performed around the city as jazz and rock pianist but he never mentioned this.

What he did like to do other than have sex was to drink. It grew progressively worse. I learned to hide my bottles of alcohol when he might come over. His capacity for drink was formidable.

The last time I saw him was at dawn on a fall morning in 1977. He had left my high-rise apartment building. I had a cozy little cocoon on the top floor.

At work that night, I saw the early edition of the newspaper. On an inside page a headline declared:

Local Man Murdered on Clayton Street.

This was the street where I lived. And then his name appeared. A group of black thugs had held him up right across the street. He had resisted and one of the attackers pulled out a knife and ripped open my boyfriend's stomach. He arrived DOA at the hospital.

When his obituary was published, I finally discovered that he was not only married, but had four grown children. None of us knew about the other. Funeral services were private. Only family members were invited.

From covering the police beat, I came across countless arrests of men who were entrapped by studly male decoys. I could barely hide my contempt at these sleazy gay imposters who wore enticing snug jeans, sleeveless tank tops. They did everything but rape the victim in order to arrest them.

Families were ruined. The arrested were jailed, some sentenced to prison and none of it made sense. One night when I left the police building, a plain looking man and woman approached me.

"Are you a reporter from the newspaper? Would you please, please not publish anything about our son, Tommy? He was arrested for indecent exposure. He wasn't doing any harm. Would you please, please not to run anything? It'll ruin us."

I saw the young man standing weeping beside a car. I had read the report that he and another man were discovered having sex in a car. The accused looked like a high school kid.

The couple was his parents. They looked careworn and decent. They said they would pay me whatever I wanted if I would just keep the name of their only son out of the newspaper.

"Okay," I said. "I won't print anything. Just tell your son to be careful!"

I was more than happy to ignore such cases although other reporters who covered the police were only too happy to write these incidents up.

When I covered court cases, I sometimes visited the aging District Attorney. He turned my stomach. I could hardly spend more than ten minutes in his company without throwing up.

He resembled an old dinosaur from the pre-Civil Rights era. He was obsessed with "nigras" taking over the country. He was passionate about wiping sex from local television and movie houses.

He was instrumental in leading a crusade that forced one of the local television stations from running any of the very popular "Charlie's Angels" episodes. The DA and his followers, of which there were many, were convinced it was programs like these that created criminals.

One visit to this washed-up old sicko had him opening up a bottom drawer and he pulled out a stack of slick, pornographic magazines.

"Just look at what some of these porno magazines are like," he said eagerly. I watched his dull, brown eyes glitter in delight as he ran his finger over the coupling bodies. Some of the pages bore suspicious stickiness.

All the mags showed signs of wear and tear. I could easily imagine this hypocrite sitting at his desk through the day, drooling over the pictures of sex, while his right hand rose and fell furiously in his lap.

While I acted myself and continued to shock many of my fellow male reporters with my high fashion and whiff of Chanel No. 5, I also knew I was playing with dynamite because of my love life.

When I visited the police station to check on a story, several of the cops made a big production of flipping their wrists and doing the usual redneck queer routine. Two detectives in particular, one black and one white, were always joking about finding somebody to "suck our cocks." Hint. Hint. They always managed to turn any of our conversations around to the "homos" in Montgomery and where did they hang out?

I bantered with them but never uttered a word that could come back to haunt me.

These cop twins were so blatant in their attempts to uncover Montgomery's gay world that I laughed in their faces. The Irish cop with the red hair was cute and hunky looking. I have no doubt that he wanted to have some fun—but after it was over, what would happen?

Although I knew a few closeted gay men, I was never involved in the homosexual scene. I knew of a few quiet little bars that catered to gay men but I was having too much fun with my straight admirers.

I didn't need to go to one of these bars and pose at the counter with my pack of Marlboro Cigarettes and nurse a beer and act so very bored with this cool, aloof expression on my face and waste hours. Besides that, my face was too familiar by this time.

I didn't want to give my enemies ammunition by having witnesses calling up the police station or the newspaper and whispering that, "Jason Fury was at the Triple X Bar last night—and he was looking for some hot fun!"

Also, because of the popularity of my movie column, I was often invited to appear on local television shows to give my opinion on what films were worth checking out and which to avoid. My face became even more familiar to thousands of viewers and potential enemies.

Lucky for me, my job gave me the perfect excuse for being alone in restaurants and coffee shops with politicians, preachers, artists, military men, telephone repair guys and former convicts.

◆   ◆   ◆

My favorite place to romp, though, wasn't in Montgomery where I was watched intensely.

No, I loved driving to Birmingham, just an hour's drive away. There, in an old, Victorian YMCA, I could let my hair down in a snug world contained in those dark, ancient rooms.

You had a rooftop, which was great for nude sunbathing and sexual pickups. You could walk by open doors and see guys going at it.

It was like a huge gay bath. Even the desk clerks were gay and often joined in the fun.

I met Amos, a beautiful truck driver, who became one of my full-time lover boys. He often stopped by in Montgomery to sleep with me. Another favorite partner at the Birmingham Y was a quiet, beautiful man with silver hair and a hunky body. After a few trysts, he told me that he was a Catholic priest from a nearby city.

Sometimes I saw him staggering around naked in the hallways, too. Booze was his real demon.

Farm boys, college professors, truckers, salesmen, and preachers—I met them all over the years at this unforgettable den of sin that was eventually razed back in the late seventies.

Back at the newspaper, I enjoyed being around the photographers more than the other workers. They seemed to always have an easy, cool attitude and their skills required being creative as well as being realistic.

One afternoon, I covered the opening of a long-delayed drug rehabilitation center in Montgomery.

This was a big event, with recognizable faces on the grandstand.

In addition to then Governor George Wallace, probably the most handsome face belonged to Reverend Luther Landau.

With a Clark Gable-like moustache brimming above full, pink lips, his powerful body encased in a paper-thin suit of white linen, he was pure macho sex.

From his chair on the stand, he glanced down at me on the front row and winked.

I smiled and winked back, slightly flustered, because I had only glimpsed him on the telly. In full, living color, he was overwhelming.

After the ceremony, I headed to my car beneath the scalding sun when my name was called out.

I looked around and this staggering, handsome male animal came up to me and grabbed both my hands.

"Jason? You're just the guy I'd love to talk to!"

His Paul Newman blue eyes glistened with delight. His white teeth startled in that deeply tanned face. Hair, the color of coal, was swept back from a square, strong face. A whiff of an expensive after-shave blended with the aroma of moist cotton and linen.

But it was that body—big, rugged, with bulging muscles that made me weak at the knees.

Would I be interested in doing an article on this Center for Special Children the minister was involved in? I could spend a weekend there with him—and others. While there had been a few mentions in the media, this project needed an in-depth feature article. He could sure use some donations from the public.

"I'll have to run it by my city editor," I explained. "The paper is pretty cautious about articles that deal with religion."

"This is a place for lil' handicapped kiddies. Religion has nothing to do with it. Could we discuss it, over lunch?"

I eventually wrote up a big article on this project and it was so gushing that I was ashamed of it after the story appeared. But this had meant my spending a weekend in a beautiful wooded locale, in one of the cabins—right next to the Reverend White Lightning.

His lovemaking was so memorable it haunted my mind for my remaining years in Montgomery. Since he was a young giant, he was physically imposing.

He used his phallus as an instrument of power to get what he wanted.

"This is my magic sword," he boasted. "It cuts through any doubt or hesitation! I use it to battle my way through life. I have only to flash it before the eyes of my critics, and they are like one struck by God. When I let them enjoy it, it's like they're eyes have been opened and God has shown them the way."

"You're damned right your cock shows them the way, Luther!" I'd laugh after his explanations. "They would have only to look at what you've got hanging between your legs and write you out a million dollar check."

The reverend howled with delight when I said such things. God had been overly generous to him when it gave him his over-developed manhood.

"God should have given some of that good stuff to other guys, Luther," I would tease. "You've got enough for four men!"

"Woo-weee!" whooped the minister. "Ain't that the damned truth!"

And he would grasp his "sword" and shake it in the air.

However, his arrogance made him careless. One day, I heard that he and his family were moving elsewhere, "to resist temptation, to start a new life, to stay away from evildoers."

He did just that, very quickly and very quietly, and telling no one, he and his clan moved to another state, at the opposite end of the nation from Alabama.

Yet, I saw him recently one early morning on television in New York City. He had gained weight, lost much of his hair, had grown pudgy around his face.

On his knees, he was pleading to God for more money. As the camera zoomed in on that once handsome face, I saw a flicker of my old lover boy.

His once dazzling eyes were buried in slits of fat. A slight pot hung over his belt. His lips quivered feverishly as he urged his worshippers to not "forget about God! He's watching you and me. Give what you can, brothers and sisters! That's what Jesus would want!"

◆　　　◆　　　◆

One of my favorite news beats was covering the state's prison system. They were in turmoil as a federal judge had ordered them upgraded and improved to a revolutionary degree.

I decided to check out all these changes and how they were being seen by both the guards and the prisoners.

I was able to do this because my numerous journalism awards had made it possible for me to pick and choose what I wanted to cover for the newspaper.

The publisher was certainly impressed with the prestige I had brought to him. Word had come down to give me a free hand.

Yet, it didn't change the rocklike resistance to my acceptance by many of the male reporters and editors. We might gab in the newsroom but they would never dare let themselves interact with me on the outside.

This bunch of rednecks loved to give parties on the weekends, with each one assuming the duties of host. Yet, I was never included on their invite list. One of them, a mush-mouthed talking loverboy who dressed all in white, considered himself God's Gift to Women.

While his patient little wife looked the other way, he screwed around with other women at an alarming rate.

He bragged about his exploits to his slack-jawed buddies in the newsroom and obviously considered himself one cool Tom Cat. He gave several huge parties each year, usually to coincide with some big football game.

He had one of the secretaries to create elaborate, striking invitations and these he handed out with much ostentation to everyone who could walk in the newsroom. That is everyone except me.

And when Monday came and everyone had recovered from the wild beer party, they would sit around and compare notes as to who had done the most outrageous thing.

This was all so familiar. This is always a familiar trick of someone in a department to utilize when they want the excluded to realize just how much they're disliked.

This never bothered me at all. I enjoyed the company of a few photographers and one particular editor. We often zoomed over to the Quinn's Club after work and enjoyed sipping beers. A few of these guys tasted better than the beer.

I began interviewing guards and prisoners and then I met some of the inmates who were just paroled. I wrote stories about their struggles to find a niche in society after years of incarceration.

Some of these men were beautiful, sexy and veterans of the sex games. To them, having sex with other men was normal. They saw nothing unusual in flirting and using their charm to gain a favor.

One of these men, in particular, was a guy I nicknamed the Silver Fox. As handsome as Cary Grant, with a body by Charles Atlas and more sex appeal than the law allowed, he enchanted—except for the cops and prison officials—with his powerful machismo...

Charlie Angel was a charismatic convict who was doing time for drug dealing and usage. As part of a work-release program, though, he became a popular speaker and counselor in the city's myriad world of the booming drug prevention programs back in the seventies.

One of my contacts, a savvy middle-aged woman doctor, called me and alerted me to a speaker who would be addressing a drug prevention program the following afternoon.

"You gotta meet this guy," gasped Laura. "The kids are crazy about him. He talks to them in their language. And cute! Ohhhh, sex appeal galore."

"My kind of guy," I joked. "I'll be there."

I met him the next afternoon.

Charlie resembled a hunky, muscular Cary Grant.

Sleeves of his summer shirt bulged from the powerful biceps. His shirt was unbuttoned halfway and disclosed enormous pectorals. The rest of his torso was just as stunning, even though he wore loose jeans.

More importantly, his face was Hollywood handsome. Square, deep-set eyes of brown, full, easy lips set off the rest of his ravishing torso. A small scar above his right upper lip added a dazzling touch of toughness to his image.

"Hey!" he grinned. "I read your movie reviews and your features. You're famous around here."

"Oh, I bet you say that to all the reporters."

"No, seriously. You've got a following here in prison."

I knew he was laying it on thick because he shrewdly detected that it certainly helped if you had a newspaper reporter on your side.

But at that time, he wasn't far off track. Despite the hostility in the newsroom from the bigoted dinosaurs, even they couldn't prevent my work from gaining me a high profile.

My Sunday movie column was the first thing many readers turned to, a fact not lost on the publisher.

I deliberately liked to create controversy, by calling popular movies and stars, like Burt Reynolds, Jane Fonda, "garbage and air-heads."

. Disc jockeys loved to read my most controversial columns on their morning talk shows to elicit listener feedback.

My articles were often bannered across the front page for I had sources in many governmental places by this time.

While people certainly discussed my proclivities, I was careful to never mix business with love affairs—or quickies. If I had fun with one of my contacts, I made sure they weren't involved in a story I was writing.

I was careful to never make the first move.

Girl reporters might screw everything that moved and the straight males certainly did as well.

But a man balling with another male?

This was something so nightmarish that it could only be discussed in hissing whispers and howls of horror.

So, I had to be very, very careful with whom I had my fun.

Charlie Angel was something else.

I watched him get in front of a group of problem kids. They worshipped him.

He looked like an authentic authority figure. With his broad chest exposed, those powerful arms bulging against his sleeves, his simple, macho way of talking, he created the image of a man who you would want to have around if anything went wrong.

He mixed street jargon in with commonsensical advice.

"You don't want to spend time on the government's dime for smoking pot and using reefer and horse. Use your brains, guys and girls. You don't wanna end up in the pen like me, especially if you're a young boy. You got big, tough guys just waiting to get their hands on you—and inside you."

I watched the wide-eyed problem boys gulp at this.

Then I saw him again, as he addressed this time the Lion's Club. These graying, middle-aged men were just as enraptured as the kids were.

Charlie made them grin as he compared his life in the pen and theirs on the outside. He appeared fearless, without nerves and sincere.

I made a point of meeting him at these gatherings for the next month. We talked a lot, over cigarettes and coffee and he told me fascinating vignettes about his life.

"Why are you in prison, Charlie?" I asked him several times.

Here, he revealed himself to be the classic con man I had been warned about.

He never told me directly. First, he had to give me a background about his life. Typically, he was raised in foster homes and abused by the staff. Then he entered reformatory schools for stealing and slashing cars.

"Stupid kid stuff."

"But Charlie—what put you into prison? Please. Tell me directly."

"Well, it's like this—" he began and then meandered again into more phases of his life, prior prison.

On my own, I was shocked to learn he was suspected of planning to gun down a State Trooper in a bank hold-up. This was major serious trouble! I knew by now that nothing could be more serious than the killing of a uniformed man or woman.

By this time, I heard that several law enforcement groups in the state were demanding the State Parole Board to never ever let Charlie enter the world as a free man.

He could do this work release jazz but he was still a state prisoner.

When I mentioned to him one afternoon that I'd love to do an article on him, he said:

"When and where? I'll be there."

"Let's do it in my apartment, Charlie. There, we'll have some privacy."

"Okay," he smiled. "I'll find a way of getting there."

Luckily for me, I had found a perfect studio apartment on the ninth floor on Main Street.

It was furnished in a cool, glitzy style. I had a knockout view of the city from the long plate glass window of my den. I could walk to work in ten minutes. You could see my building easily from any street or highway.

I don't know how he did it, but at three o'clock that Sunday, he sat just a few feet away from me in my apartment.

He looked ravishing. His short-sleeved shirt was unbuttoned all the way. It fell away to reveal his flat stomach, his large pectorals and his erect nipples.

I had served him cold beer. He sipped and smoked his cigarette and began to talk. The sense of Eros was too powerful to ignore.

I brought out my camera and told him I wanted to get some good, candid shots of him.

"You direct me and I'll pose," he grinned.

"Let's get you out of your shirt, Charlie. You've got a great a build. I want my readers to see it."

"You think so? Why not?"

Casually, he pulled off his shirt and relaxed against the sofa's cushions. I snapped pictures.

He posed in perfect he-man fashion. With his hands clasped behind his handsome head, he thrust his powerful chest out.

"You look just like a cover boy for a muscle magazine," I laughed.

"We do this a lot in prison," he said. "We pretend we're being snapped for a porno mag, or some muscle mag. One of my buddies will pretend he's snapping pictures of me."

"And do you stop at just posing?"

He laughed softly and winked.

"Ah, would you mind getting under the shower? That'd make a great shot."

"Sure, why not."

In my bathroom, I watched him undo his jeans. They fell to the floor.

He wore no underwear. I could barely speak. His flesh boasted an over-all sheen of light gold and ivory. His rump rose high and rounded.

His male equipment hung heavy and impressive, swinging lightly, as he stepped easily into my shower stall.

I shot pictures of him soaping up and lathering his privates, the crevice of his rump.

When he stepped out, he rubbed himself dry with a large towel.

"You don't have to put your clothes back on, Charlie," I said. "You look so incredibly beautiful in the nude."

"I like being bare-assed. This is how I am all the time in my cell. I've a got a jail-mate who likes me this way, too."

"Oh? Does he prove it to you?"

"Oh, yeah. He rubs lotions into my skin. And then I reward him—with this?"

He used both hands to cup his heavy, swollen equipment.

"I'd like to massage in some of my own lotion I have made for me? Would you like that?"

He smiled. "Yeah. Sounds good."

"Just stretch out here on my bed and I'll go to work."

He lay relaxed on top of my black satin comforter. Even now, I can see the stunning image of him—an amber glow to his skin, the silver hair glistening as he rested his face sideways on his powerful arms.

I rubbed in the cocoa butter and lanolin mixture that a friend of mine in Birmingham made for me. My hands moved steadily over his rippling back, then down to his hips and then over his ass.

Like gleaming light bulbs merged together, they were incomparable in their rounded perfection.

By the time he turned over on his back, his manhood rose at full staff. He pulled me hard against him.

Years in prison had made him a powerful master of the sensual arts. His intensity was stunning, as he shuddered and gasped with each lick of my tongue on his nipples, his stomach and then the pulsing masculine core between his legs.

This was a profound part of his daily life in prison, he later whispered, and men had fought over him. He had men lined up, begging to be his nightly partner. Guards were especially relentless in demanding he give them some of his time.

"They want me to fuck them," he said simply. "I do it in a way that doesn't hurt. These guards and other jailbirds can't get enough of it. Here, I'll show you."

He was sooooo right. Charlie did it in an extraordinary way. You barely felt his entry at first. And then when you did, he was already moving in and as you held onto him, tightly, he plunged his beautiful hips up and down.

But Charlie proved to be too controversial.

When my article about the city's "New Hero to Drug Abused Kids," hit the stands, an uproar was heard from all over the state by the law enforcement groups.

They were outraged that I had "glorified" a possible killer. I had only given his side of the story. There was almost nothing about the side of the survivors of the cop he murdered.

Charlie, too, got into hot water about the interview. Where had he gone for the interview? It looked like he was in someone's apartment—and that was a no-no!

I had used just the safest of the pictures—a picture showing the handsome mug of Charlie resting on his arms that clasped the back of a chair.

It was too late.

He was quickly whisked from sight and before I left Montgomery, he still languished in prison.

I received an occasional note from him—read, no doubt, by prison officials. He wished he were out in the free air. Wasn't there anything I could do? Couldn't I write just one more story about his plight?

When he was abruptly transferred to a small prison near Mobile, I knew that he was being hidden away for good.

For a long time, I occasionally wrote to the Alabama Corrections System for information on Charlie Angel. The reply was always the same: "We have no address for Charlie Angel."

◆   ◆   ◆

For eight years I lived like this in Montgomery.

Steadily, my professional reputation grew.

No matter how my enemies felt about my personae, they couldn't deny that my articles brought me more writing awards than anyone who had ever worked on a Montgomery newspaper.

Medicine, mental illness, the art scene, the drama scene, the civil rights arena, I had brought prominence to all these fields. My contacts ranged in the hundreds.

Only a very few fellow cohorts knew for sure about my private life. They were tried and true confidantes—men and women who I ate and drank with.

Yet, I became aware of a grim fact of life.

Despite my professional reputation, I was still regarded personally as a freak by many of my cohorts.

This was a result of a good ole boy network among Southern newspapers. These editors and writers were worse than any gossipy women. Some of the old guard at my newspaper, including the city editor, was members of this good ole boy group.

By phone or by mail or over drinks, names of their colleagues, names of their co-workers were diced and sliced or anointed for professional sainthood.

A woman reporter could be a lousy worker but if she put out, her chances of being hired by a fellow good ole boy executive on another newspaper was one hundred per cent.

A male scribe could be a drunk, a drug addict, a tomcat, but if members of this cabal liked him, then he never had to worry about finding work in this circle.

A very few of us—the queers, the homo's, the lezzies—didn't fare as well. In fact, word went out about our supposed proclivities and we would never ever work on these newspapers.

I had first noticed this during my fifth year in Montgomery. Although I liked my job, I didn't like the city and I didn't like my enemies. I sent resumes out to newspapers in Birmingham, Atlanta, Charlotte, Raleigh and other metropolitan hubs.

All of them sent me form rejection letters that began: "Thank you for your interest in employment with our newspaper. Unfortunately, we have no openings." I noticed this especially about the *Birmingham Post-Herald*, a newspaper in one of my favorite cities.

I loved the geographical features of this hilly metropolis and I loved the men I met there on my weekend visits.

Yet, the next month one of our staff's most incompetent male reporters was hired by this publication. This writer was notorious for getting facts and names mixed up. We had to regularly run corrections on his stories. Yet, he received the job of feature writer that I wanted.

Once more I sent in my resume to the *Birmingham Post-Herald*. This time, the publisher wrote back. His rejection was contained in one sentence: "We have no jobs here for you."

I began to keep track of these incidents. Another reporter on our staff was hired by the Charlotte newspaper to cover entertainment.

I sent out a second round of resumes to the identical newspapers and once more received the same generic rejection letter.

I might be an asset at this newspaper, but no other publication wanted me.

Several times when I attended a news conference or waited for the courtroom doors to open on a trial, I spotted a group of male reporters. They giggled and snickered as one of them impersonated me.

A limp wrist flipping in the air...eyes batting madly and rolling around in their sockets...a swishy walk...patting the hair...

On one occasion, I hurried from the newsroom to the courthouse across the street. An important trial case involving political shenanigans was wrapping up. I was to cover it for our newspaper.

I spotted the press corps in the corridor. Some of them howled at the antics of my dear ole friend, Mr. Adonis. Wearing his trademark white panama hat and his milk-hued suit, he was swishing his hips and flipping his wrists.

"Isn't thee gorgeous!" he lisped. "I'm just thoo beau-ti-fol!"

Usually I tried to ignore these incidents. My enemies were hoping for a reaction. This time, I didn't think twice.

I approached the crowd. The reporters spotted me and sheepishly became quiet.

Mr. Adonis saw me and he stared at me, grinning, his one million watt grin.

"Hey!"

I flipped my wrists at him.

"Please, Mr. Adonis, don't stop! You have me down pretty good, don't you? Only, you really need to twist your hips a little more like this"—and I humped my hips—"and you need to roll your eyes around more—like this"—and I made my eyes go crazy. "And I'm soooo sorry, I'm not married with a wife with three kids like you and five girlfriends on the side. But I'll try real hard starting today."

His grin froze. His black eyes hardened. Just then the courtroom doors opened and we hurried in. When one of the reporters later told me she admired me for sticking up for myself, I rolled my eyes.

"What good does it do? They'll be doing Jason Fury imitations long after I've left here."

My frustration grew steadily. I grew so desperate to escape this situation that I took a six months leave of absence in 1976 and traveled around Europe.

After a German freighter from New Orleans dropped me off in Hamburg, Germany, I met countless handsome, Continental men, especially in Sweden, Italy and England.

In Sweden, a dashing young psychiatrist and I met on a train to Stockholm. He invited me home to meet his wife and his two little children and then he returned to my hotel.

He proved that at least one Swedish male was phenomenal in bed. In Portugal and Denmark and England, enchanting, sexy men continued to meet me on the trains, on the sidewalks, in the lobby of my hotels.

Most were married but this didn't dampen their energies. I discovered that with these creatures, my effeminacy attracted, rather than repelled. This is what they said drew them to me.

I stayed two weeks in New York City on my way back to the Bible Belt.

My week at the Sloane House YMCA was an eye opener. I'd never encountered anything as wild. There were so many eager men who wanted sex that a voracious slut could easily go through hundreds a day.

Refreshed and optimistic, I returned to the newspaper but quickly my spirits plummeted.

Just as I arrived back, the *Atlanta Constitution,* one of the newspapers I regularly applied to but was regularly turned down, "raided" our newsroom. Anyone who could type or spell cat was lapped up and hired by this veteran institution. The *Constitution* was on a hiring binge and was even scouring community weekly newspapers for talent.

Everyone was being hired, that is, except me and a few old dinosaurs in the newsroom that were waiting to retire.

Even Allan, probably the most illiterate reporter I had ever worked with, was snapped up to work as a city reporter in Atlanta. I wasn't surprised to hear that six months later, he was fired because all of his stories were so filled with misspellings and factual errors that the copy editors screamed bloody murder.

Maybe the Atlanta people thought I wasn't interested in moving, I thought desperately. I phoned the managing editor and asked for an interview.

His response was hardly enthusiastic. "If you're around these parts, drop in."

I traveled to Atlanta the next week. To get to his office, I passed through the newsroom. Several of my old cohorts from the *Montgomery Advertiser* saw me and nodded their heads. Three of the male scribes smirked and flipped their wrists to the others. Obviously, my reputation was well known in this newsroom.

None came forward to say anything. They now worked for a cosmopolitan newspaper. They could look at me and turn up their noses because they were acutely aware of the reasons why I was overlooked.

They now watched me enter the office of this nameless editor.

Within the first minute, I realized my visit was doomed. He was a bony, shapeless man with a long face and huge, black-rimmed glasses that sat on his nose like a Kleenex box.

His thin little mouth was turned down during the fifteen minutes I sat before him. His eyes stayed frozen on my tie and then my hands and then to the blank wall. When he did glance at me, his distaste was obvious.

He agreed I had proven my professional talent and had won numerous awards attesting to my abilities. But then he said:

"I'm sorry. We just can't hire somebody like you. I mean, everybody knows you're a fag."

He said this so casually and with the tone of someone who had discussed this very subject regularly that it was like I had been slapped.

"Everybody knows I'm a fag? Who? A lot of small minds like to fantasize about my being a fag but—"

"I'm sorry," he said and stood up. "Thanks for coming by. We'll, eh, keep your resume on file—"

"Fuck it. Put it in the trash can. That's where it's going anyway."

He didn't even blink. He sat back down and ignored me. As I left, I saw from the corner of my eye a group of the deadbeats laughing with each other. One of the women I had worked with flipped her wrist again.

My bitterness was so intense I hardly knew what I was doing for the next week.

Then, just as the saying goes, while one door closed, another one opened.

◆   ◆   ◆

Montgomery's first and only adult bookstore opened.

This shocking event outraged the usual hypocrites in the church and the law enforcement circles. The District Attorney was hysterical. He gave out interviews saying that "dirty pornography destroys the minds of our young people. I promise to wipe out this scourge that can destroy our civilization as we know it."

My desire for sexual freedom and personal freedom had grown to near madness. I read of the "sexual revolution" in New York and California. It was spreading steadily across the land—but certainly not to the 'Heart of the Confederacy.' It would never come here.

My brief taste of it in New York City had proved to me that life for someone like myself was much better in a large metropolis, compared to a small Southern city like Montgomery.

None of my bed partners could understand my desperation.

They had lived their whole lives in closets and in lies. They saw nothing wrong with this. It had worked for them all this time. They would never leave 'Bama.

These men were so butch, though, that they could have both worlds without fear of being entrapped.

Because of my swishy ways, I would always stand out and be suspect.

I compared my life to that of a Jew in Nazi Germany.

I hated having to be so careful to avoid detection, of putting on a hypocritical sexless face in my professional life.

I visited the notorious Adult bookstore that first week.

I didn't care anymore how it might look. I knew there were cops photographing each customer, in an attempt to terrorize the courageous owner—who just happened to live in Atlanta.

Even today, my picture is probably in some forgotten file at the police station there as having been a customer at this unique little store.

Only a few male customers were around. The manager sat quietly behind the cash register with a bland, yet attentive expression on his face. He and I knew that the police department were bound to attempt to slip in a mature, yet underage, male to purchase some of the publications.

If that happened, the bookstore would be instantly padlocked and the owner tried in court.

In the "Male Male" section, I discovered a sleek, colorful magazine called *Blueboy.*

I brought a copy, aware that cop cars were parked up and down the street—as if a convention of serial killers was in progress.

They had no meaning to me.

I was desperate for a way out of my life there and suddenly, there it was, literally in my hands.

Instead of being printed on cheap paper with typo-ridden stories with crude layouts and wrapped in brown paper, this was the gay equivalent of *Playboy.* Sleek, good-looking, it even showcased a buffed, golden torso of a blonde male on the cover.

The stories were all gay erotica, the pictures of naked men showing everything was also an eye opener. Usually, these magazines were published under the guise of physique publications.

Men would be naked—except for a highly irritating little white pouch that hid the goodies.

But in *Blueboy,* and as a result of the sexual revolution, you saw guys with hard-ons, posing eagerly for the cameras. Ah, there must be other guys out there like me!

At last, I had discovered a way of getting into this world. After studying carefully how the fiction was written, I sat down before my typewriter at home.

I worked like a demon on a story called "Garage." I based this idea on an incident I had heard while visiting the Birmingham YMCA. One of my bed partners told me of a garage in his hometown where the owner had sex with straight male customers.

I didn't dare use my real name. Not only because I still worked on a Baptist newspaper but also because I didn't want my kinfolk to suffer from my notoriety. In the small towns where they lived, having a homosexual in their family could bring the wrath of the rednecks and the homophobes down upon them and their children.

Blanche Fury, a powerful novel of Victorian passionate love, murder and revenge by Joseph Shearing was one of my favorite novels. I had loved the name because of its dramatic image.

I wanted to keep the last name of 'Fury' but I needed something simple as the first. Not Bruce or Robert or Vernon. The name had to be classical. When watching a movie on television that week, the title rose up on the screen in blazing color: "Jason and the Argonauts."

That was it. Classical. Easy to say. Two syllables, like Fury. Ja-Son. Fu-Ry.

Within two weeks, I had received a rave letter from *Blueboy* editor, Bruce Fitzgerald, who wanted to buy "Garage" and he urged me to send him more. I wrote four more the following week and he brought them all.

These new, gay magazines were desperate for slick, readable erotica. What they got was mostly junk, written by hacks or amateurs. My stories were crisp, fast moving, with recognizable characters and I sat them all in small Southern towns.

To me, these stories were incredibly easy to write. I used the first person in all of them and since I sometimes turned out five to six stories a day for the newspaper, I was used to organizing my stories mentally before writing them fast.

Readers went crazy over my tales. Bruce said he was receiving a flood of fan mail for more stories by this new 'master of erotica,' Jason Fury. This was like Christmas. For fifteen years, nearly 200 of my short stories and ten novels had never even received a personal note from the editors and agents who rejected them.

They were pretty bad. I had tried to write about a heterosexual world that I knew nothing about. I was bored to tears by the love affairs I tried to create between my male and female characters. Gay characters were an absolute no-

no—unless they were comic relief, were secondary figures or if they were killers or child abusers.

Gleefully, I now burned them all in a ceremonial fire in my hearth. This was like a symbolic destruction of all the hypocrisy I still practiced.

My time had finally come.

Six months after selling my first batch of gay stories and receiving praise and encouragement from Bruce Fitzgerald, I turned in my notice of resignation.

Instantly, I experienced liberation.

It was like I had finally cut myself out of a suit of heavy metal armor.

I had saved up a nice little nest egg that would keep me going for several years.

By working out and lifting weights, I looked better than I ever had. I used the male centerfolds with their gleaming bodies and bronzed flesh as my models.

My stories were appearing in all the leading gay magazines. My pen name of 'Jason Fury' ran on the covers as teasers: "Jason Fury's latest Romance!…Don't Miss Jason Fury's Over-sexed Preacher!"

I was finally closing this chapter of my life and I did so with relief. I had stuck it out and given it a try and given it my best. But Alabama was definitely never going to my home.

I liked many of the people I had met there. At the newspaper, I enjoyed a number of the people I worked with, especially the photographers.

But this was a world that would be forever foreign to me. I couldn't see myself spending the rest of my days here, into old age, living a lie, waiting to have the police come pounding on my door in the middle of the night.

There were other places in the world where guys like myself could live freely, brazenly with no apologies.

New York City was the place I wanted to be.

No one was surprised when word of my resignation made the rounds.

Although it was traditional to send off a departing reporter with a round of luncheons and parties, I received zero. The few reporters and photographers I had enjoyed being with had long gone.

On my last night in the newsroom, I paused before leaving it. Several old men were hunched over their typewriters, smoking cigars or reading a newspaper. They were marking time until they could retire.

The newsroom had become a graveyard. The paper had yet to fill in all the vacancies left by the Atlanta's paper raid. I let out a sigh of relief. With my personal coffee mug in hand, a box of personal memorabilia under my arm, I left the building and walked out into the clean, fresh air.

On my last night in Montgomery, as it has been in most places I left, rain fell heavily. I watched it freezing on the street below. It didn't get this cold in Montgomery that much and it fascinated me.

I studied the empty street and thought of all the men who had made their way into the building and into my apartment.

There were all the parties I had given in my cocoon on the ninth floor and there were all the men I had slept with.

Staring at the frozen street, I could see Adam's body now—on the sidewalk further down the street. He was dead and buried now.

Never again would I have to live a hidden life in the subterranean strata of society. Nevermore would I tolerate having to live with fear of a redneck cop pounding on my door.

Or the male decoys who did everything but rape you so they could make an arrest for "sodomy and solicitation."

When I drove my packed car away the next morning at dawn, I was certain that this was a chapter of my life that I was closing for good.

It was.

I've never returned to Montgomery since that cold, wet morning in February of 1978.

This is a place I can visit comfortably only in my memories.

PART IV
The New World

❖

1979

"I love the night life
"I love to boogie…"

> *—Alicia Bridges singing "I Love the Night Life."*

Chapter Eight
The Stripper

Cigarette smoke whirled through blue, sultry air.

Whiffs of expensive male cologne combined together to perfume the darkness...*Champagne de Bain, Negretti, Creed, Aqua di Parma, Monsieur Molyneux...Candy...*

"And now," crooned the velvety voice of the hidden master of ceremonies, "all of you gentlemen settle back and applaud our first handsome number of the night—Mike!"

Chic's "Good Times" pounded out through the packed little auditorium of the Gaiety Burlesque. A bass so powerful it made the small but intimate walls of the theater tremble and the audience to nod their heads to the rhythm.

And out writhed Michael—a slender, muscular jock who wore his famous surfing outfit. Shoes, socks were quickly discarded. And as he danced down the narrow walkway that led out into the audience, his jersey vanished, then his jock strap and any remainder of his modesty.

He glistened naked, sensuous, and he stroked himself as he sexually taunted his rabid fans.

"Mike, over here!...Come'ere Mike!...Get it hard for us Mike!..."

For a year, I rarely missed a Saturday night when the legendary male burlesque house featured its "boy marathon—12 of 'em!"

I glanced around at the packed gathering: none of these guys looked gay or queer or whatever the current label was fashionable. They were ordinary men you saw on the streets of most cities.

College boys sat next to military types who sat next to salesmen who nestled close to foreign tourists. Some wore glasses, others business suits, many in casual attire. Young, old, rich, middle-class, none fit the stereotype of the "gay" male of 1979 or as portrayed in the media and the movies.

With the ease of much practice, the sweating Michael dangled his manhood close to the faces of the Japanese tourists who screeched and giggled and would have photographed him if picture taking was allowed.

Michael glimpsed me, winked and swung his toolbox as his way of a greeting. He swiveled to where I sat; his feet straddled the armrests of my seat, and squatted halfway down—enough to brush my face with his privates and to allow me to squeeze them several times for good luck.

By the time he left me, he was fully erect, a sign that he was ready to dip back behind the golden strips of lame—and to keep his fans lusting for more.

During intermission, I watched him, now dressed in loose running shorts, surrounded by older male admirers, watched some of them slip him folded money, along with messages and phone numbers of their hotels.

He winked at me and grinned.

Michael and I were sometimes bed partners because I had profiled him for a weekly tabloid, *Gay News*.

He was as delicious in bed as he was to look at. Yet, he was totally straight and had a wife and a kid. He stripped on the weekends to earn money while attending Columbia University through the week.

Rarely did he ball with a male. I was a lucky exception. He and so many of the other dancers I came to know intimately were exactly the type of men I was attracted to. Very few belonged to Manhattan's very active gay scene.

They worked other jobs by day, with many going to college or med school. Several of my favorites had girlfriends on the side. They didn't play around—but they were attracted to me.

I demanded nothing of them. I made them laugh, they enjoyed hearing about the stories I wrote and several of them made their appearances in my tales of dramatic sex and lust. The men I knew I was clean and physically fit. They had a horror of sexual disease. Some of them smoked pot, nearly all smoked cigarettes but the real stars of male burlesque knew that their bodies were their fortunes. They couldn't afford to fuck up what Mother Nature and daily workouts gifted them with.

The whole New York erotic scene never failed to thrill me.

I had never felt so free and desirable. In places like the Gaiety Burlesque, I found other men exactly like me—but none of us were slinking around or whispering about what we wanted or trying to hide it.

You were encouraged during the late seventies and early eighties to be yourself.

"*Don't live a lie!*" screamed the gay tabloids that abounded in Manhattan during that time. *Kick up your heels. Suck, fuck, have your fun. The more men you go to bed with, the happier you'll be.*

You've been locked away in the closet long enough! Now is your time to revolt and take what you want. Sex! Men! As many partners as you can cram into your life each day.

This was the credo of all the publications, gay porno films, bars and baths. You were sneered at if you timidly confessed your longing for the hunky bartender or boss of your department.

You owed it to yourself to state bluntly to your fantasy objects what you wanted to do. A strong whiff of hysteria imbued the whole isle of Manhattan. Having been "locked" away in closets for decades, the key had finally turned. Prisoners were released and now they had to make up for lost time.

I had discovered a whole universe of throbbing men who were like me. We lived for the moments we could merge into the darkness of theaters like The Gaiety Burlesque and become voyeurs.

Or we could slip into gay movie houses where you not only had a chance to see several gay porno flicks but you could have all the sex you wanted to.

You could sit in your seat, watch the movie, and if you didn't weigh five hundred pounds or were on crutches, someone would quickly settle into the seat beside you. Then you felt hands groping you, then your pants would be unbuttoned, pushed down around your knees and a mouth took over your arousal.

Or, you could go behind the screen where an even wilder cruising area thrived. You never saw who these people were. Your hands and mouth did all the communication. Yet, even in this paradise of sexual liberation, something warned me to be careful and restrain me from gorging myself crazy on all the sex around.

Rarely did I do a stranger in a theater. Never did I let them stick their hardness into me. If I knew the guys, like I did the strippers, I'd have complete fun. With strangers, I was still the bashful type.

The wildest place of all was the outrageous Show Palace off Broadway.

When you paid your five dollars, you walked up a flight of narrow steps into a small foyer. From there, you had three theaters to choose from.

The center auditorium was the biggest and the wildest.

The eight o'clock show was preceded by a sizzling warm-up. Five hunky men would come out on the narrow walkway. To pounding disco music, they quickly stripped down to a jock strap.

Then, they stepped off the stage and moved slowly along the rows of fans. The more brazen would reach out, pull out the privates and have uninhibited fun right there. What made these boy toys so attractive is that none of them were the preening, arrogant boy toys you saw as centerfolds in magazines. They looked like they had walked off the subways after playing a game of pool or basketball.

I had a passionate crush on one of the more boy-next-door types.

He resembled your neighborhood car mechanic. Beau wasn't muscular or gleaming with a golden tan.

He was beefy, fair-skinned, with the slight suggestion of a beer paunch. While he did his thing here, he casually lit up a cigarette like he was taking a break from changing a tire.

He made a point of pausing before me. With a few shots of gin under my belt to give me courage, he pulled down his jockstrap and I went to town. I had no shame. He got hard easily—and he ejaculated just as fast.

When I finished, I looked up at him. He always flashed me a grin, a wink and went on down the row until another daring fan did the same thing.

Beau was his name and again, he was super straight. He fascinated me because during breaks, I'd see him wearing only his jockstrap, while engrossed in a medical textbook. He was studying to be a doctor.

After Beau and his cohorts had "warmed" up the audience, the main show consisted of several gay porno stars that had sex with each other on stage. Many acted bored, since they did this several times a day.

But after the star attractions finished, the grand orgy began.

Ten naked men—including Beau—came out on stage.

As disco music throbbed, the emcee would urge: "Come on now, you men. Get up there and have some fun. That's why they're there. Now don't be rough. Handle their privates carefully. You can start your sucking and your rimming now!"

I always headed straight to Beau who laughed when he saw me.

"You can't get enough, eh?"

I watched young sailors, Japanese executives, and handsome straight looking guys all go crazy on the stage.

Because it really had turned into a Roman orgy.

I got to know the manager of the Show Palace, a lanky, ordinary looking guy named Alvin. He appeared more like a middle-aged office worker with glasses perched on his nose.

"You're one of our regulars," he said one night as I paid for my ticket. "Why don't you get up there and perform? I mean like one of those strippers."

"Oh, pu-leeze. I'm a little too old. I'd have to get halfway drunk."

"Do it. The performers like you. You get things started in there. You're clean and you don't get crazy. You've also got one hell of an ass and a great looking bod."

"What do I have to do?"

"Nothing. Just do what you've been doing. Except when you come here next week, be ready to strip naked and be one of our warm-up guys. All you gotta do is stand there and let the guy have his fun."

My mind was already settled. I would definitely do it.

This is what thrilled me so much about my new home city. No one hid anything. You could talk as bluntly as you wanted to. In the past, any discussion regarding gay sexuality had to be coded or restrained.

And so the following Saturday and a few more after that I became an amateur "warm up" guy—but I realized that I had much rather be in the audience, being a voyeur.

I met numerous strippers and wasn't really surprised to discover that most did this just on the weekends to make extra money for college. They enjoyed some beers, maybe some grass, but they weren't into the wild, drug-crazed lifestyle that the public expected.

A few of the younger and uninhibited strippers burned out fast. They'd get naked at the Gaiety or the Show Palace and then zoom down to the Village to gyrate as go-go boys on the wild bar scene.

Within months, they vanished into oblivion.

For in that pre-AIDS era, drugs, booze and marathon, kinky sex was the norm. If you visited any gay bath in Manhattan at that time, you always found crowds packing the fisting rooms.

Eager receivers would fit themselves into leather harnesses so that their butts were exposed. I watched men take hands, arms even feet up into their anuses. While they groaned in delight and high from poppers, they would engage in this for hours.

These men would beg more than one man to push their fists up into the greased chutes. You would see two arms twisting in and out of a man's posterior. You also glimpsed streams of blood spattering the Crisco shortening that was always around in buckets.

Some bathhouses even advertised having a nurse and doctor on hand "to stitch you up!"

That was too outré even for this now jaded New Yorker.

Another powerful factor in my physical well-being was that I had zero interest in drugs. I had tried grass on several occasions but all I got was a sore throat.

I depended on alcohol until I eventually gave that up, too, as a poison that was becoming too attractive to a basically bashful guy.

What thrilled me was to walk down Forty-Second Street and Times Square on a Saturday night.

With a warm breeze carrying the smells of cooking hot dogs and fried chicken from the greasy spoons, sidewalks were jammed with thousands of tourists.

All looked wide-eyed at the bawdy, graphic marquees of the flea-pit theaters that ran triple features: "Teenage Sex Sluts!…Boy Sluts Meet Daddy Bears!…Wild Women of Porno!…"

What really attracted the curious were the live sex theaters that jammed against each other. "Live Sex Shows! Five Different Couples! Tina and Buck Back By Popular Demand!"

Graphic color photos and posters enticed the curious. Black strands of tape blocked out the anal and oral centers of activity. I visited a few of these places but found them depressing.

While canned disco music pounded through the airless theater, bored looking couples came out and did their things. Rarely did anyone look like they enjoyed it. They were bored, pale and now and then one of them grunted or gasped, as if to prove to the audience that they weren't wound-up mechanical dolls.

Around me sat silent, ordinary men. Most had jackets or packages in their laps. Their right hands stay hidden beneath these parcels that jiggled suspiciously.

What separated these theaters and the wild Show Palace was that at the latter, everyone had a good time. Some of the male porno guys did look blank and mechanical but they were a rarity.

When Chic belted out their disco hit, "Good Times," this could have been the theme song for the popular gay entertainment dens.

◆   ◆   ◆

After a year, I had used up all my savings and needed to find work somewhere in this big city.

This idea terrified me.

I had been a success in journalism down South. But here, that meant nothing. Tens of thousands of workers with every type of outstanding background imaginable poured onto the Isle of Manhattan to seek job security.

Although my stories were all selling steadily, this still meant months before I received payment. And when it came, it was not enough to cover my living expenses.

Some of my readers pleaded for us to meet. More than a dozen demanded that I become their permanent lover boy. They would pay for everything. An apartment. All my expenses. We'd travel to Europe. I'd have an unlimited bank

account and I could shop with total abandon at all of Manhattan's most glitzy male boutiques.

I shuddered at the thought of being beholden to anyone. In the residential hotel where I had moved into, I loved having my privacy and being independent. No one told me what to do. I could lock my door and be by myself—a rare condition in Manhattan where nearly everyone was forced to have a roommate to share expenses.

So, I knew I would have to fatten up my bank account to continue this life style.

Very nervously, I signed up at several of the booming office temporary agencies that were popular back in the early eighties.

Gradually, I found myself going out each week, into a totally strange environment as an office worker. This meant filing forms, typing up documents, answering the phone—all the things I had never thought of doing before.

My first assignment was for two months at Scholastic Magazine Publishers in mid-town Manhattan.

My supervisor was a sweet, mild-mannered gay guy. Over him, though, were two huge bull dyke editors.

They made his life hell. They adored shouting and hollering at him.

They thrilled to chopping him up in front of the others. When I asked him one day why he took it, he looked surprised; "Jobs are so hard to find in publishing."

"Get a job as a stripper at the Show Palace," I joked. He paled.

From there, I took other assignments. In many ways, I totally hated this routine. I would become so nervous at getting a new temporary job that I became nauseated from anxiety. I was still a little cowed by this vast metropolis in which I was a resident. I've always enjoyed a steady routine. Anything new completely threw me.

But usually I would take these brief positions and over the years, I saw nearly all of Manhattan's executive offices.

I discovered that the very personal assets that had so repelled my enemies in the South had just the opposite effect in this jet-paced world of Manhattan.

People liked my style of dressing, my wit, my campiness. My effeminacy added to the curiosity factor. Many had never met, much less worked with, an openly gay guy, even in New York City. My type was usually found only in the fashion, publishing, and entertainment industries.

Women loved to be around me. Men were curious, too, and laughed at my acid comments and jokes. Rarely did I see any homophobia. Occasionally I

would catch some male bigot flipping his wrist and twisting his hips after I had passed him by.

This was a real rarity.

This was especially true on Wall Street. When I was assigned there, I was thrilled at the big, brawny executives I worked with.

They all looked like star athletes dressed up in expensive suits and ties.

The men I worked with liked having me aboard. I was certainly different from the usual "temps" they received. I dressed sharply, was well groomed, I could joke and banter with anyone. My journalism career certainly paid off when it came to typing, arranging meetings for my boss and handling the phone to make appointments.

I wasn't bashful or tongue-tied in their presence. Since I read three newspapers a day, I was on top of everything.

While moving around the Wall Street investment firms and banks, I finally received an assignment at New York General Bank.

I was given a private office with a window that overlooked the icy East River.

I was situated right next to a corporate big shot that needed someone to transcribe his notes on an in-house document about company protocol.

For a week, I worked leisurely as I transcribed taped recordings of my boss, Gene Adair. He was over in Europe on business and was due back anytime. His voice was attractive and intriguing. Low, smooth, it also suggested a Southern twang. His executive and possessive secretary, Margie, said Gene was actually a transplant from Texas.

The office was a hub of whining and complaints by Gene's underlings. I'd go to the coffee klatch and listen to the secretaries bickering over turf, hear the junior executives complain about their work and their salaries.

I was glad to be out of that mess. In my private lair, I found the assignment easy and very well paid. Typing up the tapes was elementary and I quickly finished them.

On my own, I put Gene's ideas into a draft and divided them into chapters. I gave each of them headings and by the end of the week; I had to admit that the booklet looked smart, cutting edge and professional looking.

I was to meet with the executive the following weekend and help him edit his words into the finished product.

That Friday morning, I had gone to the coffee klatch and overheard the usual bickering, when suddenly the main door to the area opened. The draft was cold and windy.

A giant of a man stood there.

Everyone became silent at first, then someone shouted out: "Gene! When'd you get back?"

I was spellbound. This was a man I had fantasized as running a Wall Street Bank. Hollywood could not have improved on this grand entrance.

He was big, broad shouldered and sported a beautiful head of thick, sandy hair. A lock fell over his brow.

His tie was undone and his suit was expensive but rumpled. He threw his trench coat and briefcase into a chair and swept his hands over his hair. Gene Adair could have been the exact double of movie heartthrob, Rod Taylor, who starred in *The Time Machine* and *The Birds*.

"Yeah, I'm back. Man, can I ever use some hot, strong coffee."

Quickly, I found a large cup and poured it full of Columbian java.

"How do you like it?" I smiled.

"Lots of sugar. Some cream. Who're you? I haven't seen you around here."

"I'm the famous Jason Fury. Actually, I was hired to edit your in-house booklet on corporate policy."

"You were, eh? Well, the more the merrier."

He took my coffee, sipped it and threw me a wink.

"Just right. Can you fix me another one in about thirty minutes?"

"Coming up."

Instantly, his subordinates surrounded him. They resembled school kids who've waited for a favorite teacher to return to vent.

He towered above them. As he sipped his brew, he listened; he nodded and made his way to his corner office. It was right next to mine. He looked around for me:

"Can I have my second cup now?"

"You got it!"

His secretary, the heavy, emotional Margie sidled up to me: "I get his coffee for him!"

"But—he asked me, too!"

"You're only a temp here!"

"Which means I don't have to worry about being fired like some people do."

She glared at me, gulped down air, and stood back. Her face had flushed to a tomato red. Maggie was one of these pudgy, middle-aged women you find in Manhattan's corporate offices even today.

They've been at their jobs so long they think they know everything. They like to intimidate but poor Maggie found that this temp had no patience in letting her push him around.

I felt breathless and excited. This was a kind of man I would never have met in the South. He was a prototypical Wall Street Tiger. All during that week, I heard from others that Gene Adair was a happily married with two children. He did *not* play around. A rarity in that hothouse culture.

He had been an all-star jock at one of the Ivy League schools. He had once been a movie extra in several muscle man movies while he lived the bohemian life in Europe for a year.

"He was one of the gladiators in a Steve Reeves movie," grinned Leon, a junior executive.

"I'd love to have seen him one of those little skirts."

"Skirts? I understand he wore just a tiny little loincloth."

"Yum, yum. Eat'em up!"

He howled. "You're too much."

While I put finishing touches that day on the brochure, I certainly kept eyes on The Prince.

This was an affectionate name given to this glorious macho male.

Even in the midst of all-day meetings, barnstorming sessions with his staff, listening to relentless complaints from his underlines, Gene Adair never appeared unruffled.

A lock of sun-streaked hair had a habit of falling across his forehead. His hazel eyes always looked slightly surprised. His six-feet-four torso loomed as a tower of stability and strength in that pressurized environment.

During my second week, he gave me another box of tapes to transcribe that he had dictated while on the plane home from Europe.

I noticed how several times a day, he would stick his head in my office and come in and stand there, sipping from his mug of his coffee. Someone—maybe an adoring minion or one of his kids—had hand painted the slogan across the black surface: The Chief.

"Can you understand me on those tapes?" he'd asked with a smile as I put down the earphones on the Dictaphone machine. "Can you make me sound good?"

"I've heard a lot worse," I answered. "When I was a reporter, I had to listen to tons of garbage. I think the booklet will prove to be a winner."

He was fascinated by my experiences in journalism. Even more intriguing to him was my writing career as Jason Fury. In Montgomery, my stories could have sent me to prison on obscenity charges.

In New York City, it was just the opposite. Even my straight stripper buddies had heard of me.

"*You're* Jason Fury? Wow!"

I showed him some of the latest gay magazines with my stories heavily hyped on the cover.

He laughed. "Hey, I've got a famous guy on my team!"

He didn't blink as he paged through the sleek pages of gay erotica and centerfolds. He paused as he studied one very aroused bruiser, hard-on and all.

"Whew!" he guffawed. "He looks like a tough customer."

"Maybe one day I'll see you in there, Gene—when you get bored."

"Me?" He whooped. "Yeah, I can see it now. Wall Street Banker Shows Ass and Hard-on! Maybe a few years ago."

His laugh, though, was easy and amused. I sensed that with him, he was more intrigued than repelled by my writing career.

I began meeting with him late, each afternoon, as he went over my copy and made changes and corrections. He leaned back in his chair, one leg crossed over the armrest, and discussed what he wanted to see.

"You're an editor, just polish up my words anyway you'd like to. How's your writing career coming along? Getting any new ideas from working here?"

I smiled. "I use everything in my work. There haven't been any gay stories with Wall Street as a backdrop. I'll quickly change that."

He laughed softly. "You think the guys here are good-looking?"

"Certainly! They're a different kind of beefcake fantasy. All the gay stories are just alike. Naughty boy gets the hots for coach. Naughty coach gets the hots for his jock. Or horny driver picks up horny hitchhiker. Or a horny phone repair guy comes to service more than a phone. Or horny bodybuilder gets wicked rubdown from hot masseur. I don't recall ever seeing horny Wall Street Tiger gets hot for male secretaries…"

Gene laughed at my descriptions. "Well, this is something new to me. I've never noticed that element in this business. Guess I don't look for it. I've been married for ten years. But if I weren't—who knows?"

With that enigmatic remark, he left me.

Afterwards, I thought: this would never be happening in Montgomery. There, I'd be miserable by now, going to work at a dead end job, keeping my life secret and hidden.

Here, I'm actually discussing my love life with my boss.

Sometimes I'd be at work and he'd stick his head in the door: "Time for a coffee break."

We'd go to the coffee klatch and gab a few minutes while smoking a cigarette. Yes, in those long ago days, people smoked everywhere in New York City.

"You're doing a great job. You make me sound like Winston Churchill."

"When I like working with somebody, I pull out all the stops."

"You like working for me?"

"Sure. If I didn't, I would have left here the first week."

"Why don't you work here permanently? I could get you a job easy in the public relations department."

I was pleasantly surprised at his words. But—

"That's really nice of you. But that's what I came to New York to get away from. To get out of the pressure cooker life style for a while. To create my own schedule."

"The offer stands. Anytime you change your mind. I know they'd love to have you. I'd see to that."

"You're great. I'll keep that in mind."

By this time, his secretary Maggie hated me passionately. She made fun of me behind my back. I ignored her even though I knew she was urging her boss to end my assignment there.

One day I passed her desk on my way to the elevator and she looked up with an expression of sheer hatred: "Your days here are coming to an end. Very soon. I'll see to that."

I went up to her and stared down into that pudding-like face of thick lipstick, mascara and powder.

"Haven't you ever thought about retiring, Maggie? Don't you have a life outside of here? Life's passing you by, you know. You ain't no spring chicken anymore!"

Her wet lips opened to spew something mean but my elevator door opened and I left her.

◆   ◆   ◆

I knew that the bank kept a block of hotel suites nearby, available for its senior executives who had to commute from their huge houses in Westchester, Long Island and Connecticut.

This was to make it easier for these men if they had to pull long, exhausting days. Or, if the weather created emergencies.

One afternoon, Gene came by my office.

"Would you do me a big, big favor? My secretary's out this week. I need some clean shirts. Would you mind going to my hotel room and get me some? I need to change for a big banquet this afternoon."

"Why, I'd just love to," I trilled.

He gave me his I.D. Card and told me where to look. He'd call up the hotel staff to tell them I'd be on my way.

The quiet, gray Hotel Imperial was just a few blocks away. I showed the desk clerk the I.D. and he directed me to the marble elevator banks. The hotel was legendary—an anonymous, wealthy place that reeked of money and class. Only millionaires stayed here.

I was breathless when I entered this intimate little cocoon of Gene Adair that floated near the clouds on the twentieth floor.

Like the outer image of this famed institution, the suite was dark, rich and elegant. Solid wood paneling, marble fixtures and old-fashioned windows looked out on the East River.

From the dresser smiled a framed picture of my boss and his blonde wife and two tow-haired moppets. The image didn't capture the smoldering beauty of this Wall Street mogul.

The maid had yet to clean up the room. It still bore witness to Gene's activities that morning before he walked to his kingdom.

I went to another dresser that contained his starched shirts. He wanted just any white one. He had stacks and stacks of them. Drawers bulged with them. I selected one that was so starched it felt like it were made of wood.

In another drawer, his BVDs were stacked up. I held up one and pressed it close to my face. Gene was a big man and his skivvies were plain old Fruit of the Loom.

In the bathroom, his bath towel still lay crumpled on the tile floor. His white terrycloth robe hung on the door. I embraced them both. Pressed against my nostrils, his moist aroma made me sway. They captured the elusive scent of this beautiful guy. An intoxicating elixir of Dial soap, Colgate toothpaste and clean flesh.

A hairbrush with a wooden back contained several tendrils of his hair. This came from Gene. The same light brown that always gleamed like a dark gold. On the glass shelf crowded a modest array of his toiletries.

He didn't care much about these things.

A bottle of Old Spice Aftershave, a razor and a can of Bristol-Meyers Shaving Cream. A stick of Mennen's Deodorant.

This was all he needed to fight his daily battles with management.

I stood by his large bed. The pillow was hallowed out where his head had lain. I'll bet he sleeps in the nude. I could see so easily that beautiful, tall form curled up there at night.

Reluctantly I left his room. I felt like he was there, watching me and approving of my visit.

Ironically, *New York Magazine* ran a playful feature that week on the 'Boys of Wall Street.'

Several pages were filled with photos of the most handsome of the Wall Street Tigers.

Gene Adair was voted by "secretaries and female executives" as one of these beautiful creatures. He was shown smiling in sweater and slacks, in a beautifully cut business suit at his desk, and one showed him shirtless, as he played golf.

He looked so Hollywood beautiful, with his gleaming helmet of hair, his square face and strong jaw, those white teeth and those boyish looking eyes.

His body was that of a Roman gladiator—broad shouldered, powerful chest, strong arms and thighs. The article had been written long before I entered his world so I was thrilled to see my hero emblazoned on those pages.

Everyone joked about his sudden burst of fame. He laughed charmingly, blushed and I thought: the pictures couldn't capture that irresistible charm of masculine sweetness.

◆   ◆   ◆

"You mind if we move our base of operations from here to my hotel suite? I've got to relax and lay down some. My back's killing me. I want to get out of here before they close the building. Looka that snow!"

Outside, a blizzard raged. It was late February 1980 and his staff was already scurrying to get the hell out of there and catch their train's home.

He stood in my doorway. His shirt was unbuttoned halfway down his chest and his hair was unusually mussed.

He had endured nonstop meetings all day, since dawn.

"No problem. You ready?"

"Sure you don't mind? I don't want you to get stuck here."

"The subways always run. I'm just a block away from my stop."

Our department was completely empty. It was only four o'clock but it looked like night outside.

Everyone had gone. Even my nemesis, Marji. Her face remained an ugly red most of the day—so red that others had commented on it.

She was calling in sick a lot now and Gene was having me to do the things his love-blind old secretary had done.

As for the in-house booklet, it was nearly completely.

I had worked hard to type up more corrections on the manuscript for him. This is before we had computers that could easily take care of any errors. We still had to rely on white out and the manual typewriter.

He grabbed his trench coat and I put on my fur-lined coat of red fox and a matching hat.

"Hey, you look like a movie star!" he smiled. "You always look sharp, striking."

"I'm a frustrated actor. I always felt I shoulda been a film legend."

I was thrilled, and nervous, to finally be really alone with this guy.

Snow had already settled several feet on the sidewalk when we made our way to the few blocks to the hotel. With him beside me, his big form blocked out the ferocious winds, the blinding snow.

He's like a powerful bear, I thought, and would protect anyone he loved.

In his room, he threw his briefcase and coat on the sofa. It was snug and cozy in here. Heat purred through the ventilator and the wide windows revealed a Christmas card scene of whiteness.

We saw a dark barge inching through the frozen surface of the East River.

"I could sure use a drink. There's the bar. Let's have a snort of something strong."

His bar was fully stocked by the hotel staff. I prepared gin and tonics, explaining that when living in Montgomery, this was one of the most useful talents I had learned.

Over drinks and cigarettes we settled down on the sofa and we went over the rough copy of the publication. He kept yawning.

"You look exhausted," I said. "Why don't you stop?"

"Yeah, I am a little tuckered," he sighed. "I've got to get the first part of this thing ready by tomorrow morning and fax it out to the board members. You think you could do that?"

"No problem. It'll look great. I promise you."

He winced and gasped as he stood up and rubbed his back.

"My back is giving me hell. My usual hotel masseur went home early. I hurt my back during my football days at Yale. It's never been the same."

"Let me give it a try. Why don't you take a hot, steaming shower, and I can't hurt it."

"Sure you don't mind? It's nothing fancy. Just massage my lower back. That's where the pain's centered."

"You'll feel like a new man when I've finished."

"I'll bet you've had plenty of experience in making new men out of old," he laughed.

My breathing had quickened. This was a scene I had run through countless times through my mind. Gene and I alone, in bed, having passionate sex. This was also the most popular and trite plot device in countless tales of gay erotica.

Panting gay guy gives aroused straight man a sexual massage.

Yet, from all the office gossip, everyone agreed that Gene Adair simply did not play around. He might flirt mildly as male executives did everywhere but that's as far as it went.

He winked and went into the bathroom. I listened to the shower running.

He came out draped only in a towel. Instantly, the vibes of the room intensified. He looked incredible.

His muscles were perfectly proportioned to his height, with dark hair shadowing his broad chest. His pectorals resembled two half moons, each capped by a thick nipple.

His hair was freshly washed and swept back from his face.

He smiled and stretched out on his bed. He had brought along a bottle of rubbing alcohol.

Unlike the super-heroes of gay tales, Gene looked so damned natural! His beautifully shaped torso was that of a real man and not one who spends hours in a gym, with every hair shaved off his flesh.

I hardly knew what I was doing. Here I had my hands literally on the most magnificent looking Wall Street Tiger of them all. Everything about him was perfect. His powerful thighs were slightly parted.

Lower my hands went and when I murmured: "Do you mind if I lower your towel a little? I need to get to the base of your spine?"

"Oh, just take it off. I'm not modest."

He lifted his hips and yanked the towel away. His perfectly shaped ass was only inches from my face. Like the rest of him, his skin was flawless, as if it had been draped with a paper-thin sheen of ivory silk.

When he settled his hips against the bed again, I saw his legendary male package pressed firmly against the sheets. I use the word "legendary" here because in the New York article, the writer had made sly references as to who of the Wall Street Tigers were the sexual beneficiaries of a generous Mother Nature. Gene's name was at the top of the list.

His sac gleamed like a dark pink pouch. Not a hair marred its surface. It was so large it had extended halfway down his thighs.

And beneath that bulged his manhood. Its length gleamed with power and thickness. An overhang of thick flesh protected the enormous tip, which had pushed halfway out, like a small pink apple.

My hands continued to edge lower until they covered his buttocks. He muttered: "Yeah, that's where I hurt."

My fingers slid into his inner thighs and he stirred slightly. His phallus was steadily growing—thicker, longer and more taut.

When he turned over, he smiled and he winked.

"You're making me forget my pain and exhaustion. Don't stop."

His arms went suddenly around me and pulled me hard against him. His mouth felt incredible: soft, warm, firm and he kissed me expertly. Quickly, I slipped out of my clothes, too.

My mouth replaced my hands as they tasted his nipples, his chest, his flat stomach and then to the center of his power.

Both my hands grasped the stalk and there was still more than enough to mouth. For long minutes I savored and feasted on him, never forgetting that I had the Prince of Wall Street literally within me.

Gently he began to probe me and gradually he entered me a few inches at a time. I gasped and thought he would never end entering me until he whispered into my ear: "Ah, I'm there! Hold on to me, baby."

I became dizzy as his mouth stayed on mine—and his hips steadily rotated, with each thrust nearly lifting me off the bed. Now and then he would pause, gasp, "Eh! I just came. That's only the beginning."

For an hour or more he plunged into me and several more times he experienced orgasms. When he finally pulled out, his mouth stayed on mine. Incredibly, I felt his erection growing steadily against my stomach and when I took it in my mouth, he was rampant again.

The aftermath of a sexual coupling can be awkward but Gene made it as pleasant and delightful as he had at work.

He held me in his arms and kissed my face. We lit up cigarettes as he still nestled me in his arms.

"I've wanted to do that with you since I saw you standing there in the doorway that day. You looked so damned nice and pleasant and sexy."

He had never balled with a guy before and after he married, he had never had fun with another woman.

"I kicked up my heels before marrying," he said, "but most guys do. I read your stories. I brought one of those magazines from a newsstand in Chicago last

month. Wooo, that story of you and the convict got me hard and lathered up. Maybe you'll do one about me. But change my name."

Gene kept me on the book project for another two months. We could have finished it in weeks but I was delighted that he continued the project—because it meant that he and I got together several times in his hotel room.

Never was their any embarrassment between us after that first and memorable night. He was charming, powerful and tender in the work area just as he was in bed.

When he asked me to stay "late" and work on the project, he asked this with an impish smile and a wink. This said everything. He knew I was staggered by his lovemaking but I also adored him as a person. He wasn't just a great quickie.

By this time, his real secretary had nearly vanished from the scene. She was now on medical leave. I hoped I was the cause of it.

One night, we lay in bed together. A wintry rain fell steadily and coated the windows of our hotel room with glistening ice.

"I want to take care of you," he said again. He sat up against his pillows and smoked a Marlboro. I ran my hand over his broad chest and caressed the light shadow of hair. My fingers made his nipples hard. "Let me get you an apartment close by here. A nice one-bedroom at Battery Park. You wouldn't have to work. I'd give you a weekly allowance. I'd create unlimited accounts at Bloomingdale's, Verranoes, Testoni's, anyplace you'd like. I just want you to be there for me."

We had gone through this before. Although flattered and intrigued, I had turned him down. I did so, again.

"Gene, you're fabulous. I love you for thinking of me like that. But—I'm just too independent. I don't like strings. I like going my own way."

He pulled me close and stared down at me.

"You're the weirdest guy I've ever met," he said quietly. "I don't like someone I love living on the edge like you do."

"This is what fate had in store for me," I joked. "Seriously, I don't object to you. No way do I object to you. I'm used to taking care of myself. I like to meet other guys. You're the jealous type."

"Me?" he teased. "I can't believe I'm saying all this to another guy. But then—you're not like other men."

"You're just now discovering that?"

"You say the word—and I'll have you an apartment ready to move into within a week."

I never said the word and many times since then I wish I had.

A month after this offer, I was getting dressed to return home. Gene looked up from the morning papers. Room service had brought us a large breakfast and *The New York Post*. Dressed in a blue silk robe, he resembled even more movie star, Rod Taylor.

"Are you sure you don't want that job in public relations?" he asked me.

"Would I work closely with you, Gene? If not, I'd rather not."

"I've not told my staff this yet, but we're closing down our operation here and moving up to Westchester. That's in upper New York."

I had buttoned up my fur coat and looked at him in surprise.

"You'll be staying up there then?"

"Yeah. I don't want being away from my wife and my kids. They hardly see me anymore. I want to watch my children grow."

He talked a lot about his wife and children. He adored them. I was horrified by this news. Although I knew there would have to be an end to my job there, I had dreamed it would last for many more months.

Word went out to his staff that Gene's department was being relocated up to Westchester. Many were shocked. This meant having to completely change their lifestyles, of closing down their houses in New Jersey, Long Island, Staten Island and finding new homes in upper New York.

My assignment ended there in late 1981. Gene took me back to his suite on that last day and we never left the bed through the night. Before I said my good-bye that morning, he walked naked to his closet.

"Here, I've brought you some things. To remember me by."

A stack of beautifully wrapped boxes in silver paper and sequined ribbons were revealed. From the top one, I removed a spectacular long overcoat of black leather, lined in fox with a large fur collar.

Another box contained a gleaming decanter of Creed Perfume. I knew how expensive this scent was for I had mentioned it to Gene one day as "the perfume I most wanted."

Glistening next to it was a bottle of the precious Aqua Di Parma perfume, another rare fragrance.

There were other boxes: of Lady Godiva chocolates, beautiful sweaters in black and white and pink cashmere. Handmade boots by Verona of Italy, silk briefs in gold and silver hues.

But before I left him on that final morning, he held me close, we kissed and for the final time, I used my mouth to travel over that unforgettable terrain of Wall Street flesh and muscle.

His last kiss lasted for a long time. We stared at each other for a long time, our eyes wet, and then I left quietly, carrying my expensive souvenirs of an affair now ended.

Gene and I sent each other postcards for a while, talked on the phone, but gradually, life re-arranged itself to the changes in our lives and we faded apart.

I was startled one morning recently to open the New York Times and right there on the business page was a picture of my old boyfriend with several other executives of his bank.

With his hair thinner, his face heavier, Gene smiled along with his cohorts because they had all been promoted to the pinnacle of their banking complex.

Of the three men, his smile dazzled more than the others. He was still Hollywood handsome and radiated a glowing charm and pure sensuality. What would have happened if I had become his kept boy?

Better to move on before an affair ends. Age plays no favorites.

Chapter Nine
Gay Author

My stories now sold steadily to all the new gay magazines that had exploded like comets with the emergence of the gay power movement of the late seventies.

Each month, I received a batch of these publications as complimentary copies with my work in them.

This new breed of magazine editor was often fun, brash, sassy and impish.

Their predecessors were few. Until now, being known as the editor of porno wasn't something an editor wanted on his resume. And to have worked on a "queer" publication would have been the final end.

But now, these bright, young men of the new Gay Pride days were proud to edit these magazines. They were clever and in no way tried to hide what they were doing. None displayed any interest in being mainstream. Their roster of tens of thousands of readers bolstered their sense of independence.

A few still harangued me about shoe horning more sex into my tales. The majority, though, sensed what I was trying to do. Readers obviously approved, too, since most of the mail they received was devoted to my work.

When I opened these magazines, the first thing I looked for was my contribution. I never tired of seeing how Jason Fury was presented. The cover promo's alone whetted the appetite of readers to thumb to my story first.

My dramatic and sometimes comedic tales of love between men, and my show-biz articles had become so popular that editors depended on my name to help sell their publications.

One day I walked by a newsstand on Forty-Second Street and Broadway.

On display were four gay magazines. I had short stories in each one.

One cover shouted: "Jason Fury's Unforgettable Love Affair!"

Another screamed: "Jason Fury's Christmas Story! Don't Miss It!"

A third one screeched: "Big Bill Gets Down!"

A fourth proclaimed: "Jason and the Preacher!"

I had to smile. Thousands of people passed by these newsstands all over Manhattan. They had to see my pen name on the cover of these colorful, gaudy magazines.

And if they chanced to read them, they would see that my stories were different than the others.

I worked hard to avoid the hackneyed clichés that filled much of gay erotica. From being exercises in sheer sex tales, I gradually added touches to my Jason Fury personae so that he became a unique creation.

Starting with the narrator, I added blonde curls, a swimmer's build, large blue eyes and a charismatic personality.

His profession was that of a writer and then a famous drag queen who performed at the Ritz Male Follies on Broadway. Over the years, he enjoyed a wondrously changing resume: professor, ballet dancer, teacher, author, reporter, nurse and trapeze artist.

Time meant nothing to this extraordinary creature. In one story, "Burnt Oranges," I put him aboard the Titanic where he watched his hunky and powerful father go down with that legendary ship.

In "White Gods," he found himself in Hawaii in 1941 where his much-decorated father became a victim of the attack by the Japanese on Pearl Harbor.

In "They Won't Forget," Jason Fury was a reporter in Boise, Idaho in 1956 during that city's notorious purge of homosexuals. In "Children Not Allowed," my literary alter ego became an employee of a day care center in Edenton, North Carolina, which became the focus of hysterical charges of child abuse.

Increasingly my stories became mini-novels. I worked hard plotting them and fleshing them out with realistic people. I ignored the iron walls of erotica "musts" and had my characters emerge as bigger-than-life.

I refused to trap them into the over-used milieu that marred most of homosexual story telling at that time.

In "King of the City," Jason's swarthy brother becomes a Mafia don who is obsessively in love with his yellow-curled sibling.

"Animal," finds Jason Fury as a college professor who murders a brutal male hustler. My stories could be either sharply dramatic or light-hearted. In "Bastard of the County," a cross-dressing Jason is shipped off by his parents to New Orleans to visit his handsome cousin. After much turmoil, the two run away together to the shock of the horror of Mrs. Fury.

In "Wild, Wild Young Men," Jason again wears make-up while visiting the beach in 1956. He meets two sexy young brothers and they become lovers.

I used my mother in many of these tales. It gave me a kick to finally twist the knife in her through my stories—repaying her for the countless times she had stabbed me in real life.

I felt no guilt. I knew that she would rather cut her throat than to read any of my work.

Nearly all my stories were based on fact—either inspired from my own personal journals or from some historical event, like the Boise, Idaho homosexual witch hunt, the Edenton, North Carolina, child care abuse hysteria, the attack of Pearl Harbor, or the over-the-top lives of New York City's Mafioso.

Death played a role in numerous stories. In "Barbed Wire," the handsome Vietnam vet commits suicide. In "Forbidden Fruit," the beautiful mental patient who Jason cares for takes poison and dies. In "Poochie Woochie," the sexy young jock dies of a heart attack.

Readers were jolted by these realistic depictions of gay life. FirstHand Magazine was the publication that encouraged me to explore the realms of erotica outside sheer sex. The editors of this wildly popular little magazine forwarded me fan mail, encouragement, witty little notes about story ideas—until a new policy was enforced where my stories were no longer welcomed. But that was still in the future.

There were still some editors, though, who continually carped about the way my Jason Fury stories were going.

They hated the way I dressed up my ravishing young dream boy. Instead of having him wear the uniform of all gay guys that consisted of jeans, tennis shoes and sweatshirts, I attired him in striking fashions—leather, furs, cashmere, and tweeds.

And when he wore drag, his gowns were stunning creations of glittering sequins, mink coats and dazzling jewelry.

To satisfy these complaints, I created new, super macho personae: 'Big' Bill Jackson. While he became exactly what my editors wanted, I also enjoyed imagining how it must be to be an incredibly muscled and endowed man who lived the life of pure hedonism.

Big Bill loved his beer, stogies, being naked, having sex with men and doing it in public. I merged men I had known and fantasized about into this one boyish satyr. Readers flipped out over him.

Fan mail poured into the magazines. Readers—and editors—begged me to send them naked pictures of both Jason and 'Big' Bill. In all of his Bill's tales, Jason Fury made a cameo appearance so there was little doubt that these two bigger-than-life characters were living together.

Now, I often saw not only my Jason Fury stories being showcased on magazine covers but often 'Big' Bill Jackson was there as well.

◆　　　◆　　　◆

While my work was popular with readers, the incestuous and intimate little circle of gay literary powerbrokers in the city did not share their reaction.

These were the ones who got together to dish, to discuss what new gay author was up and coming and who to promote and eventually to push for book contracts. This cabal saw to it that their favorites were showcased on national television shows like *Good Morning, America*, got interviews with magazines like *People* or *Time* and were reviewed by *The New York Times Book Reviews, New York Magazine*.

None are remembered today. Few readers, except friends of the authors, could get far into these self-conscious attempts to write literary work with a gay theme.

These new book authors were the ones who wrote boring, flat stories about losing their "lover" and which no one but their boyfriends and supporters would enjoy. Someone in these stories had to have AIDS. If you brought this subject into your work, and tried really hard to slavishly follow *The New Yorker Magazine* style of boring, nasal literature, then you might have a chance at having your book published.

You found these attempts at serious literature in little read magazines like *The James White Review* or other, smaller ones whose aim was to "publish serious gay literature." Other cliquish publications like the *Lambda Book Review* gushed over these quickly forgotten exercises in tedium and mediocrity.

Fiction that I wrote was ignored. It was considered gay erotica, a genre so beneath contempt and so abysmal that this small circle of hacks deemed it a grave embarrassment to the "gay" movement.

Why, it merely reinforced the public's idea of gay people as being over-sexed!

Sensuality was a no-no in this faddish little circle. These very serious tales must not possess any emotional edge and with minimal description of the characters. You struggled through these empty stories where the narrator whined about life's problems. Fifteen minutes later, you couldn't remember the words.

To make my writing career even bleaker, I was forced to stop writing for the gay magazines.

◆   ◆   ◆

During the mid-eighties, my favorite editors gradually left the gay magazines and went on to other things. The pay was never that great, anyway, and they took more lucrative jobs in public relations, teaching, advertising.

One editor who left told me that at one time he was editing not only Blue Boy, but Numbers and Playguy as well—a staggering amount of work for one man with a tiny staff.

A brash new breed of editorial hot shots replaced these literary pioneers.

These new kids on the block had zero interest in publishing the unusual or the different. They wanted pure, unadulterated pornography. They wanted no fancy dialogue, plot or ambiance. There could be no death, no emotional scenes, no sense of the characters as being real or—God forbid—sensitive.

Their story formulas were inflexible.

Sex had to begin in the second paragraph and it had to be repeated many times before 'The End.' You had to stuff each paragraph and sexual episode with tried and true expressions like "hard, raging cock…big, wide asshole…gobs of man juice…gorge on his man root…"

I discovered this harsh fact as my mailbox now began to fill with rejected manuscripts, rather than amusing, affectionate notes of acceptance from my former buddies.

The new editor of *Advocate Men* was blunt when he rejected my story, 'The Comeback of Mighty Mike': "Drop all the drag shit and making Jason Fury look like a weenie. Butch'em up! He comes across as just a sissy-britches."

His predecessor, the delightful Stuart Kellogg, was just the opposite. With the checks he sent me, he often scribbled brief, funny remarks: "Will the over-sexed Jason Fury and Big Bill Jackson stop their coupling for a few seconds and send me some more stuff?"

My favorite magazine to write for, *FirstHand*, also started rejecting my work.

"Sorry, there's just not enough sex in your submission."

Another note observed: "Get Jason out of drag and put him into jeans and work boots!"

And then, the rejections became generic, with impersonal form letters: "Thank you for your submission. Unfortunately…"

Now, I saw the handwriting on the wall and concentrated again on writing books.

I had already sold one before even arriving in New York City.

Before leaving Montgomery, I wrote in three days an exercise in pure erotica: *I Love My Daddy*.

I did it mainly to see if I could parlay my burgeoning magazine story career into books. The story moved fast and filled with countless sexual adventures by the heroic young football player and his father. I threw in every fantasy I could come up with. I wanted to entertain the reader with the most feverish sexual tome he had ever read.

Yet, I wanted to avoid the worn-out expressions and plot devices. I based the idea on a real life story I had heard from one of my preacher boyfriends: in a small Alabama town, residents were horrified to discover that a coach was having a torrid sexual affair with his own son!

A trial was held but before it could begin, the father and son committed suicide together.

I gave the plot a happy twist, though, yet I wanted *I Love My Daddy* to be the most arousing, exciting, fast-moving gay book ever written.

As a now seasoned reporter, I knew how to channel my thoughts into a fast-paced reading experience.

Since I had been unable to sale any of the countless straight novels and stories I had written over the years, I was thrilled to receive a contract and a letter of acceptance from Green Leaf Publishers.

They loved the book and wanted more.

When the novel appeared six months later, it was re-titled, *Daddy Stud* and for some bizarre reason, bore the pen name of 'Jerry Tucker,' when I had specifically requested the non de-plume to be that of 'Jason Fury.'

It sold out its first printing in two months. Through the years, I saw it on newsstands with different cover designs as it continued to fly off shelves.

Now, I decided to try the mainstream book-publishing world again.

From the nearly two hundred and fifty stories published under my pseudonym of 'Jason Fury', I selected twenty and compiled them into a collection that bore the title of *Eric's Body*. I was stunned by the often-violent reaction to these tales.

Over a two-year period, over one hundred and fifty agents and editors rejected my proposal. One agent, whose last name rhymes with 'Fuck', actually phoned me one night and screamed abuse at me for sending him "a pile of pornographic shit."

"What are you complaining about, you two-bit hack?" I screamed back. "My stories are a hell of a lot better than that last pile of shit you represented."

I knew that this same agent had successfully sold, with much fanfare, the pornographic memoirs of a female author whose graphic descriptions of sex made Jason Fury and Big Bill Jackson look like Mary Poppins.

Before I threw my manuscript into a drawer, I tried one more agent. Lyle Steele of New York liked my story collection—very much.

In just two months he sold it to maverick Publisher Richard Kasak who specialized in presenting classy erotica to the public. He published lesbian, bi-sexual, gay, heterosexual, bondage and the classics of Oscar Wilde and others. His imprints were wildly popular, especially Badboy Books that represented gay erotica.

Six months later, *Eric's Body* appeared under the Badboy imprint, and it became an overnight sensation.

The first printing of three thousand copies sold out within six months. A second printing, then a third and a fourth were ordered. A paperback was considered successful, in any genre, if it 1,000 copies.

"Jesus, what did you do?" Richard Kasak cried in excitement on the phone. "We can't keep any copies on the shelves."

Lyle Steele then sold to Kasak a collection of my 'Big' Bill Jackson stories. *Eighth Wonder* became another success, with its first 3,000 copies vanishing from bookshelves within three months.

Another printing followed, and then another.

Lyle and I had very different ideas as to what I should be submitting and we came to an amicable parting of ways.

On my own, I worked feverishly on a novel set in contemporary Manhattan.

For months, grim snippets appeared in the gay tabloids about a strange and new type of disease that was infecting only homosexual men. Quickly, the story grew until the mainstream press was sending out shock waves about this infection: AIDS.

I coupled this New Age horror with an actual incident of serial murders.

I had often heard of a killer who butchered blonde-haired go-go boys in the Village. The lunatic was never found.

I worked both themes into my suspense novel, *The Rope Above, the Bed Below*.

Richard Kasak loved it. Once again, my book joined the other best-sellers on the gay book lists. My books succeeded despite the total absence of publicity or hype. None of the gay magazines even mentioned the titles.

The new magazine editors were contemptuous of my type of erotica and made certain their readers knew nothing about them.

What made the sales of these books so unusual is that in the early nineties, bookstores refused to stock erotica—unless it was straight and it came from a big name publisher.

If the sexual activity was heterosexual in nature, then the bookstores had no problem. Gay sexuality was still considered an abomination.

Masquerade Books was the first publisher of gay erotica to be carried by a major chain like Barnes and Nobles. I was thrilled to see my titles all around Manhattan.

Yet, the very few queer bookstores in the city treated my work like embarrassing intruders into their racks of boring titles.

For instance, A Different Light Bookstore, on East 19th Street, had book signings and author appearances every week. On their store windows, they touted the appearance of anyone who had written anything with the word "gay" in it.

I went in to browse one afternoon and saw that my books, like those of other authors of male-male sensuality, were hidden away near the bathroom in the back. A garbage can and the Men's Room were just a few feet away.

It reminded me of the old days when dirty books were arranged out of sight of the conventional customer.

The manager, a slender man with thinning hair, clad in the requisite uniform of faded jeans, flannel shirt and tennis shoes was gushing over the spotlighted poetess who had arrived for her book signing.

She was a skinny lesbian wearing the identical outfit of the store manager.

The author could have been a Bowery bum who had wandered in from the street. I had never heard of the poet but the manager acted as if the Queen of England had suddenly appeared.

I discovered that in this tony little book store, like others in America, if you had composed a poem about your dog becoming gay, or if you had written a boring "gay literary" tome, you were invited to appear among their unknown luminaries.

Authors of gay erotica were the perennial outcasts. You see, writers in this genre perpetuated the stereotype of homosexual men as nothing more than sex-obsessed animals. Or so the thinking went, and still continues, today.

Windows of this little store that day were cluttered with posters announcing the date and the time of a gay author signing. You found even more signs within, above tables of the current favorites, and announcements that "_____ will be here at 3:30 p.m. sharp August 3! Don't Miss it! A book reading will be followed by a book signing."

With all three of my books receiving their second and third printings, I contacted the manager of A Different Light the next day and asked if I could come by one day and autograph my books.

His reply wasn't very enthusiastic: "If you're around, drop by."

I told him I would be there on Tuesday of the following week at three o'clock sharp.

When I appeared, no one was even expecting me. No signs were in the window announcing my signing. The clerk said the manager was busy. I saw his door cracked open and he was sitting there, yakking it up on the phone.

I dragged a chair to my books that were still hidden at the rear of the store near the bathroom.

After I signed my volumes I went to the cashier and said I had finished.

"Did the manager know I was here?" I asked dryly.

"I think so. He said he was very busy."

"Oh, sure. I can see that."

I looked at the door that was open. The manager lounged in his chair, clad in his jeans and flannel shirt and tennis shoes, as he read through *The New York Post*. He'd never even come out to shake my hand. He glanced up, saw me at the front, and quickly shut his door.

Bookstores like A Different Light wanted so desperately to be like their straight counterparts. But in this case, even mainstream book emporiums like Barnes and Nobles put books like mine in brightly lit areas where readers could find them. When I told one of the Barnes and Noble clerks that my books were on their shelves and could I sign them, she acted thrilled.

After I signed all the copies of *Eric's Body, The Rope Above, the Bed Below* and *Eighth Wonder*, the young woman and other workers put special signs on the shelves: "Autographed Copies by the Author!" There was no hypocritical snobbery here.

I wasn't surprised to hear that A Different Light Bookstore closed down several years ago. The manager said that major book chains had drained away his customers.

No, I thought. It was hypocritical arrogance that did you in.

◆   ◆   ◆

My novel, *The Rope Above, the Bed Below*, appeared in 1994, five years after the first nuggets of grim news began to appear in the flashy gay tabloids in New York City.

A growing number of queer men were reporting an unidentifiable illness. Signs of it were ominous: victims suffered severe weight loss, relentless flu-like symptoms, and mental illness. Most of the cases were accompanied by ghastly visual signs: red rashes and purple blotches on the skin.

These snippets of news caught the eyes of all readers. *Gay Times* and similar weekly newspapers were usually hysterical in their advocacy of all readers finding as many partners as they could.

"You deserve it!" the tones proclaimed. "You've been locked up in the closet long enough."

But now, here were these headlines about a sinister disease that struck swinging gay guys!

Even the *Village Voice* and then *The New York Post, the New York Daily News* slipped into their columns ominous articles about this devastating disease.

More stories began to appear about The Gay Plague and although I didn't hang out at the bars, I did frequent the gay movie houses and baths so that I grew increasingly nervous.

Within a year, mainstream media was reporting that homosexual men were becoming infected—and many were dying—from this Gay Cancer. A name was finally given to it: AIDS.

New York City panicked. Both straight and gay people could pick up AIDS, the media warned. You caught it by kissing, by saliva, by handshakes, some columnists warned. You were warned to beware of toilet seats, faucets, eating utensils, pens, and paper, everything—if a queer person had used them.

Hangouts like the gay theaters, bathhouses, sex clubs, bars were described by the media as incubators for this dread disease. Photographs of dying men splashed across newspaper and magazine pages every day.

The New York Post ran a series inflammatory articles of "queer dives" being breeding grounds for AIDS. Screaming headlines warned the city that everyone was at risk—all because of these "pervert paradises!"

I joined other activists on a freezing February morning to protest their rabid accusations.

The reporter of these shrieking true-life experiences portrayed himself in breathless detail as a reluctant visitor into Dante's Hell. He recounted in shocked gasps how some men had actually approached him and invited him into their cubicles—gulp, to have sex!

And then the City ordered all popular gay hangouts like the Show Palace, the Ramrod Cinema, the gay baths to be padlocked.

All the places I had haunted over those wild, feverish years vanished overnight.

No longer could I kick up my heels at the spectacular Show Palace. When I visited it one night after the scare began, I was horrified. Bright lights glowed everywhere. Men came out to dance and to strip down to G-strings. Stern-looking men with flashlights cruised the aisles, looking out for any sign of sexual activity—even masturbation.

"Keep it in your pants!" they'd holler to some uninhibited soul. Just a year before, you'd find guys not only jerking off but doing each other, getting screwed and fisted right there in the seats.

I witnessed male beauties vanishing mysteriously for several months. When they reappeared they were nightmare versions of their former selves. As they shambled along the sidewalk, they resembled escapees from a leper colony.

Yellow skin, dull, watery eyes, baldheads, curved spines, saliva drooling from their thin lips.

Death had enveloped the wild, Disco days of Manhattan's gay scene.

PART V
Manhattan Twilight

✦

September 11, 2004
I Walk Alone

The Last Man

The knock on my door was followed by a shout:

"Open up! Police!"

"What do you want?"

"You've got five seconds to open up or I'm breaking down the door."

I threw open the door.

The police officer was rugged, powerful in his trim uniform. Dark shades hid his eyes. Across his palm, he slapped a billy club.

"Trying to keep the police out, eh?"

"Yeah, you bastard! I'm filing a complaint of police brutality with your commanders."

"Oh, you are, eh? Well, let me show you what I think of queers like you?"

He tore off his hat, his shades and his hat.

I grabbed his crotch and he grabbed me.

"You are some fuckin' weirdo!" he muttered before kissing me roughly. From long practice, my fingers quickly unbuttoned his shirt and he kicked off his boots.

When he stripped off his trousers, his manhood was already ready to explode. It hung outward, like a smaller version of his wooden nightstick.

He picked me up easily and threw me on my bed.

We had just enacted a favorite fantasy of his: bad ass cop rapes swishy cocksucker.

Either dressed in his cop clothes or bare-assed naked, Roberto Devereaux was one hell of a great looking guy.

His black curls gleamed wet from sweat and from Charles Worthington conditioner. His ever-present stubble cast his chin and jaws in shadow. His juicy mouth was pressed against mine and as we connected sexually and passionately, I still thrilled to his young torso as it rippled with power and brute strength.

A blue shadow of an eagle and the American flag covered his right shoulder. His body was solid, touched by the sun, and gleaming in its power.

"I don't want you flirting with all those guys tonight," he threatened me. "I hate to share your ass with those fire eaters and other tough cop sumbitches."

"They're my fans," I smiled and ruffled his curls. "I've gotta be nice. They're great guys, too. You act so selfish!"

"Fuck selfish," growled my gorgeous young warrior. "When I go with somebody, I want it to be just me."

"You sound like an Italian high school kid talking about his girlfriend. I don't want to be tied down. Remember? We've talked about this. And you told me you didn't either. You play around—with girls."

Roberto was so passionate and intense that he quivered when we were pressed close together. When my mouth traveled over his warm, tense torso, his strong hands gripped the bed board and his hips rose slightly.

I loved to watch him getting dressed. Every movement made the muscles of his stunning proportioned torso dance. His back, his legs and his shoulders—they interlocked like a dancer's.

His butt stuck out in a most attractive way.

"Come on. Get dressed. We don't want to keep your fans waiting."

Although he joked, an undertone of seriousness marked his words. He lived with his two older brothers, who were also policemen, in Brooklyn. They dated nice, Italian girls and they planned to marry them after Christmas.

Their hotheaded kid brother, though, still wanted to play around.

Some of my faithful readers had planned a small coffee gathering in my honor in a café in the Village. My new book, *His Eyes Were Dark, He Licked His Lips*, had just appeared.

This was my first novel in a year and word had spread that it would be special. My old boyfriend, Gene Adair of Wall Street, had already ordered a dozen copies. I had hinted to him that he was the inspiration for my ravishing Wall Street tiger—David Darling.

I didn't know what sexual orientation my party hosts or guests that night enjoyed. This question never interested me. The men who intrigued me were usually very straight, macho and ordinary. I never wanted to segregate myself into a particular niche.

Roberto and I had met when I was browsing in the Barnes and Noble Book Store in the Chelsea section of Manhattan several months before.

A fan had recognized me, then several others, and they crowded around me in a corner of the enormous room.

Roberto had noticed the small mob and watched me autograph some of my books. One of the men was a retired military guy from Queens, two were college guys who lived near Harlem, and two of them were visitors from Oregon.

The college boys wanted me to join them for drinks but I couldn't make it that night. I had a deadline for my new book and only had two more days to get it in final shape.

As I put on my new black fur coat, this handsome, charming Italian policeman came up to me.

His eyes swept my face. "You think I might enjoy your books? I'm straight. I'm just curious."

I had heard that line many times before. I smiled and pulled an earlier favorite from my briefcase. I always carried extra copies of my work—in hopes it might convert someone handsome into someone closer than a friend.

"You don't have to be anything to enjoy a book of love stories. Here. Why don't you try my first story collection, *Eric's Body*?" Everybody seems to like this one. Gals, guys. Bi's. Tri's. Gays. Straights. If you don't like it, throw it away."

"You really think so, eh? Would—would you autograph it for me?"

"Of course. What's your name?"

"Roberto. Just Roberto."

"I like your name. It's got a musical quality about it. I've always loved Rudolph Valentino, the old movie star. What shall I inscribe for you?"

"Oh, anything."

"How about—to my new friend, Roberto—in hopes, that you'll become a fan of Jason Fury."

His dark eyes had such long lashes. They touched his cheeks as he looked down at my hand with the pen. A slight blush made him look as innocent as a young Italian choirboy.

"That'd be very nice," he said quietly. "Would you like me to see you home? I'm off work. I could give you a ride in the cop car out there?"

"Would you really? I've never ridden in a police car. Will you promise to handcuff me and beat me up? I simply love pain."

He squinted his eyes, as if startled by my words. Then he saw I was joking. He grinned: "Hey, for you, anything you want, pal."

Customers in that crowded Barnes and Noble turned to stare at the unusual sight of a man wearing a black fur coat being escorted through the aisles by a handsome young policeman.

His buddy, Kevin O'Connor, an Irish policeman, was funny and bawdy.

When I settled into the back of the patrol car, Kevin called out: "Better watch out for my buddy here, Jason. If he gets the hots for you, he'll jump you right here in the car."

Roberto made a good-natured protest but I joked: "Hey, my kind of guy! I'd prefer to do it on the sidewalks and give everybody a real thrill."

Roberto held up his copy of *Eric's Body*. The cover was from the original edition that showcased a sultry, boy-toy who symbolized perfectly the Eric of my book. He lay naked on his back with an arm across his forehead.

"Maybe you could put Kevin here on the cover of your next book."

"I'll put you both. And the only thing you'll be able to wear is a big grin."

This time they both laughed.

And that's how Roberto connected to me.

◆　　　◆　　　◆

He called me up the next week and said he had read my book.

He liked it. A lot.

"Did it get a rise out of you?" I teased.

"Uh, well, yeah, I did get hard," he said softly and giggled. "You've probably heard that a lot."

"Maybe. But I'm especially glad you said it."

"You are? Why?"

"You're very attractive. I mean, a uniform is always good looking. But when it's filled with something nice looking like you—that helps."

He didn't say anything for a moment. Then: "Hey, you're a cut-up. I know you're teasing. But—thanks."

I suggested we get together for coffee near the hotel where I had lived for twenty years. He met me that night. We discussed the stories, all the different men I had written about.

"Wow, you've known a lot of guys," he said. "Or did you make it all up."

"Nearly all the stories were based on real men. I changed the locales now and then and some of the guys are a combination of several. And those stories that took place back in 1954 in Boise, Idaho and at Pearl Harbor, well, I naturally recreated those."

"You must have a secret ingredient to get all these guys in bed," he grinned.

"I don't have any. When I'm really interested in a guy, I don't pretend."

"Maybe you could write a story about me," he said quietly, with an impish grin.

"It'd have to be very sexy, Roberto."

"Well, I've never swung with a guy before."

"You don't have to swing. Just have some innocent fun. It doesn't make you gay or bi or whatever the label is. My stories are always about straight guys."

His dark eyes widened.

"Yeah, you're right. All the guys you wrote about were just plain straight guys, right?"

"That's it. If they liked it, they did it."

"Well, I don't know. That'a big, big jump for me. To have some guy feeling me up. My brothers would kill me."

"What's the difference between a human hand? If you closed your eyes or were in the dark, you wouldn't know whose hand it was."

"Yeah, maybe. But for me, that'd be too big a leap."

He smiled sweetly and gave me a shy glance.

◆　　　◆　　　◆

From the fan mail that came my way over the years, a healthy percentage was fire and law enforcement guys.

State troopers, detectives, rookie cops, firefighters—they got a kick out of my tales. One of their favorites was "The Bull of the Blue Ridge Mountains." This account of lusty romance involved Jason's torrid weekend with a ravishing young state trooper. They're both snowbound in a mountain cabin.

Another great favorite was "Miracle on 55th Street." This was a wildly popular account of Jason performing as a drag queen at the Ritz Male Follies on West 55th Street. In the climatic finale, his crippled cop lover struggles down the aisle to be with him on Christmas Night.

Among these uniformed fans were several from New York City.

Gradually I met some of these handsome, take-charge guys. We'd have coffee in a small shop or we'd talk on the phone. These men were wonderful lovers—passionate, intense, sensitive and when they told me they had never "done it" with another guy, I believed them.

So I wasn't really shocked that a dashing young rookie like Roberto was among my fans.

◆　　　◆　　　◆

He lay naked on my bed, smoking a cigarette. I kissed his thighs, his package, and his flat stomach and rested my face against his brawny chest.

"My brothers want me to get married," he murmured. "They keep asking me why I'm not seeing any girls."

"Tell them the truth. You're seeing me."

"Oh, sure," he snorted. "They'd really love that."

His brothers weren't bigots, but they simply had no interest in knowing men who were strictly homosexual. They had to tolerate them on the force because the NYPD even had a gay association of men and women.

Officers took sensitivity training because their work threw them directly into situations that comprised a problem resulting from a "gay" factor—like fag bashing.

Roberto's buddy, Kevin, had also read *Eric's Body* and was turned on by it. With Roberto's knowledge, Kevin and I got together several times. With him, it was more like being with a good ole drinking friend. We had fun, we laughed, and we enjoyed each other.

With Roberto it was much different. He reminded me in some strange way of Billy Dragon and of Eric the patient. He could be quiet, thoughtful and adorable.

Although thoroughly macho, he didn't preen or swagger or make a big deal about it. Like many Italian guys I had known, he possessed a sweetness and tenderness about it that made a startling contrast to his rugged virility.

He stubbed out his cigarette and pulled me close to him and we kissed again. Wind and snow ticked-ticked against my window as winter passed into spring and then summer.

◆   ◆   ◆

I was on the subway, heading toward the Wall Street area.

I glanced at my watch. I was already running late. I was supposed to meet Roberto and Kevin for our weekly breakfast.

I loved to hear what my old buddies were up to and they were fascinated in the characters I was creating for my new book. I was using them as primary figures—although I had promised to change their names.

By the time, I arrived at the coffee shop my friends were in their usual rear booth.

"Hey, what'd ya mean keeping us two guys waiting, huh?" joked Kevin.

"Yeah, we kinda thought you were mad or somethin' at us?" Roberto grinned.

"Sorry, sorry. The subway was so damned late."

We ordered a big, old-fashioned breakfast of scrambled eggs and buttered toast and bacon. Like me, they had no patience for dieting or picking delicately at food. We three were large breakfast consumers.

Roberto looked impossibly gorgeous. His jet curls were tousled and that slight blush made him look so innocent and young. He was laughing with Kevin over some street person they had to arrest. The woman had stripped off all her clothes on Forty-Second Street.

"I don't think they'd want her to star at The Love Pit," Kevin mocked, referring to a popular strip joint that off duty cops liked to visit.

As we now bantered and ate, I glanced around me and everything looked so incredibly sharp—and strange.

Something eerie occurred just then.

Like one of those old "Twilight Zone" episodes, for less than a split second, everyone froze. No sound penetrated this extraordinary pulse beat of time.

Roberto and Kevin were immobile in that surreal instance and I thought again how like two affectionate puppies they were.

Their mouths were stretched into grins and laughter. Roberto looked sideways at Kevin who had his hand around a mug of coffee. Beyond their handsome heads, the sky glowed a cobalt azure.

A cool breeze snapped away at the remnants of summer.

It was September 11, 2001. Waitresses, diners, traffic—all appeared to stop dead.

Suddenly, a strange "boom" exploded somewhere near us. The table shivered. That sinister spell of stillness disappeared.

Both my buddies looked around. Others glanced up from their meals, as if they were waiting for something else to happen.

"Jesus Christ!" gasped Kevin. "What the fuck was that?"

"Explosion!" Roberto muttered. "Something fuckin' big blew up!"

Through the window, the steady throng of people had stopped in their tracks. All eyes stared upwards. The Twin Towers of the World Trade Center rose up like cubistic castles into the sky. Smoke streamed from one of them.

People outside screamed. They pointed to a jagged hole that gaped hideous and horrible against the gleaming veneer of glass and steel.

"A plane hit!" someone out there shouted. "A plane flew right into the tower!"

Now, everyone in the café had rushed to the windows, out the doors, to see what had happened. For only a few years before, a terrorist group had tried to bomb the two towers that left dead and wounded in its wake.

"Gotta go, gotta go!" shouted Kevin. "Man, it's the fuckin' Towers!"

He and Roberto both jumped up, making the table shake.

Roberto grabbed my neck, squeezed it, and then and he and Kevin hurtled out of the restaurant and into an inferno.

They were never seen again.

◆   ◆   ◆

Three years have passed since that nightmarish day.

I remember it like it had happened a minute ago.

After my two buddies raced away, I had rushed outside with the others to stare upward. That glistening, smooth tower belched black smoke from the enormous wound in its side.

As we watched, someone screamed:

"There's another plane!"

We couldn't believe it at first. A huge, passenger jet raced toward the second tower.

And against that incredible blue sky, we saw the plane slam into the structure, right in the middle of it, like a bizarre alien knife slicing into a gigantic bar of crystal.

This time, the explosion was louder and flames exploded out and upward.

Thousands of people surrounded me now. We all saw things falling through the air from the windows. Burning furniture, papers—and then the bodies.

"They're jumping!" a man shrieked. "People are jumping outta the windows!"

Like thousands of others horrified spectators, I kept muttering: "No, no, this can't be happening! It can't be happening!"

But it was.

On that beautiful, surreal day of azure beauty, this horrific nightmare was happening just blocks away.

We listened to the screams of the fire trucks converging from everywhere. We saw the hundreds of people at the windows above the roaring flames.

Many waved shirts, sweaters, and coats. Some had burst open their windows. They crowded there, shrieking silently above the roar of the flames.

The horrible sight of falling bodies from above grew.

We covered our mouths as we watched the living people knife through the air and explode on the ground. So many had jumped that a faint mist of red gradually arose off the ground. Blood saturated the air.

And then suddenly, there was a roar, thousands of shrieks as the first tower suddenly shook, shivered and then it collapsed.

We ran madly to escape. I lunged into a crowded doorway where others huddled. Many more smashed up against us. The bank doors were locked. But quickly they crashed open as dozens more frantic people hurled against us.

We fell inside, onto the broken glass and still more people jumped inside as an Atomic shaped cloud of darkness roared by for long, long minutes.

Gray ash covered everything and when we finally emerged, we couldn't breathe. I pulled my coat over my head and could still barely see where I was going.

And then, more screams and then another tower fell. An even bigger cloud exploded upon lower Manhattan. We ran for cover and this time I escaped most of it. A large man I'd never seen before grabbed my arm and pulled me along with him. We both fell gasping into a restaurant jammed with other escapees.

I looked up at my hero and nodded my head. His face was black with soot and ash. He closed his eyes and fell backwards. It was only then I saw the jagged bolt of glass protruding from his back. He was only one of the many who died that day.

An hour later, I moved out of that restaurant, as the clouds of ash thinned out, and moved away from it, walking along Broadway.

I looked back and saw a scene from hell.

Much of lower Manhattan had vanished within minutes.

Our Twin Towers were no more. Billowing smoke and flames covered the cityscape.

It was as if we had been hit with an Atomic Bomb.

Everything was covered with the ash from destruction and death.

This wasn't supposed to happen. Not on this dazzling, blue day of early autumn.

I wandered around in a daze for hours. Somehow I made it home by darkness. When I turned on the television, it was as if a movie played on the screen.

The planes crashing into the Twin Towers…the mushroom clouds racing up the city canyons…people running and screaming…

I showered, scrubbing myself raw and collapsed in bed with a sleeping pill.

But when I awoke the next morning, the hell of a cataclysm was only worse.

It really did happen. None of it had been a terrible fantasy. I had only to turn on the television and watch it again and again and the aftermath. I walked over to Broadway. I had to be with other people.

A surreal silence hung over everything. No horns screamed, people talked in subdued voices, even the tourists had a vacant, stunned look on their faces.

I visited Union Park on 14th Street where I'd heard there was an observance. Thousands of people wandered around there, candles lit, tears gleaming on many faces.

Strangers would stop, say a few words and then embrace. A group sang the words, "Nearer My God to Thee," and we all joined in. And then another bunch of stragglers began the words to "Amazing Grace."

A group of young college girls sang "America, the Beautiful." We sang along and somehow hands locked with those close by.

Strangers connected briefly in that terrible moment. For weeks and months afterwards, pictures of the missing hung everywhere—from lamp posts, from subway walls to the outside of buildings.

Heart-breaking messages accompanied the smiling faces of the doomed. "If you've seen _____, please call this number."

I studied them all. Women, men, policemen, firemen, emergency workers.

A whole community of people destroyed by a group of lunatics. Their Muslim supporters both in New York, New Jersey and other parts of the nation, celebrated by dancing and holding parties.

Many Muslim workers and school kids had mysteriously stayed home the day of the attack. Rumors had it that they knew ahead that something was to happen that day.

The New York Times ran an editorial that day admonishing Americans to not single out Muslims for revenge. Yet, it was Muslim men who had perpetrated the worst terrorist attack on American soil in its young history.

And young Muslims in America, when interviewed on television, were arrogant and smug about the massacre.

My two boyfriends were never seen again. They had been the first to respond and they became members of the doomed.

◆   ◆   ◆

Dark clouds clotted the sky yesterday.

September 11 had rolled around again. I had to get out and away from all the television memorials about that horrendous occasion. On East Twenty-third Street, I approached a gray, anonymous building.

A small group of people studied something on the outside wall. I paused to look and saw that in observance of the September 11 massacre, the building owners had created a large display window.

Against an American flag, a memorial was filled with the photos of the hundreds of firemen and policemen who had perished that day. All those eyes, staring back at me and all them dead. Two of the faces were the ones I had known.

A policeman's hat covered that mass of crazy red curls that belonged to Kevin. None of the others in this small group of pedestrians had any idea of his crazy, bawdy sense of humor.

A row lower, I spotted the shy, handsome image of my cop boyfriend. Roberto looked solemn in his picture but I recognized the suggestion of an impish grin that tugged at his beautifully shaped mouth.

His brothers wouldn't have to worry about finding a good wife for their younger brother. Would Roberto have followed their demands that he marry and settle down and raise kids?

Or would he have actually defied them, as he told me he planned to do. And would he have remained single, choosing a different lifestyle that he really wanted?

The small crowd gradually left except for one young woman who raised a Kleenex to blot the tears that flowed down her face.

My face was wet, too, and I used my fingers to wipe away the sadness.

"How many are there?" I asked quietly, not looking at her. "Is there a number?"

"I don't know. It's too many of them. Hundreds of them."

"I knew two of them," I said. "They were wonderful men."

"They were all wonderful," she said. "Not just one. All of them…"

"That's what I mean."

"Three years ago it happened," she said quietly. "It's just like it was yesterday. Everybody—" she gestured toward the passing people, "has forgotten about it."

"Not me. I'll never forget."

She put her wet tissue into a coat pocket and pulled up the collar of her overcoat.

"Sometimes I wish I'd died that day, too. My husband was a fireman. He was killed."

She pointed to the face of a rugged man with strong face and kind eyes.

"Everybody's forgotten them," she repeated. "If they had lost someone, like you, like me—they'll never forget it."

"I'll never forget. Never ever."

She left but I stayed for a few minutes more. All those hundreds of faces, staring back at me, as if they were trying to tell me something.

All those thousands who perished that day, in the towers, in Washington, in a remote field in Pennsylvania.

Vanished forever.

Rain started falling again. A gray, chilling wetness made the sidewalks resemble tombstones knocked down by a powerful wind.

Then I left, too. I wanted no one with me.

These days, I walk alone.

Jason Fury
September 11, 2004
New York City

About the Author...

'Jason Fury' is the pen name of cult author, Jery Tillotson.

Using this *non-de plume*, he has written seven best sellers, beginning with *Eric's Body* in 1993 and which was hailed as a "timeless classic of gay erotica". In 2000, both *Eric's Body* and *The Rope Above, the Bed Below* were reprinted by the Authors Guild Back-in-Print series of American classics.

About *Nights of Fury*, he says: "This book was terribly hard to write. I don't usually think of the bad times that we all have but in trying to make my words honest, I had to do a lot of remembering."

Although he visits his home state of North Carolina several times each year, he has lived on Manhattan's Upper Eastside for nearly twenty-two years.

Tillotson invites readers to visit his website at: www.jerytillotson.com

0-595-32356-1

www.ingramcontent.com/pod-product-compliance
Lightning Source LLC
Chambersburg PA
CBHW032059280526
45784CB00012B/203